INCULTURATING NORTH AMERICAN THEOLOGY

ℛ

American Academy of Religion
Studies in Religion

Editor
Lawrence S. Cunningham

Number 54
INCULTURATING NORTH AMERICAN THEOLOGY
by
Donald L. Gelpi, S.J.

INCULTURATING NORTH AMERICAN THEOLOGY
An Experiment in Foundational Method

Donald L. Gelpi, S.J.

Scholars Press
Atlanta, Georgia

INCULTURATING NORTH AMERICAN THEOLOGY
An Experiment in Foundational Method

by
Donald L. Gelpi, S.J.

Library of Congress Cataloging-in-Publication Data

Gelpi, Donald L., 1934—
 Inculturating North American theology : an experiment in
foundational method / by Donald L. Gelpi.
    p.   cm. — (Studies in religion / American Academy of Religion
; no. 54)
 ISBN 1-555-40210-0 (alk. paper). ISBN 1-555-40211-9 (PBK. : alk.
paper)
  1. Theology—Methodology.   2. Theolody. Doctrinal—North American.
3. Christianity and culture. I. Title.   II. Series: Studies in
religion (American Academy of Religion) : no. 54.
BR118.G43   1988
                                                          230'.01'8—
                                                          dc19
                                                             87-33965
                                                          CIP

Printed in the United States of America
on acid-free paper

TABLE OF CONTENTS

AUTHOR'S PREFACE

Every book of theology, even one which deals with theological method, organizes the verbal precipitate of some religious experience. Some branches of theology focus on the past: they evoke the experiences that have blended into the shared religious heritage of a people. Foundational theology, the branch of theology with which the present volume deals, probes the religious experiences of living human beings in order to derive from them a normative insight into the experience of conversion. Of course, no responsible theology of conversion ignores the past; for contemporary religious experience needs to be interpreted in the light of the developing traditions of religious communities. Nevertheless, by probing the experiences of living persons in order to derive from them principles for authentic religious growth and development foundational theology uses the insights of the past in order to understand the present and to advance toward a future more solidly rooted in God.

In this volume I propose to study the methods of foundational theological thinking. These pages, then, concern themselves only secondarily with the experience of conversion itself and primarily and proximately with the techniques of theological thinking that lead to a sound understanding of Christian conversion.

A treatise on theological method must seem at first pretty far removed from experience. But not so. Rather treatises on theological method attempt to put into words the experience of achieving conscious self-understanding in faith. Studies of method attempt to describe fruitful ways of achieving such self-understanding and of avoiding erroneous interpretations of the human encounter with God. They should then interest not only professional theologians but also any reflective person interested in understanding the word of God.

In the present volume I have attempted to reflect on ten years of my own personal search for religious self-understanding. I joined the faculty of the Jesuit School of Theology in Berkeley, California a little over ten years ago. I came to Berkeley with a fairly ambitious program of theological research and writing in mind. I held a doctorate in philosophy from Fordham University. During my doctoral studies I had concentrated on North American philosophy. After receiving the doctorate I had spent three years teaching philosophy and researching the development of the North American philosophical tradition at Loyola University in New Orleans. I came to Berkeley determined to test my own ability to use the best insights of that tradition to create an inculturated Catholic theology, one which not only drew its categories from North American culture but also challenged that culture to repentance and authentic Christian faith.

When I came to Berkeley I had another important item on my theological agenda. While at Loyola I had studied and taught Bernard Lonergan's *Method in Theology*. The more I pondered his reflections on method the more convinced I felt that he had pointed the way to doing the kind of inculturated theology I ambitioned. On arriving at Berkeley I was asked to contribute three basic courses to the master of divinity curriculum: one on the theology of the human person, one in sacramental theology, and one in the theology of the Holy Spirit. I determined to transform all three courses into studies in theological foundations in Lonergan's sense of that term. All three books have been published. In the present volume I would like to try to share with others what I have learned in the course of writing them about the practice of foundational theology.

Method in Theology prescribes a largely untested formula for thinking theologically, especially in those areas of theological specialization which Lonergan calls mediated theology. Mediated theology, as we shall see later in more detail, comprises four specialties: foundational theology, which ambitions a normative theology of conversion; doctrinal theology; systematic theology; and communications. Foundational theology grounds the other three specialties. It provides the doctrinal theologian with norms for distinguishing sound from unsound doctrines. Systematic theology tries to show the relationship among sound doctrines. Communications tries to use the insights of foundational theology in order to diagnose and remedy breakdowns in communications within a living faith community.

Probably because *Method in Theology* provided a largely untested formula for doing mediated theology, Lonergan himself manifested extreme reticence concerning the operational procedures of the very theological specialty I was most interested in pursuing. In discussing the method of foundational thinking Lonergan had largely contented himself with describing three "nests" of categories which foundationnal theologians needed to use.

To a great extent, therefore, in the actual pursuit of foundational speculation, I very often had to make up my own rules as I went along. As my work advanced I not only understood more and more about the complex experience of initial and ongoing conversion but also grew in my understanding of the techniques of foundational speculation.

The pages which follow attempt to articulate some of those techniques and to reflect on the adequacy of the operational procedures I employed. This book asks, then, a straightforward question about theological method: namely, *how does one go about the task of formulating a normative theology of Christian conversion?* In the course of writing it I have come to recognize some significant methodological oversights in the three books I have published, oversights I will attempt to remedy in subsequent volumes.

I have decided to make these reflections public partly because I believe that they contribute some novel insights into the contemporary pursuit of theology but primarily because I hope that many more will be willing to join in the effort of formulating an inculturated North American theology of conversion that speaks with a Yankee idiom even as it challenges the religious inauthenticities in North American culture.

In the course of the pages which follow I have indulged in a literary conceit that I have employed in other books I have written. I refer to the third person of the trinity as the Holy Breath and designate Her as She. I avoid the term "spirit" because of its many misleading philosophical connotations. The term "breath" seems to me an acceptable translation of the Hebrew term *ruah*. Moreover, as I have attempted to show in *The Divine Mother: A Trinitarian Theology of the Holy Spirit,* both the Bible and Christian tradition sanction imagining the third person of the trinity as feminine. Anyone interested in pursuing these matters further is referred to that volume.

I owe a special debt of gratitude to the other members of the John Courtney Murray Group who have criticized and helped improve the pages which follow. A post-doctoral research seminar dedicated to the fostering of an inculturated North American theology in dialogue with the classical American philosophical tradition, the Murray Group gathers each summer for shared scholarly work. Several of the chapters which follow have been much improved by their friendly criticisms. Among the members of the Murray Group I would like to thank especially Francis Oppenheim, S.J., John Stacer, S.J., William Spohn, S.J., and J.J. Mueller, S.J. I also owe a debt of gratitude to Walter Conn for his careful critique of the manuscript. With the assistance of such colleagues, I must take full responsibility for any inadequacy in the chapters which follow.

Donald L. Gelpi, S.J.
The Jesuit School of Theology at Berkeley
July, 1987

CHAPTER I:

TOWARD AN INCULTURATED NORTH AMERICAN THEOLOGY

The term "culture" first entered the English language in the latter part of the nineteenth century as a neologism borrowed from the German. Once introduced it found a variety of definitions and descriptions. Scholars attempted to catalogue the contents of culture. Monographs contrasted culture and instinctive behavior. Students of culture generally agreed both that it possesses some kind of structure and that it engages habitual human responses. They characterized it as the social and historical heritage of a group, as a way of life. Some anthropologists looked on values as constitutive of culture. Others probed its psychological and human sources.[1]

Neologisms differ from slang expressions. In slang a familiar term acquires an unusual meaning. Police are renamed "fuzz." Money becomes "bread." A bumbling fool is dubbed a "turkey." Neologisms, however, attempt to expand the panoply of symbolic tools available to thought. They bespeak therefore the dawning of a new shared awareness.

The term "inculturation" has recently surfaced as a contemporary neologism. It has entered the English language almost a century after the term "culture." Its emergence also bespeaks an expansion of social consciousness. Moreover, the term "inculturation" enjoys both theological and anthropological connotations. Its popularization signals more specifically therefore the emergence of a new kind of faith awareness.

As a theological term, "inculturation" characterizes an ideal of sound evangelization. An inculturated proclamation of the gospel recognizes both the fact and the legitimacy of cultural pluralism. It acknowledges that groups within distinctive historical and cultural heritages lay legitimate claims to equally distinctive hopes and aspirations correlative to their situation and traditions.

Inculturated evangelization aspires to ecumenical openness and sensitivity. It respects the diversity of Christian traditions. It seeks to engage

---

[1] A.L. Kroeber and Clyde Kluckhohn, *Culture: A Critical Review of Concepts and Definitions* (New York: Vintage Books).

non-Christian religions, secular society, and even atheism in meaningful dialogue.

Inculturated evangelization seeks an "incarnational" proclamation of the gospel. The divine Word, it argues, took flesh in a particular people and drew upon the religious heritage of the Hebrews to interpret to others His person and mission. In the same way the proclaimed word of the gospel must find embodiment in a variety of nations, peoples, and traditions.

But inculturated evangelization also seeks to avoid narrow nationalism. It voices concern with universal, planetary values, even as it strives to preserve cultural pluralism. It seeks the communion of all nations in the same religious faith; but it finds true union in the freedom of individuals to respond directly to the action of the Holy Breath of Jesus in ways that express and reflect their distinctive cultural heritage.

Finally, inculturated evangelization ambitions the Christian transformation of culture. In the words of Pedro Arrupe, S.J.:

> Inculturation is the incarnation of Christian life and of the Christian message in a particular cultural context, in such a way that this experience not only finds expression through elements proper to the culture in question (this alone would be no more than superficial adaptation), but becomes the principle that animates, directs, and unifies the culture, transforming and remaking it so as to bring about a "new creation."[2]

Contemporary theological use of the term "inculturation" suggests a metanoia on the part of western Christians. Its emergence tacitly acknowledges the fact that occidental nationalism and colonialism have in the past suffused the proclamation of the good news with a kind of cultural totalitarianism. Since the papal suppression of the Chinese rites, non-Christian nations have until recently been expected to submit to Europeanization or Americanization as a condition for Christianization. Those who speak of "inculturation" ambition therefore a return to the pioneering missionary methods of men like Bartolome de las Casas, Francis Xavier, Matthew Ricci, and Robert di Nobili.

Any attempt to engage in inculturated evangelization risks cross-fire from a number of conflicting historical concerns and interests. Because it insists that the gospel reach embodiment in different cultural contexts, inculturated teaching needs to find a way of mediating between the original proclamation of Christ in Hebraic thought patterns, its many subsequent incarnations in Graeco-Roman, medieval, and modern sym-

---

[2] Pedro Arrupe, S.J. "On Inculturation," *Acta Romana Societatis Jesu* (1979) XVII, ii. p. 257. Hereafter this work will be abbreviated as OI.

bols, and the contemporaary cultural contexts in which evangelists announce and Christians try to live the gospel. An inculturated theology must strike a balance between church unity and local diversity, between the concerns of the developed and the developing nations. It must steer between the scylla of relativism and the charybdis of artificial uniformity. It must deal not only with broad, typical, cultural movements and patterns but also with the survival and evangelization of deviant sub-groups within a dominant cultural system.

Despite generations of Americanization, the Catholic community in this country still lacks genuine inculturation. Three events in the history of the Catholic church in the United States have conspired to alienate its theological speculation from serious dialogue with problems and issues raised by North American secular culture: the immigrant status of the Catholic community in the nineteenth century, the autocratic suppression of creative theological work in the United States in the wake of the modernist crisis, and the regrettable but frequent failure of the American Catholic theological community to take North American culture seriously.

The Catholic immigrants who swarmed ashore on Ellis Island and similar ports of debarkation brought with them strong ethnic ties to Europe. Economically poor by and large, as foreigners and Roman Catholics they faced a doubly hostile world. The Catholic community responded to Protestant anti-Catholicism with an equally virulent form of Catholic anti-Protestant prejudice; but in response to the charges of Nativists that as foreigners immigrant Catholics had no place in the American dream, our religious forebears in North America set out to out-American any Yankee. Often they succeeded. Often too the result fell short of inculturated Christian living. In the lives of second and third generation immigrant Catholic families, religious and secular values sometimes remained merely juxtaposed rather than theologically or religiously integrated. Habitual and uncritical acquiesence in secular, North American values constitutes then the first serious obstacle to inculturated evangelization in the United States.[3]

Although the term "inculturation" emerged only in the twentieth century, Catholic leaders in the nineteenth century already showed concern with the reality. By the turn of the century American Catholicism under the leadership of men like Orestes Brownson, Isaac Hecker, John Cardinal Gibbons, and Archbishop John Ireland had begun to produce something like an indigenous American Catholicism. The systematic suppression of that creative effort in the wake of the modernist crisis

---

[3] Cf. Sydney E. Aholstrom, *A Religious History of the American People* (New Haven: Yale, 1972) 330–342, 537–568; John Tracy Ellis, *American Catholicism* (Chicago: University of Chicago Press, 1969) 1–123.

marks one of the saddest chapters in the intellectual history of American Catholicism.[4]

The immigrant Catholic Church left an enduring monument in the American Catholic educational system. At first that system was founded to preserve popular Catholic belief intact in a hostile Protestant environment. By and large it succeeded; but Catholic institutions of learning have also served as powerful instruments for fostering the Europeanization of the American Church. Since Vatican II the situation has changed somewhat, but even to this day American Catholic theology like American oil tends by and large to be imported from abroad. Except for stirrings in Catholic feminist circles and in the field of Catholic moral theology serious contemporary educational efforts to deal theologically with the religious issues raised by American culture remain relatively rare.

One may, of course, name notable exceptions to this pattern. Most North American Catholics live blissfully ignorant of the philosophical and theological achievements of Orestes Brownson. Through his books and his *Quarterly Review* during the nineteenth century he patiently laid the speculative foundations for an indigenous American theology. In the twentieth century John A. Ryan applied Catholic social teaching to North American social and economic issues, while John Courtney Murray, S.J. wrestled with "the American Proposition." Murray's pioneering work eventually bore fruit in the decree on religious freedom endorsed at Vatican II. That document constitutes perhaps the only significant theological contribution of the North American church to the work of the Council.

Matters stand, of course, somewhat differently with Protestant theology in this country, for it helped engender American secular culture. The foundations of secular American life were laid in part by Unitarian ministers in full flight from the Calvinist doctrines of predestination and natural depravity. The Protestant Enlightenment created the political structures which govern American life. Moreover, Protestant theologians like H. Richard Niebuhr, James Gustafsen, and Langdon Gilkey have drawn more freely and consciously on American cultural sources than do most of their Roman Catholic counterparts.

In his letter to the Society of Jesus on the subject of inculturation, Pedro Arrupe lists eight attitudes which should motivate any attempt to inculturate the gospel: docility to the Breath of Christ, a unifying vision of salvation history, freedom of heart both to give to others and to

---

[4] Ahlstrom, *op. cit.*, 825–831, 124–263; Michael V. Gannon, Before and After Modernism: "The Intellectual isolation of the American Priest" in *The Catholic Priest in the United States*, edited by John Tracy Ellis (Collegeville: St. John's University, 1971) 293–383.

receive from them, discernment, interior humility, persevering patience, discrete charity, and a loyal *sensus ecclesiae* (OI, 256–263).

In addition to sound personal attitudes, however, inculturated evangelization stands in need of a speculative method for dealing theologically with the problems, issues, and challenges which Christianity poses for any given culture and which the latter poses for Christianity. Among the current theoreticians of theological method Bernard Lonergan has perhaps raised the question of theological inculturation most explicitly. In his method, the confrontation between a religion and its ambient culture sets the speculative agenda for theological thinking. In the first sentence of *Method in Theology* he writes: "A theology mediates between a cultural matrix and the significance and role of a religion in that matrix."[5] In a sense the rest of his book attempts to explicitate the implications of that statement.

In the pages which follow, I shall try to determine whether Bernard Lonergan's method can in fact revive the dream of Brownson and of Hecker, of Gibbons and of Murray, the dream of an inculturated North American Roman Catholic theology. In the present chapter I shall examine Lonergan's own understanding of culture and some of the philosophical presuppositions on which it rests. I shall also explore the ways in which his method would seek to facilitate the dialogue between a religion and a culture. Finally, I shall begin to examine how thinkers who have given decisive shape to American secular culture might criticize some of Lonergan's own methodological presuppositions.

(I)

In *Insight* Lonergan concerned himself only superficially with culture. There he grounded cultural development in the human capacity to ask, to reflect, and to reach an answer. He described culture as the food of practical intelligence, and he identified it as one of the forces that can counteract social decline, even though human culture can also be made to serve crudely utilitarian ends.[6]

In *Method of Theology,* however, Lonergan focused directly on the interface between religion and culture. His approach to culture rested on three fundamental distinctions. He distinguished between a classical and empirical understanding of culture, between religion and theology, and between faith and belief.

---

[5] Bernard Lonergan, *Method in Theology* (New York: Herder and Herder, 1972) xi. Hereafter this work will be abbreviated as MT.

[6] Bernard Lonergan, *Insight* (New York: Philosophical Library, 1958) 236–238. Hereafter this work will abbreviated as I.

The later Lonergan defined "culture" as "a set of meanings and values informing a common way of life" (MT, 301). He distinguished, however, two possible attitudes toward culture: classical and empirical.

A "classical" view of culture claims normative validity. It ignores cultural pluralism, recognizes only one standard for measuring cultural achievement, and assumes both the permanent and universal character of that standard. The classicist mind opposes culture and barbarism. Because it believes in the fixed and immutable nature of things, it regards its philosophy as perennial and the verities it values as eternal. In religious matters it opposes doctorinal pluralism.

Cultural classicism manifests as a consequence the same totalitarian tendencies which the search for inculturated evangelization abjures. Not only does it fail to anticipate shifts in speculative interpretations of the nature of reality in general, but it feels free to impose its own conceptions forceably upon others in order to free them from the blindness of barbarism (MT, xi, 301–302, 315, 363).

The empiricist, however, conceives of culture in pluralistic and developmental terms. The empiricist recognizes the existence of as many kinds of culture as there are sets of meanings and values informing distinctive ways of life. Empiricism acknowledges too that cultural changes always involve shifts in meaning. Cultural empiricism remains open and sensitive to the processes of cultural development, stasis, and dissolution. In religious matters it fears no threat from doctrinal pluralism and development. It recognizes the need for inculturated evangelization.

Lonergan's sensitivity to the need for unculturated evangilization leads him to judge correctly that only cultural empiricism grounds adequately a contemporary pursuit of theology. His method, therefore, seeks to mediate not merely between a religion and a culture but between a religion and a culture empirically conceived (MT, xi, 30, 78, 301, 326, 363).

The ability of theology to mediate between a religion and a culture presupposes that all three differ. In the case of Christianity Lonergan regards the distinction between religion and theology as an historical *fait accompli*. In the earliest expressions of Christian faith, theology and religion, he suggests, blended indistinguishably; but the speculative developments within Christianity that led to the Council of Nicea forced a differentiation between the two. Lonergan describes religion as transcendent falling in love and Christian theology as critical reflection on the historical self-revelation of God in Jesus Christ (MT, 106, 138–140, 296).

Faith he defines as "knowledge born of religious love." Faith roots itself in feelings that respond intentionally to values, values which make absolute claims. Human love becomes religious when it consists of God's own love flooding our hearts (MT, 115–116).

Because religious faith engages the heart it precedes religious belief. Nevertheless, faith needs to be verbalized in order to grow and develop. It needs three kinds of words. The word of proclmation announces the good news that God loved us first and revealed Himself to us in the fullness of time. The word of tradition expresses the accumulated wisdom of a religious community. The word of fellowship unites those who share in the gift of divine love (MT, 113, 118–123).

Clearly, the distinctions Lonergan draws between religion and theology on the one hand and between faith and belief on the other imply one another in his method. His method presupposes that the transformation of religious faith into belief moves through different stages of meaning: common sense, theory, interiority, and mystical self-transcendence. As common sense religious beliefs become a religious theory or a systematic account of religious interiority, they are transformed into a theology (M, 114, 170).

Moreover, in Lonergan's method concern with religious interiority differentiates mediated from mediating theology. Mediating theology envisages the systematic retrieval of a religious tradition; mediated theology envisages its creative reformulation and communication to others. The former makes the latter possible and in this sense mediates it. Mediating theology embraces four functional specialities: research, interpretation, history, and dialectics. Mediated theology consists of four other functional specialities: foundations, doctrines, systematics, communications. Let us reflect briefly on the scope of each of these eight foci of theological inquiry; for their relationship to one another casts practical light on the way Lonergan's method might be used to foster inculturated evangelization (MT, 134–135).

Theological research gathers the data needed for the pursuit of theology. It includes religious archaeology, the editing of sacred texts, the study of sacred languages. Interpretation offers an account of what the religious data unearthed by research meant originally to those who created and formulated it. History tells the story of a religious community. Dialectics seeks to distinguish real from merely apparent conflicts in the course of that community's development (MT, 127–130).

Mediating theology studies the past. Such study creates the possibility of reaching the new insights into the authentic meaning of a religious tradition ambitioned by mediated theology. Foundational theology effects the shift to mediated theology through its explicit concern with religious interiority. It attempts to elaborate a normative account of conversion. It also tries to unmask the religious inauthenticities that motivate dialectical conflicts within a religious community. Foundational theology thus supplies the criteria that allow the doctrinal theologian to distinguish between authentic and inauthentic religious doctrines. Systematic theology seeks to understand the relationships that unify the authentic expressions of faith identified by doctrinal theology. Finally, communications attempts to translate the results of technical theological speculation into terms that will transform the faith experience of non-theologians (MT, 130–133).

Among the functional specialities, the normative character of foundational thinking endows it with special importance. Foundational theology provides the criteria for diagnosing the inauthenticities within a religious tradition that cause doctrinal breakdowns and the dissolution of religious communities. As a consequence, foundational theology bears special responsibility for dealing with questions raised by the confrontation between a religion and its ambient culture. For religious inauthenticity commonly results from an uncritical acquiescence in culturally motivated attitudes and values which contradict those demanded by an authentic and integral conversion to gospel living. As a consequence, Christian theology will successfully foster inculturated evangelization only when theologians begin to apply the techniques of mediating theology to secular culture as well as to religious traditions.

The dialectical examination of the American tradition shows that it offers rich resources for pursuing an inculturated foundational theology. Foundational thinking probes the dynamics of conversion. Written in the eighteenth century, Jonathan Edwards' *Treatise Concerning Religious Affections* remains to this day a classic in religious psychology. Moreover, the thought of this puritan divine first focused attention on many themes that would preoccupy North American philosophy during the nineteenth and twentieth centuries, issues relevant to a theology of conversion. Among those issues we discover an insistence on the primacy of experience and on the analogy between religious and aesthetic experience, the centrality of affectivity to human religious experiences, the abandonment of scholastic patterns of thinking, the attempt to establish a dialogue between religion and science, the religious search for synthetic insight.[7]

American Transcendentalism was born in the eighteen thirties, but the movement spanned the rest of the nineteenth century. It attempted to vindicate the primacy of intuitive knowledge within human religious experience. Crusty New England individualists, the leaders of this move-

[7] Harry Miller, *Jonathan Edwards* (Toronto: Sloan, 1935); Conrad Shay, *The Theology of Jonathan Edwards* (New York: Anchor, 1966); Roland Delattre, *Beauty and Sensibility in the Thought of Jonathan Edwards* (New Haven: Yale, 1968); John Gerstner, *Steps to Salvation: The Evangelical Message of Jonathan Edwards* (Philadelphia: Westminster, 1959); David Levin, ed., Jonathan Edwards (New York: Hill and Wang, 1969).

ment offered sharply differing accounts of religious intuition. A dialectical analysis of the issues dividing Ralph Waldo Emerson, Theodore Parker, and Orestes A. Brownson would offer the contemporary foundational theologian instructive insights.[8]

The critique of intuitive religion mounted by Chauncey Wright and by C.S. Peirce inaugurated important speculative impulses in the final phase of Transcendental speculation.[9] It alerted Francis Ellingwood Abbott, a convinced Emersonian, to the need to reconcile the religious claims of Transcendental intuitionism with those of positive science. The scholarly community has almost totally neglected Abbott's work; but his *Scientific Theism* and *Syllogistic Philosophy* anticipate many of the insights of twentieth century process speculation. His philosophy, especially his *Scientific Theism,* also exercised a significant influence on the mature thought of C.S. Peirce, the founder of American pragmatism.

Peirce wrote the final chapter in the development of American Transcendentalism. Peirce's dissatisfaction with the speculative imprecision of other self-styled pragmatists eventually caused him to dissociate himself from pragmatism as a movement. He changed the name of his philosophy from pragmatism to pragmaticism and eventually to critical common sensism. Moreover, the logical terms on which he attempted to reconcile religion and science cast important light on the dynamics of conversion.[10]

[8] David Edgell, *William Ellery Channing: An Intellectual Portrait* (Boston: Beacon, 1955); Octavius B. Frothingham, *Boston Unitarianism: 1820–1850* (New York: Putnam's, 1890); Conrad Wright, *The Beginnings of Unitarianism in America* (Boston: Beacon, 1955) and *The Liberal Christians* (Boston: Beacon, 1970). Cf. Johathan Bishop, *Emerson on the Soul* (Cambridge: Harvard, 1964); Sherman Paul, *Emerson's Angle of Vision* (Cambridge: Harvard, 1952); Stephen Whicher, *Freedom and Fate: An Inner Biography of Ralph Waldo Emerson* (New York: Barnes and Co., 1961); Gay Wilson Allen, *Waldo Emerson: A Biography* (New York: Viking, 1981). Theodore Parker's Transcendentalism was of a different character from Emerson's: Cf. John Edward Dirkes, *The Critical Theology of Theodore Parker* (New York: Columbia, 1948); H.S. Smith, "Was Theodore Parker a Transcendentalist?" *New England Quarterly,* 23 (September 1959) 351–368. Orestes Brownson developed his transcendental vision largely after his conversion to Catholicism. Cf. Bertin Farrell, *Orestes Brownson's Approach to God* (Washington: Catholic University Press, 1950); Arthur Schlesinger, *Orestes A. Brownson: A Pilgrim's Progress* (Boston: Little, Brown, & Co., 1939); Leonard Gilhooley, *No Divided Allegiance: Essays in Brownson's Thought* (New York, Fordham University Press, 1980) and *Contradiction and Dilemma: Orestes Brownson and the American Idea* (New York: Fordham University Press, 1972).

[9] Alfred Ayer, *The Origins of Pragmatism: Studies in the Philosophy of Charles Peirce and William James* (San Francisco: Freeman and Cooper, 1968); John E. Smith, *Purpose and Thought: the Meaning of Pragmatism* (New Haven: Yale, 1978).

[10] Francis Ellingwood Abbot, *Scientific Theism* (Boston: Little, Brown, & Co., 1885); *The Syllogistic Philosophy* (Boston: Little, Brown, & Co., 1906); D.D. O'Connor, "Peirce's Debt to F.E. Abbot," *Journal of the History of Ideas,* 25 (October, 1964) 543–564; T.A. Goudge, "The Conflict of Naturalism and Transcendentalism in Peirce," *Journal of Philosophy,* 44 (July, 1947) 365–375; Charles Hartshorne, "Charles Sanders Peirce, Pragmatic

Though Peirce authored the pragmatic maxim, William James launched pragmatism as a movement. His classic study of religious psycholocy, *The Varieties of Religious Experience,* laid the foundations for his distinctive application of the pragmatic maxim to religious questions. In addition, the philosophical dialogue that developed between James, Peirce, and John Dewey offers a number of enlightening insights into the dynamic structure of human experience, insights useful for a systematic account of conversion.[11]

An inculturated North American theology must deal not only with the issues raised by American pragmatism but also with those raised by the religious idealism of Josiah Royce. His greatest work, *The Problem of Christianity,* offers a searching philosophical analysis of the enduring relevance of Christian belief to human culture. Both his philosophy of loyalty and his analysis of community consciousness offer important insights into the social dimensions of religion.[12]

American naturalism offers other resources for the pursuit of foundational thinking. John Dewey launched a systematic assault on the dualisms that have infected religious thinking for centuries. His insights into the fields of ethics, esthetics, logic, and epistemology illumine human experiential development; and with proper qualification they can cast light on human religious experience as well.[13]

Process theology offers a useful contemporary point of entry into the American philosophical system. It too deals with issues that address religious experience. Alfred North Whitehead founded American process theology, which already counts three generations of thinkers. Though born and raised in England, he did his most significant and influential philosophical work while teaching at Harvard University. He

---

Transcendentalist," *New England Quarterly,* 14 (March, 1941) 49–63; Murray G. Murphey, *The Development of Peirce's Philosophy* (Cambridge: Harvard, 1961); Vincent Potter, *Charles S. Peirce on Norms and Ideals* (Worchester: University of Massachusetts, 1967); Francis E. Reilly, *Charles Peirce's Theory of Scientific Method* (New York: Fordham, 1970); Edward Madden, *Chauncey Wright and the Foundations of Pragmatism* (Seattle: University of Washington, 1963); W.D. Gallie, *Peirce and Pragmatism* (Edinburgh, Penguin, 1952).

[11] Julius Steelye Bixler, *Religion in the Philosophy of William James* (Boston: Marshall Jones, 1926); Josiah Royce, *William James and Other Essays on the Philosophy of Life* (New York: Macmillan, 1911); Edward C. Moore, *American Pragmatism: Peirce, James, and Dewey* (New York: Columbia, 1961); and *William James* (New York: Washington Square, 1966).

[12] James H. Cotten, *Royce on the Human Self* (Cambridge: Harvard, 1954); Gabrielle Marcel, *Royce's Metaphysics,* tr. by Virginia Ann Gordon Ringer (Chicago: Regnery, 1956); John E. Smith, *Royce's Social Infinite: The Community of Interpretation* (New York: Liberal Arts Press, 1950); Mary B. Mahowald, *An Idealistic Pragmatism* (The Hague, Nyhoff, 1972).

[13] Edward C. Moore, *American Pragmatism: Peirce, James, and Dewey* (New York: Columbia, 1961); Thomas R. Maitland, *The Metaphysics of William James and John Dewey* (New York: Philosophical Library, 1975); George R. Geiger, *John Dewey in Perspective* (New York: Oxford, 1958).

describes his most ambitious work, *Process and Reality,* as an attempt to transform the thought of James and of Dewey into a philosophical system.[14] The later Santayana influenced his thinking in significant ways.

Whitehead's thought dealt with questions that have fascinated American thinkers since the eighteenth century. He transformed "experience" into a metaphysical category. He offered an account of the anatomy of feeling that avoids the pitfalls of philosophical dualism. Like Jonathan Edwards, William James, Francis Ellingwood Abbott, and C.S. Peirce, he attempted to wed religion and science. His philosophy of organism systematized themes present in the work of Emerson, Abbott, and Royce.[15]

A dialectical analysis of the issues that have preoccupied North American thinkers discloses six recurring themes that have shaped the philosophical tradition in this country and which taken collectively yield a distinctively North American way of perceiving the human condition.

(1) North American philosophy rooted itself in European and derived from it initially many categories; but speculation in this country quickly came into conflict with the dualistic cast of much European thinking. Dualism conceives two interrelated realities in such a way that their relationship to one another loses its intelligibility.

Already in the eighteenth century, Jonathan Edwards's phenomenology of religious experience resisted the attempt of his theological critics and adversaries to divide the faculties of the soul into lower, sensible powers distinct from and opposed to the higher, spiritual powers of intellect and will. Edwards depicted the will as the highest expression of human affectivity. Early in the nineteenth century Orestes Brownson denounced dualism as the chief bane of Christian thought. Later in the same century C.S. Peirce launched an all-out speculative attack on the spirit of Cartesianism together with the multiple dualisms

---

[14] Alfred North Whitehead, *Process and Reality: Corrected Edition,* ed. by David Ray Griffin and Donald W. Sherburne (New York: Macmillan, 1978) xii. Hereafter this edition will be abbreviated PR.

[15] William Christian, *An Interpretation of Whitehead's Metaphysics* (New Haven: Yale, 1959); Nathaniel Lawrence, *Whitehead's Philosophical Development* (New York: Greenwood, 1968); Ivor Leclerc, *The Relevance of Whitehead* (London: Macmillan, 1961) and *Whitehead's Metaphysics* (London: Macmillan, 1958); Victor Lowe, *Understanding Whitehead* (Baltimore: Johns Hopkins, 1962); William Palter, *Whitehead's Philosophy of Science* (Chicago: University of Chicago, 1960); Paul Arthur Schilpp, *The Philosophy of Alfred North Whitehead* (New York: Tudor, 1951); Delwin Brown, Ralph E. James, Jr., and Gene Reeves, eds., *Process Philosophy and Christian Thought* (Indianapolis; Bobbs Merrill, 1971); Ewert H. Cousins, *Process Theology: Basic Writings* (New York: Newman, 1971); Jack R. Sibley and Peter A. Gunter, *Process Philosophy: Basic Writings* (Washington: University Press of America, 1978); John R. Cobb and David Ray Griffen, *Process Theology: An Introductory Exposition* (Philadelphia: Westminster, 1976).

that mar that particular philosophical system. The writings of Abbot, Dewey, and Whitehead offered a relational account of reality that sought to replace dualistic constructs of the real with a more or less systematic philosophy of organism.

A persistent resistance to dualism in any form—whether individualism, subjectivism, substantial or operational dualism—typifies, then, a Yankee perception of the real. Instead North American thinkers on the whole tend to conceive reality in organic, relational terms that insert developing human persons solidly into their environments. American thinkers tend to resist language that suggests the hierarchical superiority of spiritual to material powers. They prefer to focus on the continuities that shape reality while thinking in relational categories that attempt to do justice to both the continuities and discontinuities of human experience.

(2) One also discovers in American philosophers a tendency to question the speculative utility of the category "substance." Although their polemic focused primarily on John Locke's philosophy of substance, dissatisfaction with the language of substance eventually produced some suggestive attempts to forge alternative language systems for understanding the dynamic structure of the real. Chauncey Wright dismissed the category "substance" as scientifically useless. James criticized it as pragmatically meaningless. Whitehead attempted to replace it with the category "experience."

(3) Moreover, as the North American philosophical tradition developed one discovers there a growing preoccupation with the dynamic structure of experience as well as a growing tendency to invoke the category of "experience" in order to unify speculative perceptions of reality as a whole. Edwards in his *Treatise Concerning Religious Affections* anatomized the experience of Christian conversion. The American Transcendentalists explored the realm of intuitive experience. William James's philosophical psychology probed the varieties of human and religious experience. Josiah Royce explored the sources of religious insight and the conditions for the possibility of a conscious, communal experience. John Dewey's philosophy examined the esthetic, rational, and moral dimensions of human experience. In the process philosophpy of Alfred North Whitehead "experience" achieved the status of a transcendental category: Whitehead's reformed subjectivist principle taught that any reality may be conceived as a concrete instance of experience.

(4) From the time of Jonathan Edwards on American thinkers have tended to assimilate religious and esthetic experience. Edwards understood religious conversion as cordial consent to the divine beauty incarnate in Jesus and in people who resemble him. Emerson assimilated religious experience to artistic and poetic creativity. In his article "A

Neglected Argument for the Reality of God," Peirce discovered the lure of beauty as the chief motive for initial religious assent. Royce held that religious loyalty engages the affections and binds them to a cause that makes absolute moral claims. Even the atheistic naturalism of Dewey and Santayana portrayed the religious dimensions of experience as esthetically enhancing. In Whitehead's philosophy of organism not only is the growth of experience esthetically conceived but God functions also as the lure for feeling and as the ultimate source of creative novelty.

(5) American thinkers from Emerson on tended to resist the speculative attempt to portray human reason as virtually infinite. Instead they insisted on the finite, dialogic character of all human thought. At the height of his Transcendental optimism Emerson believed that each individual has access within subjectivity to infinite, divine creative energy, but the mature Emerson depicted the individual mind as a thoroughly finite bias toward a specific kind of creativity. James, Peirce, and Dewey all professed a "contrite fallibilism" in their account of human thinking. Moreover, Peirce's fallibilism led him to insist more strongly than James on the social, dialogic character of human symbolic activity. Royce, who began his philosophical career obsessed with the fallilbility and finitude of individual human experience, eventually developed Peirce's social construct of inquiry into a theory about the conditions for the possibility of shared, communal awareness.

(6) A North American account of the growth of human experience manifests a concern for consequences. Edwards looked to Christian practice as the ultimate test of the authenticity of any alleged conversion. His concern with practice foreshadowed the pragmatic cast of American logic. Peirce formulated the pragmatic maxim, which equates the meaning of an idea with its predictable practical effects. James used Emerson's polemic against retrospective thinking to elaborate a brand of pragmatism that looked away from first things, principles, and categories toward last things, fruits, consequences, the future. Concern with consequences motivated John Dewey's instrumentalism. Even Royce's idealism took on a pragmatic tinge in his attempt to portray every idea as driving toward concrete embodiment in action; but Royce also manifested more concern than any other North American thinker to counterbalance a pragmatic orientation to the future with a systematic retrieval of the past.

Anyone therefore who perceives the human condition with Yankee eyes will gravitate toward an organic, relational construct of experience as a fruitful way of understanding reality as a whole. Anyone with a Yankee mind-set will avoid dualistic categories, will eschew substance philosophy for a philosophy of experience, and will tend to assimilate religious experience to esthetic. A convinced fallibilist, one concerned to think as a North American will insist on the finitude and dialogic character of all human thought and will counterbalance a future-oriented concern for consequences with the systematic retrieval of the past.

(II)

We have then reason to believe that a dialectical analysis of the American philosophical tradition could indeed yield important insights into the experience of conversion and that it offers significant resources for engaging in inculturated foundational thinking. Nevertheless before using Lonergan's method to inculturate theology, we must deal critically with an important speculative claim which the method itself makes. The method claims to rest on a transcultural epistemological foundation. By means of what he calls "transcendental method," Lonergan claims to have reached an insight into the human mind itself, to have grasped an unchanging transcultural dynamism of the human spirit which lies at the basis of every cultural achievement. Hence, Lonergan's method presupposes that the human mind produces culture but is not produced by it.

Lonergan defines method as "a normative pattern of recurrent and related operations yielding cumulative and progressive results" (MT, 4). Transcendental method studies the pattern of operations normative for any human act of thinking. It objectifies the data of consciousness, i.e., those acts which ought to structure any human attempt to experience, understand, judge, and decide about any reality (MT, 13–20).

At this point we need to distinguish two kinds of normative thinking. Contemporary philosophy tends to blur somewhat the classical distinction between "is" and "ought" propositions. To grasp what a thing "is" one must understand how it "ought" to behave; for we understand what a thing is when we have reached a verified insight into the laws that allow us to predict what it will or will not do. In this sense, an "is" proposition, when it explains reality, yields a normative insight into the thinker's world.

Normative thinking, however, takes on a different character when I reach an insight into how I myself ought to behave. I bear no personal responsibility for the consequences of the actions of realities other than myself, but I do stand accountable for the consequences of my own decisions. Insight into personal behavior involves, then, more than the normative grasp of reality present in explanatory thinking. It attempts to measure the predictable effects of human choices against criteria personally acknowledged as morally, religiously, intellectually, or emotionally binding. In the future I shall call this second use of the term "normative" "strictly normative."

Both explanatory and strictly normative thinking can attempt universal generalizations. I can predict that a particular chemical or element will always behave in a specific way; or I can prescribe responsible behavior for every human. In any matter of complexity, however, both kinds of generalizations labor under the constraints of human fallibility; for in dealing with complex questions, I must hazard my generalization without any certitude that I have taken into account all the pertinent data. As a consequence, in complex, problematic situations one can never rule out the possibility that new data will emerge that will force the revision of earlier hypotheses, of the frame of reference in which they were formulated, or of both.

As a consequence, in its attempt to deal with complex problems of explanation, the human mind must rest content with working hypotheses. Hypotheses work when they allow us to resolve problematic situations by predicting accurately the course of events in ways that allow us to direct them to some desired goal or satisfaction. In dealing with complex behavioral problems, the human mind must rest content with working norms for responsible behavior. Behavioral norms work when they promote healthy emotional growth, the validation of beliefs, mutual concern and mutual respect for rights and duties in social intercourse, and progressive transformation in religious hope, faith, and love.

Lonergan recognizes the fallible, tentative character of explanatory hypotheses. Nevertheless, I have come to believe that his account of strictly normative thinking creates inflated claims for transcendental method. Transcendental method, as Lonergan describes it, seeks through critical reflection on the structure of human intentionality to discover norms for sound speculative, moral, and religious development. Transcendental method, however, claims much more than the discovery of a set of working norms for human thought. It claims to have uncovered *unrevisable* norms for thinking that disclose universal transcultural cognitive dynamisms (MT, 15–25). In other words, not only does Lonergan exempt his methodological hypotheses from the kind of fallibility that attends scientific generalizations, but he also uses transcendental method to hazard an explanatory generalization about the nature of the human mind as such, namely, that it transcends culture.

In his search for unrevisable methodological norms of thinking Lonergan attempts laudibly enough to avoid philosophical relativism. He is searching for a solid rock on which to construct a speculative edifice, one that resists the erosion of doubt (MT, 19). He concedes that his normative account of the unrevisable basis of all human speculation can be reached through the self-correcting process of learning. He also concedes that once reached, this unrevisable foundation can always be rendered with "a greater exactitude and a greater fulness of detail." He does exclude, however, "the radical revision that involves a shift in the fundamental terms and relations of the explanatory account of the human knowledge underlying existing common sense, mathematics, and empirical science" (I, 335).

In what then does this invariant foundation of all knowing, this knowledge "underlying" other forms of knowing, consist? It consists in the fact that the "cognitional process falls on the three levels of presentation, intelligence, and reflection." In other words, "underlying" every human attempt to understand lies the invariant pattern: experience, understanding, judgment, decision. This pattern *understood in the "fundamental terms and relations" which Lonergan uses to describe them* allegedly provides all thinking with its unalterable presuppositions, even though the unrevisable presuppositions of all thought justify the endless revision of empirical (or explanatory) hypotheses (I, 336). Lonergan states his fundamental argument for unrevisability clearly and succinctly in *Method:*

> . . . at the root of all method there has to be presupposed a level of operations on which we evaluate and choose responsibly at least the method of our operations.
>
> It follows that there is a sense in which the objectification of the normative pattern of our conscious and intentional operations does not admit of revision. The sense in question is that the activity of revising consists in such operations in accord with such a pattern, so that a revision rejecting the pattern would be rejected itself.
>
> There is then a rock on which one can build. But let me repeat the precise character of the rock. . . . The rock . . . is the subject in his conscious, unobjectified attentiveness, intelligence, reasonableness, responsibility (MT, 19–20).

The "rock" also includes the subject in an experience of religious self-transcendence (MT, 19, note 5, 101ff).

Moreover, with the aid of transcendental method, Lonergan draws some important conclusions concerning the contours of this rock. The fact that the normative pattern of operations which "underlies" all human thought culminates in a judgment discloses to transcendental method the essential orientation of every human mind toward Being. Lonergan describes judgment as an inferential act, as the grasp of the "virtually unconditioned." By that he means that in every judgment the mind grasps some conditioned reality, the link between the conditioned reality and its conditions, and the fulfillment of those conditions. In Lonergan's theory of knowledge Being is grasped as such only in true judgments. Moreover, the infinity of Being entails that the mind spontaneously oriented to It of its nature enjoys an "unrestricted desire to know." A thirst for infinite Being, the human mind also enjoys a virtual infinity (I, 271–316, 348–364).

Anyone who concedes the legitimacy of Lonergan's overall definition of method must of course also concede the necessity of reflecting on
the operations that structure human cognition. Such a concession, however, simply asserts the tautology that one cannot reflect on the mind's
operations without reflecting on the mind's operations.

One may, however, concede Lonergan's overall approach to method
without simultaneously conceding the unrevisability of his explanation
of "the fundamental terms and relations" that govern the human search
for a true account of reality. That explanation labors under the same
kind of fallibility as any other strictly normative hypothesis.

In point of fact, anyone can legitimately challenge Lonergan's account of the normative pattern of operations that allegedly "underlies"
all human cognition and can do so without contradiction, as long as one
does not repeat the cognitive operations Lonergan describes *in the precise
terms in which he describes them.* One will achieve this allegedly impossible
feat by the simple expedient of offering a more accurate account of
human cognition than Lonergan's own and by exemplifying it in one's
own thought processes.

In the chapters that follow I will suggest that Lonergan's account of
the terms and relations that govern thinking needs revision at several
critical points. More specifically, I will argue in Chapter II that the North
American philosophical tradition offers a more adequate understanding
of the term "experience" than the one Lonergan proposes. In chapters
III and IV I shall attempt to prove that such a redefinition of experience
not only forces a contrasting account of affective, intuitive awareness
from the one Lonergan proposes but also revises Lonergan's theory of
judgment. I shall argue more specifically that in addition to the inferential judgments which Lonergan describes in his theory of knowledge the
human mind also grasps reality in non-rational judgments of feeling that
require coordination with rational, inferential judgments. In Chapter V,
I will attempt to demonstrate the inability of intentionality analysis alone
to generate an adequate theory of method; for any theory of method
which rests on intentionality analysis alone fails to take into adequate
account the need of any method to supplement the analysis of intentionality with situational analyses.

For the moment it suffices to reflect on two important points. (1)
Transcendental method lacks the resources to demonstrate the unrevisability of any theoretical account of human cognition. (2) No human
attempt to interpret reality transcends culture. Let us examine each of
these points in order.

Those cognitive operations which Lonergan describes as an act of
"understanding" can and should be separated into two inferential moments. In the first, the mind formulates an hypothesis (sometimes called
an abduction); in the second it predicts deductively the abduction's
consequences.

Every human hypothesis is derived from a finite and therefore fallible survey of data taken as relevant to a question of interest. The data comes to be recognized as relevant in the process of classification. In abductive argumentation initial classification rests on principles assumed to be true. All such assumptions are, however, open to subsequent question and revision. They remain in a word fallible.

Moreover, the abductive formulation of an hypothesis terminates the initial amassing of data. In human attempts to resolve problems of any complexity, initial data gathering must then be terminated before one can certify its completeness. For the human mind, being finite in every way, has limited time and resources available for the investigation of any complicated question. Unavoidably then, in technical inquiries of any complexity every initial hypothesis could well be based on insufficient evidence.

Darwin's formulation of evolutionary theory illustrates how abductive thinking proceeds. When Darwin embarked on the *Beagle* he did not set out initially to formulate evolutionary theory. He was charged with gathering data about biological species around the world. The more data he gathered the more dissatisfied he became with the accepted explanations of how they had originated. He began to suspect that they had evolved through natural selection; but he delayed for years publishing his hypothesis because he did not believe he had sufficient facts to prove his case definitively. Nor did he have sufficient data when he published.

Deductive thinking predicts factual consequences of a fallible hypothesis, consequences not in immediate evidence. Deduction seeks to prepare the inductive testing of the assumed principles that ground an abductive classification of gathered data. Deductive inference argues that if an abductive inference holds, then the things it has classified in a particular way will behave in the same way as other members of that class. Their failure to do so calls into question the legitimacy of their initial abductive classification. Successful prediction has the opposite logical effect. It suggests that the assumptions which grounded an abduction enjoy validity.

Inductive inference seeks to verify or falsify deductive predictions. Inductive inference corresponds to what Lonergan calls the moment of judgment. When predicted consequences occur, inductive argument infers that the rule or principle which allowed their prediction obtains in reality. When predicted consequences fail to occur, induction draws the opposite conclusion.

Once again evolutionary theory illustrates how the inferring mind functions in its deductive and inductive moments. Having hypothesized that natural selection explains the origin of species, Darwin spent years amassing further data in support of his case. He did so on the assumption that if his hypothesis held true, other species than those he had examined aboard the *Beagle* would show evidence of evolutionary development. As other scientists subsequently subjected his theory to scrutiny, however, they began to question whether natural selection alone adequately explains evolution. Some believed that cataclysms could inaugurate new evolutionary developments. Even to this day scientists question the verifiability of Darwin's theories.

Induction like abduction remains fallible. Other facts than the ones I take inductively into account may turn up, facts which may call into question both my initial hypothesis and my present inductive conclusions. Moreover, every inference occurs within a frame of reference. In a question of any complexity, another mind may well construct a frame of reference more adequate than the one in which I am accustomed to think. When that happens, my inductive conclusions will stand in need of logical revision.

Transcendental method attempts at one and the same time to construct a strictly normative hypothesis about how human beings ought to think and to offer an explanatory generalization about the universal, *a priori* structure of "the human mind itself." Both hypotheses rest in part upon Lonergan's personal reflection on his own thought processes. They also rest on an attempt to survey how the mind works in mathematics, science, common sense, philosophy, and theology.

In point of fact Lonergan conducted a finite survey of human cognition. It dealt almost exclusively with abstract, inferential forms of knowing. It considered only cursorily intuitive, artistic and mythic insight. As a consequence, it underestimated and undervalued the mind's capacity to grasp reality through feeling and through image.

Moreover, Lonergan's theories also give evidence of cultural conditioning. The kinds of epistemological issues that preoccupied him arose from Roman Catholic attempts to wrestle with post-Kantian European philosophy and with the historical residue of the Enlightenment in a church in which every theologian and philosopher was (until Vatican II) expected to think like a Thomist. Like Joseph Marechal, S.J., whose thought influenced his own, Lonergan concerned himself primarily with philosophical issues raised by the first Kantian critique and only secondarily with *The Critique of Practical Reason*. He virtually ignored *The Critique of Judgment*.

In principle, a culturally conditioned hypothesis about the way the human mind functions, a hypothesis formulated on the basis of a finite survey of the kind of rational thinking that goes on in the industrialized nations, might or might not enjoy validity. Even if true, however, transcendental method as Lonergan practices it lacks the wherewithal to settle the matter one way or the other, because for all practical purposes, it arrests inquiry at the abductive stage of inference. While trancendental method recognizes the need to clarify deductively and verify inductively all explanatory hypotheses about "the data of sense," in dealing with "the data of consciousness" it eschews systematic verification or falsification and rests content with inviting others to reflect on their own thought processes in order to see whether or not those processes advance in the ways that Lonergan says they do. A positive answer joins one to the ranks of faithful disciples. A negative answer signals the end of any further discussion of the dynamics of human cognition.

The same impasse does not, however, occur when critical reflection on human thought processes is balanced by experimental studies of the way people actually think. Then the validity of one's epistemological generalizations can be tested systematically against the evidence supplied by human cognitive behavior.

Moreover, not only do experimental studies of human cognition disclose the existence of cognitive acts which Lonergan either ignores or undervalues; they also call into question any attempt to project trans-cultural cognitive dynamisms into human thought processes.

Transcendental method discovers at the basis of culture a spon-taneous orientation of the mind towards Being. Lonergan calls it "the unrestricted desire to know." The assertion that such a drive exists in every human being needs validation in human cognitive behavior. Un-fortunately, however, one can more easily discover a spontaneous resist-ance to truth in human cognitive acts than an unrelenting drive to grasp the real. Experimental studies of human consciousness establish its spon-taneous egocentrism and finitude. Its interests begin limited and remain limited. Far from tending to explore the unknowable endlessly, most people prefer to live within the familiar. The questions we raise arise not from the pure love of truth, but from limited personal interests. We resist, sometimes violently, any challenge to our presuppositions or biases. Indeed, egocentrism and ego inertia would seem to pervade human cognitive impulses far more than Lonergan's unrestricted desire to know. Even culivated minds enjoy at best only restricted speculative interests. Their window on the world, their cognitive "horizon," remains irreducibly finite and specific.

More specifically, experimental studies of human consciousness show that for almost two years the human mind cannot think beyond the things it senses. It lacks the capacity to imagine a world. When that capacity emerges, it does not bring with it the ability to reason abstractly. That ability emerges only around eleven years of age. In other words, judged by its ability to operate, the human mind can be said to possess only a finite, if potentially expandable, "horizon."

Moreover, as the conscious ego matures, it becomes increasingly focused on one or other realm of experience: sensation, intuitive imag-ination, imageless feelings, or abstract thought. Once again, radical finitude rather than virtual infinity characterizes its operation.

In addition, the conscious ego stands stretched between its limited capacity to think and understand and its unconscious fears and anxieties. The latter severely circumscribe the mind's capacity to deal realistically with its world. This failure plus the fallibility of its hypotheses and inductive judgments make the mind's dynamic orientation toward the real partial, haphazard, variable, and conditioned, not universal and uniform. The only cognitive dynamisms we can verify in human behavior correspond to habitual patterns of evaluation which the mind has acquired in the course of its finite history.

Finally, the postulation of fixed, essential dynamisms in the human mind fails to do justice to its evolving, historical, linguistically conditioned character. If this or that mind experiences a speculative orientation toward being as such, one may be sure it has enjoyed the metaphypsical education of a Lonergan. If it aspires to God, it has acquired the habit of faith through contact with religiously significant persons and events.

In other words, to the claim of transcendental method that every human mind experiences an essential orientation toward Being that transforms it into an unrestricted desire to know, we can on the basis of the evidence furnished by human behavior at best only respond: "not proven." At worst we must confess that the hard evidence points in a different direction. Moreover, any account of religious experience that postulates (as Lonergan's does) universal *a priori* tendencies as the ground of human religiosity, labors under a similar criticism.[16]

---

[16] The empirical evidence provided by the developmental psychology of Jean Piaget supports the interpretation of the human psyche here suggested. The child's earliest thinking remains sense bound. After eighteen months children engage in "transductive," irrational thinking governed by image, affect, and free association. Not until eleven does the capacity for abstract thinking emerge. In other words, the human cognitive horizon begins finite. It can be expanded, however, and in healthy minds actually expands. If one claims that the advance of childish thought from sensory motor to transductive to abstract thinking expresses the innate drive of the reasoning intellect toward Being, one must also explain why we lack operational evidence for asserting the existence of any such drive prior to the age of eleven. One must also explain why it is that the intellectual drives people manifest in their behavior give every evidence of having been learned. Moreover, Piaget's studies of children indicate that childish thought is initially spontaneously and innocently egocentric. Cf. John H. Flavell, *The Developmental Psychology of Jean Piaget* (New York: Van Nostramb, 1963); Hans G. Firth, *Piaget and Knowledge* (Englewood Dliffs: Prentice Hall, 1969).

Although the ego-centrism of childish thought patterns is diminished through socialization, the fact that conscious thinking remains rooted in unconscious processes makes ego inertia inevitable. Threatening insights are resisted, suppressed, or avoided. Inevitably, the resistance to new understanding leaves the mind's horizon limited and circumscribed. Clinical psychology offers ample evidence of the power of ego inertia as well. Cf. Donald L. Gelpi, *Experiencing God: A Theology of Human Emergence* (New York: Paulist, 1978); Gordon Allport, *The Nature of Prejudice* (New York: Doubleday, 1958). Jungian personality theory

Nevertheless, can we not name elements in human experience that transcend culture? In a sense we can. Humans have similar needs: the need to survive and to maintain a supportable mode of existence. Wherever human beings exist, they depend on some kind of environment and upon one another. They enjoy at birth the potential to learn, to create, and to use symbols as well as some capacity for development in behavior modification. They experience consciousness and self-awareness, finitude, and egocentrism. Still, these common constants in human experience would be better characterized as pre-cultural rather than transcultural, since they precede human symbolic behavior in ways that the cognitive dynamisms Lonergan describes do not.

Symbolic behavior defines the realm of culture. As a consequence, every concrete development of human intelligence transpires *within culture*. The human mind begins to undergo linguistic conditioning from the neonate's first experience of human speech; and speech shapes understanding. The emerging mind acquires through education a supply of traditional beliefs and attitudes before it develops through further education a limited capacity to modify them creatively and critically. When creative modifications occur, they may or may not advance culture; but they never transcend it. In other words, nothing in the human mind's symbolic response to the infra-cultural variables that shape experience can be characterized as transcultural. Culture creates each human mind as much as the mind transforms culture.

Not even the existence of international cultural organizations establishes the presence of transcultural cognitive drives within the human psyche. International organizations exemplify a certain kind of culture. Membership presupposes its own form of acculturation. Even the human ability to communicate within limits across cultures is most probably explained by the common infracultural variables that shape experience. Because humans share common generic needs and the same generic means to fulfill them, they can with effort begin to understand how and why people in different cultures go about things in the way that they do; but they must grope their way painfully to such insights. Only

---

hypothesizes that as the conscious ego consolidates itself, it becomes increasingly focused and circumscribed in attitudes of introversion and extraversion and in one or another of four dominant psychological functions: sensation, intuition, thinking, and feeling. C.G. Jung, *Psychological Types* (Princeton: Princeton University Press, 1974). The Myers-Briggs test has provided some empirical validation of his theory.

In other words if we eschew the *a priori* argumentation of transcendental method and prefer to judge the human mind by the way it acts and develops, we are led by the evidence to assert the finitude rather than the virtual infinity of the mind. Since the virtual infinity of the mind is inferred from its *a priori* orientation toward Being, its finitude calls into question as well the existence of any such drive.

through prolonged exposure to another way of life can an individual acquire even a working mastery of its presuppositions.

Only one personal intelligence can claim to transcend human culture: God's. For only the divine intellect completely transcends space and time. The evidence furnished by human behavior suggests, however, that every finite, developing, spatio-temporal mind not only creates culture but derives all of its powers of symbolic interpretation from cultural intercourse.

If, however, the reality of God transcends culture, must we not also recognize within religious aspiration a transcultural dimension? Here we need to distinguish natural attempts of the human mind to assert or demonstrate the existence of God and religious faith. Natural proofs of God's reality, when they occur, are formulated in complete abstraction from God's historical self-revelation. The response of faith consents to some historical, revelatory self-communication of God on the terms God has set.

Natural proofs of God's existence, when and if they are formulated, transpire within the limits of ego consciousness. They engage self-reliant habits of thought and communication formed in abstraction from divine revelation. Those habits are acquired through dynamic interaction with the world and with the persons and things that inhabit it. They express human hope and belief in the reality of some ultimate cause, unifying principle, or cosmic source of intelligibility. They may or may not culminate in commitment to that reality. When they do, that commitment expresses rational self-reliance rather than the experience of self-transcendence in authentic religious faith. Because they express an interpretation of reality constructed by a finite, natural ego relying on its naturally acquired powers of evaluation and communication, such proofs may aspire, albeit self-reliantly, after a reality that transcends space, time, and culture; but they transpire within culture. They may challenge, advance, or subvert a culture; but as self-reliant creations of the finite, natural mind they do not transcend culture.

Faith responds to some concrete, historical act of divine revelatory self-communication. In touching the individual believer either directly or through the instrumentality of others, God enters efficaciously into some human experience, becomes initially a part of it, transmutes it, and thus creates within it the capacity to respond in ways that transcend natural ego processes. We experience the divine touch in moments when we sense that we stand in a receptive relationship to a Reality that transcends ourselves and our world even as it invites our consent. We experience the invitation to Christian faith when we encounter that Reality in Jesus and in people who resemble Him because they have already submitted in faith to the God historically revealed in Him and in

His Holy Breath. The consent of faith establishes an initial, habitual, finite openness to a self-revealing, self-communicating God. That openness needs nourishing through prayer that expands receptivity to the Holy Breath's illumination.

As faith grows, it acquires an enhanced capacity to transform and re-evaluate the believer's natural and sinful tendencies. Faith changes the human character. It reorganizes it by ordering its habitual responses toward the transcendent reality of God. As the process of transvaluation advances, faith dependence on God heals egocentric self-reliance and centers the believer's life more and more in God. In other words, through the action of grace human experience draws its life and vitality increasingly from the world-transcending reality of a self-communicating God. The graced heart yearns increasingly for total transformation of its finite longings in the infinite ocean of the divine.

The categories we use to interpret the graced encounter with God in faith and its transforming consequences, however, engage culturally conditioned habits of interpretation and communication. Any image or concept we apply to God emerges from a particular cultural matrix and reflects that matrix. When we apply such images and concepts to the God encountered in faith, we use them to describe a transcultural reality that exceeds them. As a consequence, when we approach God from within ego-consciousness we are forced to use any such culturally conditioned notions analogically, for they both express and do not express the divine reality to which they refer. Moreover, as faith deepens into mystical union, the mystic senses with increasing keenness the inability of any concept or image to encompass or express the reality of God.

We spoke earlier of mere natural attempts to prove the existence of God as cultural events untouched by the transcendence of faith. Often, however, rational approaches to God spring from religious faith more or less directly. Some arguments for God's existence collapse under close scrutiny because, while posing as purely rational proofs, they actually express a tacit faith commitment masquerading as pure reason. Such arguments share of course the same cultural conditioning as creedal affirmations.

The experience of authentic religious transcendence offers us, then, no justification for positing any natural, transcultural, intellectual dynamisms that lie at the basis of human thought and culture. Nor have we any reason to posit within humans an unrestricted desire to know. Even the "horizon" of faith opens only a finite window on the transcendent reality of God, an expandable "horizon" to be sure but a finite one nevertheless. Humans may, of course, learn with pain to love the truth, even transcendent divine truth; but that habit must be acquired with difficulty and sustained with sacrifice. It results not from an inbuilt drive but from patient growth in knowledge or in faith.

Perhaps at this point we should summarize the results of the preceding suggestions. We began our reflections by noting the contemporary need for a theological method that would foster inculturated evangelization. We discovered that Lonergan's method aspires to do just that and that it gives initial promise of success. Nevertheless, our examination of Lonergan's attempt to establish a transcultural basis for human culture has led us to a number of conclusions that call into question some of the presuppositions that ground Lonergan's method. They include the following:

1. No epistemology can claim unrevisability in principle, including Lonergan's own.
2. One may revise an epistemological theory without self-contradiction provided one's revised theory of knowledge offers a more accurate interpretation of human thought processes than the theory it criticizes.
3. Any epistemology which aspires to deal with the issues raised by inculturation must offer an adequate interpretation not only of the abstract inferential thought processes that fascinate industrialized cultures, but also of the kind of intuitive, mythic thinking which enjoys an enhanced importance in preindustrial cultures. That Lonergan's method can do so without critical revision can legitimately be questioned.
4. Lonergan's transcendental method does not yield an insight into universal transcultural dynamisms of thought but only a set of fallible, working postulates about how humans ought to think inferentially.
5. Every explanatory interpretation of the human mind needs empirical verification in human cognitive behavior.
6. The human mind does not transcend culture. Rather minds are created by culture and can within limits modify culture.
7. A close observation of human cognitive activity suggests that finitude, ego inertia, and ego-centrism constitute more spontaneous human intellectual tendencies than any fictive "unrestricted desire to know."
8. Because symbolic behavior is transmitted culturally rather than genetically, all the identifiable dynamisms of the human intellect can be plausibly explained as the result of personal acculturation.
9. Only God completely transcends both history and culture.
10. While faith orients us consciously toward and roots us in the world-transcending reality of God, neither intuitive doctrinal expressions of faith nor rational statements about God, whether or not they are inspired by faith, transcend culture.

(III)

The preceding criticisms of Lonergan's epistemology need not, however, cause us to abandon his theory of method in general and of
theological method in particular. Indeed, one can argue that his very
conception of method forces such a critique. Lonergan, as we have seen,
defines "method" as "a normative pattern of recurrent and related operations yielding cumulative and progressive results." His approach to
method focuses upon cognitive operations, not upon theories about
them. The operations which structure a method ought to answer questions and solve problems. They ought to yield a cumulative grasp of
reality. Any theoretical account of those operations which blocks the path
of inquiry must be either revised or replaced. In other words, in an
operational approach to method, procedures and presuppositions justify
themselves pragmatically, by their ability to advance inquiry.

Moreover, one may justify the need for functional specialization
within theology without accepting the details of Lonergan's epistemology. Lonergan himself attempts somewhat artificially to establish a
rough correlation between his eight functional specialities and his theory
of the normative operations that ought to structure human cognition.
Nevertheless, the order of the functional specialities as he describes
them also corresponds to speculative exigencies within the theological
enterprise itself: the need to assemble, interpret, contextualize, and
evaluate theological data; the need to reformulate a religious tradition in
the light of a sound insight into the claims it makes upon the believers;
the need to reach a unified understanding of those claims; and the need
to translate the results of technical theological explanation into terms
that can be grasped by non-theologians.

Among the functional specialities foundational theology is specially
and legitimately charged with the critique of the presuppositions that lie
at the basis of theological method. Foundational theology discovers the
warrant for mounting such a critique in its own purpose. It seeks to
construct a normative theory of conversion. Unless foundational theology can deal with the presuppositions that motivate theological reflection, it cannot deal with the intellectual dimensions of conversion.

The ongoing, foundational critique of the presuppositions that motivate theological reflection ought to proceed in dialogue with the culture
which this or that foundational theologian seeks to address. Such criticism transpires as a religio-cultural event; for since religion too grows
through symbolic acts, it stands within human culture, neither opposed
to it nor outside it. Any dialogue between religion and culture should
then be characterized as a dialogue between the religious and secular
forces that shape a given culture. Moreover as the dialogue advances, we

may anticipate that it may well force the revision of Lonergan's culturally conditioned epistemology at more than one point.

One may, moreover, argue that without the systematic pursuit of foundational theology, no theology can ever achieve the ultimate purpose of inculturation: namely, the transforming Christianization of human culture. Inculturated evangelization demands much more than the translation of traditional symbols into their local cultural equivalents. It ambitions, as Pedro Arrupe correctly insists, that Christian faith animate, direct, and unify every culture from within. Theology will remain helpless to foster such evangelization until it reaches a sound insight into the practical exigencies of Christian conversion. To such an insight foundational theology aspires.

We have already seen that the American cultural tradition offers resources for formulating an inculturated theology of conversion. It also offers resources for expanding our understanding of the operations that ought to structure foundational thinking. In the chapters which follow we will attempt to tap those resources in order to correct and complete Lonergan's own innovative, ground-breaking description of the scope and function of foundational theology. We propose then an experiment in theological inculturation. If Lonergan's method can facilitate the dialogue between religious and secular culture, its systematic application to an understanding of foundational method itself in the light of the American cultural tradition ought to yield an inculturated instrument for constructing a theology of conversion that speaks to North American culture.

Let us clarify as far as possible the terms of our experiment. We propose to invoke Lonergan's method in order to reflect on the meaning of foundational method, its presuppositions, and operational procedures. We propose to do so in a North American cultural context. In the process we hope to put foundational method into dialogue with sources in the North American speculative tradition which Lonergan himself largely ignores. In this manner we will attempt to test whether Lonergan's method enjoys enough flexibility to correct and develop its own presuppositions and operational procedures. If so, the method will have established its preliminary validity. A successful experiment should also yield an insight into the procedures that will foster the pursuit of an inculturated North American theology of conversion.

Here we should recall that one cannot engage in critical reflection on foundational method without in some measure engaging in foundational thinking itself; for any strictly normative hypothesis about the procedures for pursuing an inculturated theology of conversion must coordinate those procedures with the very realities they attempt to understand: namely, the variables, the constants, and the dynamics of conversion itself. Our experiment proposes, therefore, more than just an academic discourse on method. It proposes to probe the human experience of conversion for the light it throws on the way in which theologians ought to appproach theorizing about it. Our experiment seeks, then, to answer the following question: what operations ought to generate a strictly normative account of conversion?

Chapter II

THE DYNAMICS OF PERSONAL CONVERSION

(I)

All thinking advances through self-criticism. Theology exempts itself from this rule only at its own peril. In the preceding chapter we began a critical inquiry into prospects for elaborating an inculturated North American theology. We noted that Bernard Lonergan's theological method aspires to inculturated theological thinking. That very claim, however, forced us to examine critically a further claim his method makes. It boasts of having identified a transcultural reality that gives rise to human culture. Lonergan calls that reality "the human mind itself" and describes it as "an unrestricted desire to know," as an insatiable cognitive appetite for Being. One is supposed to discover this dynamic, transcultural tendency within oneself by a reflective process called transcendental method, which investigates the data of consciousness rather than the data of sense.

We found reason to question the operational adequacy of transcendental method and its characterization of the human mind. Its practitioners face a fundamental speculative option. They must either concede or deny that human consciousness can be investigated not only through personal reflection on one's own thought processes but also through experimental methods that test theories about the human capacity to think against human cognitive behavior. If they deny the possibility of such investigation, they close their eyes to the very existence of experimental psychology. If they admit the legitimacy of experimental studies of human consciousness, then they must further concede that those studies call into question Lonergan's characterization of the human intellect as possessed of a virtually infinite horizon and as unrestricted in its desire to know. The neonate's horizon on the world suffers from an almost humorous egocentrism and lacks the ability to think either imaginatively or inferentially. This finite horizon expands through the processes of socialization and acculturation but never achieves the virtual infinity of Lonergan's "unrestricted desire." The mind's capacity to question, understand, and judge always labors under the constraints of the finite human ego's interests and skills. The fallibility of human thought processes reveals that the human mind's relation to Being, to reality, remains not only haphazard but emotionally and educationally conditioned.

Moreover, the fact that the human mind grows through symbolic interchange with other minds situates it within culture. It does not transcend culture; for culture, which emcompasses every deliberate symbolic act, creates the mind. That creation advances as a cultural event, as does any limited, creative transformation of symbolic behavior that any given mind can effect.

This discrepancy between Lonergan's characterization of human cognition and the hard evidence furnished by experimental investigations of human cognitive behavior points to operational inconsistency and inadequacy within transcendental method itself. Transcendental method discovers within human cognition a normative pattern of operations that corresponds to experimental, hypothetico-deductive thinking, but it fails to apply systematically to the data of consciousness the very operations it recognizes as normative for human thought. Instead it rests content with inviting individuals to reflect on their own consciousness in order to discover whether their minds work in the same way that Lonergan says they do. Nevertheless, as William James noted almost a century ago, notorious fallibility attends any attempt to analyze one's own thought processes. Hence, theories with such a tenuous speculative foundation need to be tested against systematic studies of the way the psyche actually functions.

Moreover, we found that Lonergan's own hypothesis concerning the structure of conscious intentionality, despite its claims of having discovered a transcultural basis for theological method, manifests clear evidence of cultural and historical conditioning. First formulated in the days when Roman Catholics were forced to think in Thomistic categories, it acquiesces tacitly in some of the assumptions of medieval faculty psychology. Among these assumptions one must name the belief that stable, essential dynamisms impervious to historical influence lie at the basis of human behavior and that the human intellect enjoys an essential orientation to Being. The first belief confounds the structure of reality with the way in which we perceive it. Essences exist, of course; but they do not function as dynamic principles of Being. Rather they are simply human conceptions abstracted from the realities the mind senses and perceives and from the self who does the perceiving and sensing. Moreover, the fallibility of abductive and inductive thinking effectively subverts any philosophical attempt to portray human judgments as a privileged grasp of Being.

In other words, the culturally conditioned scholastic origins of Lonergan's epistemology combine with his endorsement of transcendental method in order to invalidate important facets of his account of human cognition. These realizations forced us to conclude that despite his claims to the contrary, Lonergan has failed to provide an unrevisable starting point for human inquiry. We shall return to this point in another context. In a later chapter we shall attempt to show that the turn to the subject demanded by transcendental method does not do full justice to the transactional character of human knowing.

Despite these negative conclusions concerning the epistemological presuppositions that underlie Lonergan's theory of method, we nevertheless found reason to hope that his overall conception of method as well as his theory of functional theological specialties might still provide means for pursuing an inculturated North American theology. By focusing on the operations that lend dynamic structure to theological thinking, Lonergan's theory of method invites critique of the epistemological presuppositions on which it rests. Moreover by charging theology with the task of mediating between the religious and secular elements within a given culture, Lonergan's method also invites a critique of its own operations, a critique that advances in dialogue with a specific cultural tradition.

In the present chapter we will attempt to begin to lay the foundations of a North American theology by reflecting on the dynamics of personal conversion. We will try to derive from that reflection new insights into the specific operations that ought to structure foundational theology, insights that go beyond Lonergan's own cryptic account of foundational procedures. Moreover, since we ambition a method that engages North American culture, our argument will advance in dialogue with North American thinkers whose reflections address the kinds of methodological issues that confront us.

Our argument advances in four stages. First, we will attempt briefly to clarify the meaning and implications of the term "conversion." Second, we will contrast Lonergan's understanding of the term "experience" with another suggested by the North American philosophical tradition. Third, we will suggest that the latter conception of experience offers a fruitful context for understanding the dynamics of conversion. Fourth, we will attempt to reflect on the operational consequences entailed by substituting our own construct of experience for Lonergan's and by the insights into the dynamics of conversion that flow from that substitution.

(II)

We first need to clarify the meaning of the term "conversion." Lonergan characterizes a conversion as a decision that creates a horizon. Lonergan means by "horizon" the kind of interpretative frame of reference which results from the attempt to engage in critical self-understanding. He correctly regards such thinking as normative in ways that an explanatory account of one's world are not. He contrasts a cognitive horizon with a cognitive perspective. The latter orients one, not toward reflective self-appropriation, but toward a cognitive grasp of one's world (MT, 103, 131, 189, 192, 216–219, 235–236, 250).

Unfortunately, other thinkers besides Lonergan have used the term "horizon." In existential philosophy and theology a horizon of knowing can never be grasped as such. Only things within the horizon can. Because a horizon resists verbalization, it is associated with the idea of absolute mystery. As a consequence, one finds a tendency in existential theology to speak of an infinite God as the horizon of human experience and to characterize that horizon as both virtually infinite and absolutely mysterious.

We have already found reason to question the virtual infinity of the human intellect; but further difficulties attend the existential attempt to describe the horizon of the intellect as an orientation toward an infinite and absolutely mysterious God. Paul Tillich has stated the problem most clearly. He has argued that an infinite and absolutely mysterious God who functions as the horizon of human aspiration can never be revealed in space and time; for spatio-temporal symbols lie within a horizon they can never grasp or express. As a consequence, Tillich's God cannot become incarnate or be historically revealed as triune.[1] In other words, not only does the term "horizon" connote an unverifiable conception of the human mind, but it also implies a conception of God which contradicts the historical revelation we have actually received. For both these reasons I prefer to avoid the term "horizon." "Frame of reference" offers a neutral enough substitute.

At the level of inferential thinking, we should distinguish three kinds of frame of reference: "descriptive," "explanatory," and "strictly normative." Descriptive frames of reference characterize the way in which things appear prior to explanation or strictly normative insight. An explanatory frame of reference attempts to formulate an applicable and adequate causal account of one's world. A strictly normative frame of reference evaluates self-critically human behavior against norms personally appropriated as binding.

Every conversion establishes a strictly normative frame of reference. We have defined conversion as the decision to assume responsibility for one's subsequent development in some area of one's own experience. Let us also postulate four distinguishable moments in personal conversion corresponding to distinguishable realms of experience. Affectivity, speculation, moral deliberation, and religious faith engage different kinds of responsive habits, or laws. Because we can decide to assume respon-

---

[1] Paul Tillich, *Systematic Theology* (Chicago: University of Chicago Press, 1967) I, 63–289, 141; II, 97–180; III, 283–294.

sibility for one set of habits and ignore another, we can experience conversion in one or more of these four experiential realms but not necessarily in another. Absence of conversion in any realm of experience breeds inauthenticity. By inauthenticity I mean the performance of irresponsible acts that contradict one's professed intention to act responsibly.

Let us therefore define affective conversion as the decision to assume personal responsibility for one's subsequent emotional development, intellectual conversion as the decision to assume personal responsibility for one's subsequent speculative development, moral conversion as the decision to assume personal responsibility for the motives and consequences of one's subsequent decisions, and religious conversion as the decision to assume personal responsibility for one's response in faith to God's historical self-communication.

We can also distinguish initial and ongoing conversion. In initial conversion one first opts for a life marked by personal accountability in some realm of experience. In ongoing conversion one faces and acknowledges the consequences of that initial option. Finally, let us postulate that an insight into the meaning and consequences of conversion engages strictly normative thinking.

(III)

Ever since the days of Jonathan Edwards, American thinkers have shown a fascination with the structure of experience. Moreover as the American philosophical tradition advanced, some of its creators began to use the term "experience" in ways which contrast with Lonergan's own usage.[2]

In *Insight* Lonergan allows for a broad sense of "experience" which lets one speak of an experience of intellectual understanding and rational judgment. Nevertheless, in his own technical use of the term Lonergan consistently opposes "experience" to both "understanding" and to "judgment," and implicitly to "decision." For Lonergan "experience" in the strict sense designates the most elementary form of knowing. We experience a reality only as long as we fail to ask ourselves about its meaning or fail to pass judgment on the interpretations of it which the mind suggests. At one point he asserts, for example, that the verification or falsification of an hypothesis cannot be experienced, presumably if we use "experience" in the narrow sense. Moreover, even when we broaden the term "experience" to include an experience of the data of con-

---

[2] For a fuller discussion of this matter see Donald L. Gelpi, S.J., *Experiencing God A Theology of Human Emergence* (New York: Paulist, 1978). Hereafter this work will be abbreviated EG.

sciousness and therefore of acts of understanding and of judgment, we are justified in so doing only if the conscious acts in question have never been described, distinguished, compared, or related (I, 361, 272, 393).

Because experience supposedly precedes the abstract insight born of understanding, Lonergan describes it as concrete. Its content consists of what we observe, of whatever is presented to us to be understood and judged. It includes concrete images and utterances (I, 273–274, 331, 342, 357, 371). The realm of experience is therefore equated with the realm of "empirical consciousness." Empirical consciousness enjoys a primitive kind of differentiation, like the concrete difference between seeing, hearing, and imagining. Even memory moves beyond experience into the realm of understanding by offering an interpretation of experience.

The later Lonergan shows more sensitivity to the diversity and complexity of human experience. In *Method in Theology,* for example, he discriminates more explicitly between personal experience and reported experience. His new fascination with conversion causes him to approach even God in experiential rather than in abstract metaphypsical terms (MT, 41, 105–106, 109, 112–114, 119, 177, 242). He recognizes an historical dimension to experience (MT, 105–106, 117). In *Insight* he describes experience as "ineluctably private" (I, 215); but in *Method* he insists that the intimate, personal character of experience does not deprive it of a social dimension (MT, 118).

Still, despite his new openness to the complexity of experience, the Lonergan of *Method* reiterates the technical understanding of "experience" he elaborated in *Insight.* Knowledge moves in a linear progression from experience to understanding, from understanding to judgment, and from judgment to decision (MT, 106–181). Each new stage in the growth of cognitive differentiation sublates the preceding.[3] One can speak of an experience of understanding and of judgment, but only on the condition that the understanding and judgment remain unreflective, uncritical (MT, 8, 14–15). As soon as we attempt to question experience it ceases to be experience. It becomes instead first understanding and then

---

[3] Robert Doran, S.J. has grasped this point clearly: See Robert Doran, S.J. *Subject and Psyche: Ricoeur, Jung, and the Search for Foundations* (Washington, D.C.: University Press of America, 1977); *Psychic Conversion and Theological Foundations: Toward a Reorientation of the Human Sciences* (Chico, CA: Scholars Press, 1981). I approach affective conversion somewhat differently from Doran. He accepts transcendental method and the unrevisability of the terms and relations of human cognition as Lonergan describes them. He therefore interprets psychic conversion as an extension of intellectual conversion into the unconscious in such a way as to bring disordered emotions to therapeutic healing and thus transform them into experiential matter fit to be sublated into a judgment of value. His theory of psychic conversion expands Lonergan's position creatively but dramatizes to my thinking the inability of Lonergan's epistemology to deal adequately with appreciative forms of knowing.

judgment. The world of experience remains, therefore, the world of the given as given. It has nothing to do with the given as interpreted and judged (MT, 9, 76, 104, 106).

The writings of John Dewey and of Alfred North Whitehead offer hints of an understanding of experience that differs from Lonergan's. Dewey speaks of both artistic activity and logical insight as forms of experience. For Dewey every human cognitive response provides an instance of experience. Dewey, however, in contrast to Whitehead opposes the reality that is experienced to experience itself. Whitehead, inspired in part by the work of Dewey, extends the term experience to include experienced realities as well. He thus transforms "experience" into a transcendental category in which all reality divides into what is experienced and the way experienced reality is experienced. Transcendental categories apply in intent to any reality whatever.[4]

The construct of experience invoked in these pages, however, draws not only on the thought of Whitehead and of Dewey but broadly on the American philosophical tradition as a whole. With Dewey it discovers within experience a felt, qualitative unity grounded in an experiencer's perception of reality. Those perceptions grow through an ongoing transaction with one's world, a transaction punctuated by achieved satisfaction and the search for satisfaction. Experience grows therefore through the alternation of activity and receptivity. We interact not only with persons and things but with symbol systems used as instruments for understanding both. Symbol systems help us to shape our situation, to change and control our world. We perceive ourselves and our world both affectively and appreciatively on the one hand and rationally and inferentially on the other. Indeed, we may discover within experience a continuum of evaluative responses stretching from sensation to imageless feelings to remembered and imaginative responses to description to inference. We express our affective, intuitive perceptions in art and literature, in prophecy, in esthetic and prudential judgments, in judgments of discernment. We express our inferential perceptions of things in logical propositions.

Our construct of experience also draws on the thought of Charles Sanders Peirce in order to render Dewey's descriptive account of experience more terminologically precise. With Peirce we distinguish within experience three interrelated realms. The entire spectrum of human evaluative responses defines what I call the realm of Quality. Decisive action, reaction, and collaboration define the realm of Fact. I call the tendencies that shape experience the realm of Law. When a tendency, or

[4] John Dewey, *Experience and Nature* (New York: Dover, 1958) 3A; Alfred North Whitehead, *Process and Reality*, edited by David Ray Griffin and Donald W. Sherburne (New York: Free Press, 1978) 157–167.

law, functions autonomously I call it a self. If in its autonomous functioning it manifests susceptibility to conversion, I call it a human person.

While the construct of experience I defend endorses largely without
qualification Dewey's analysis of esthetic experience, it replaces much of
his propositional logic with Peirce's logic of inference. Moreover, I
qualify Dewey's account of experience in other ways as well. I embellish
his esthetic theory with insights from Emerson. Because in a religious
encounter with a self-revealing God, we experience the supernatural in
ways that Dewey overlooks, I replace his naturalistic account of the
religious dimensions of experience with the kind of experiential approach to supernatural faith which one discovers in the writings of
Jonathan Edwards and Orestes Brownson. I draw on William James and
other psychologists to describe the psychodynamics of religious experience. I invoke the religious philosophy of Josiah Royce to describe the
experience of shared faith consciousness. I derive my philosophy of
essence from the later Santayana.

If one accepts the construct of experience I am proposing, any
attempt to understand oneself and one's world or to make judgments
and decisions with regard to both modifies the way one experiences
reality. In such an understanding of experience, all reality, as Whitehead
saw, can indeed be divided into two realms: what is experienced and the
way what is experienced is experienced.

Moreover, in an experiential theory of knowledge every evaluative
response endows experience with presentational immediacy. I have borrowed the term "presentational immediacy" from Alfred North Whitehead, but I use it in a slightly different sense from his. Such
terminological piracy may dismay strict Whiteheadians. It can, however,
be justified in any developing cultural tradition. The term as I use it
describes two important functions which evaluative responses perform
within experience. First, evaluative responses enable one to become
present to oneself and to one's world. Second, evaluation grounds one's
experience of the present moment. The reality to which I am present
sensibly, affectively, or inferentially may eventually display traits that call
into question either the truth or adequacy of my evaluative response to
it. In that case the way I am present to it should be appropriately
modified (EG, 80–83).

With Whitehead I also conceive experience in both relational and
esthetic terms. That is to say, every element within experience consists of
a feeling of some sort. Every feeling consists of some kind of relationship. In contrast to Whitehead, however, I would want to distinguish
three fundamental kinds of feeling rather than the two of which he
speaks. We experience conceptual relationships among affections, images, and ideas, factual relationships in moments of decisive interaction
and collaboration with other selves, and habitual relationships or tend-

encies which constitute and structure each developing self and orient it toward its future. These habitual tendencies I call laws.

The introduction of a novel feeling into a developing experience changes its felt constitutive structure, much as the addition of a new patch of color changes the felt, esthetic character of a painting. For a new relational element has been integrated into the pattern of the whole thereby changing the totality of its constitutive relationships.

How then does this modified conception of experience affect our understanding of the dynamics of conversion?

(IV)

The relational, esthetic model for experience which I have just proposed, in which every feeling transmutes every other by changing the felt, relational structure of experience itself demands that the different moments within a conversion experience be conceived as simultaneously transvaluing and transmuting one another. As we shall see, a novel feeling transmutes experience when its introduction into experience forces a readjustment of the way in which the feelings that already constitute the experience relate to one another. An experience undergoes transvaluation when a sensation, feeling, image, or concept is introduced into a novel frame of reference that endows it with new meaning. Let us begin to reflect in more detail on how this occurs. Let us do so in dialogue with the North American speculative tradition.

When one form of conversion conditions another, it introduces a dynamic into the total process of conversion. I discover five identifiable dynamics within personal conversion. (1) Religious conversion mediates between affective and moral conversion. (2) Intellectual conversion seeks to inform affective, moral, and religious conversion. (3) Religious conversion graciously transvalues affective, intellectual, and moral conversion. (4) Moral Conversion orients affective and intellectual conversion practically to realities and values that make absolute and ultimate claims. (5) Affective conversion animates intellectual, moral, and religious conversion.

(1) *Religious conversion mediates between affective and moral conversion.* American thinkers since the time of Jonathan Edwards have repeatedly insisted on the importance of affectivity within religious forms of knowing. That insistence has also helped motivate their assimilation of esthetic and religious experience. Attention to the dynamic structure of religious experience suggests the soundness of both tendencies. Christian assent to God resembles the assent to beauty more than anything else. It does not, as Vatican I correctly insisted, result from argumentation or human reason (DS 3041). It expresses a leap of a heart confronted with the beauty of God's revelatory self-communication to us in Jesus and the

Holy Breath. Edwards also correctly insisted that "Christian practice" provides the most basic test of the authenticity of religious aspiration. In other words, within the total experience of Christian conversion, religious conversion ought ideally to mediate between affective and moral conversion.[5] It begins in repentant confrontation with one's own disordered affectivity and ends in practical consent to those religious realities and values which endow Christian morality with absoluteness and ultimacy. By the moral absoluteness of a reality or value, I mean the ethical need to affirm it in every circumstance. By its moral ultimacy I mean the willingness not only to live but, if necessary, to die for it (EG 259–323). One form of conversion mediates between two others when it sets them in a relationship they would not otherwise enjoy.

(2) *Intellectual conversion seeks to inform affective, religious, and moral conversion.* Peirce's theory of the normative sciences suggests a second important dynamic within personal conversion. Peirce recognized three normative sciences: esthetics, ethics, and logic. Esthetics he defined as the science of the *summum bonum.* It studies the kinds of habits one must form in order to be able to respond affectively to supreme beauty and excellence. Ethics studies the kinds of habits one must form so that one can order one's choices to supremely beautiful and valuable ends. Logic studies the kinds of evaluative habits one must form in order to think correctly about reality and about the choices one must make concerning it.[6]

For Peirce, then, the normative sciences all study the habitual patterns that ought to shape one's own growth processes. Strictly normative thinking engages in self criticism. One may then argue that the pursuit of what Peirce calls esthetics presupposes affective conversion. The pursuit of what he calls ethics presupposes moral conversion. The pursuit of what he calls logic presupposes intellectual, or cognitive, conversion; for Peirce meant by "logic" pretty much what Lonergan means by "method": namely, self-critical insight into the kinds of habitual mental operations that advance thought. We shall return to this point in Chapter V.

The relevance of Peirce's theory of the normative sciences to a theology of conversion becomes more obvious when one reads it in the light of his Neglected Argument for the Reality of God. In the Neglected Argument, Peirce like Edwards before him acknowledged the esthetic character of initial religious assent. We consent initially to God, he argued, because the beauty of the divine exercises a spontaneous attraction over the musing, healthy mind. Religious assent, however, fixes a

[5] Jonathan Edwards, *A Treatise Concerning Religious Affections,* edited by John E. Smith (New Haven: Yale, 1959).

[6] See Vincent Potter, S.J. *Charles S. Peirce on Norms and Ideals* (Worcester: University of Massachusetts, 1967), 452–493.

number of basic beliefs about the nature of the *summum bonum*. Ethics then orders concrete choices to the supreme good religiously conceived, while logic attempts to inform every human effort to think about religion, affectivity, choice, or thought itself by providing them with sound operational procedures. If, however, the pursuit of logic in Peirce's sense of that term presupposes intellectual conversion, then we have identified a second dynamic within the conversion process: namely, intellectual conversion seeks to inform affective, religious, and moral conversion by providing sound logical and methodological principles for judging their authenticity.[7]

(3)*Religious conversion transvalues affective, speculative, and moral conversion.* In speaking of the development of experience Whitehead frequently uses the term "transmutation." He speaks of different feelings transmuting one another. As used here, the term "transmutation" has a specific meaning. An experience is transmuted when: (a) It develops in continuity with a preceding experience but (b) incorporates within itself one or more novel elements (c) that are then integrated into its relational structure in such a way that the resulting new experience constitutes a more or less successful unity.

For example, every new decision transmutes experience in some way; for it creates a new habit, re-enforces an old one, interrelates previously independent habits of action, or dissociates previously interrelated habits. The pianist who learns a new piece or practices an old one emerges from the exercise a better pianist. The child who first inserts its thumb into its mouth by that act coordinates its sucking instinct with its ability to control physical movement in a way that produces long hours of subsequent pleasure. Such decisive acts emerge from a matrix of feeling which they express. They therefore stand in vital continuity with earlier experiences. Once taken they not only endow experience with new concreteness but also change in some way habitual patterns of behavior. They therefore transmute experience.

The term "transmutation" implies another: "transvaluation." An experience undergoes transvaluation when it is conceptually transmuted in a particular manner. More specifically, an experience is transvalued (a) when the frame of reference in which a concept, image, or affection had functioned is replaced by a different frame of reference and (b) when the same affection, image, or concept is employed in the novel frame of reference in such a way that (i) some of its former meaning is preserved (ii) despite the fact that its use in a new frame of reference endows the former affection, image, or concept with new denotative, connotative, or inferential meaning.

[7] C.S. Peirce, *Collected Papers,* edited by Charles Hartshorne and Paul Weiss (8 vols.; Cambridge: Harvard, 1931–1958), 6.452–467.

For example, humans once believed that the earth is flat. That belief created a context for understanding the hazards of human travel: presumably, one could sail off the edge of a flat earth. Once explorers like Columbus and Magellan established the earth's roundness, the term "earth" acquired new and important theoretical and practical connotations, even though it continued to mean the hard surface of the planet on which we live. In other words, the term "earth" underwent an important transvaluation.

Three other terms need clarification before our argument can advance: namely, "nature", "grace", and "sin." Many contemporary theologians resist speaking about nature apart from grace. They reject the concept "pure nature" as a scholastic abstraction. The fact remains, however, that we experience a realm of nature that gives no evidence of having been touched by grace.

Faith divides the realm of grace from the realm of nature. Animals, plants, rocks, minerals, elements give no evidence of religious consciousness or of the capacity to respond in faith to God. In a world of developing experiences, decisions derive their character from the conscious and unconscious evaluative responses they terminate even as they specify the habits to which they give rise. Natural reactions or responses prescind from faith in God's historical self-communication in Jesus and the Holy Breath. A graced response by contrast is informed by faith in some historical act of divine self-communication which creates possibilities of collaboration between the divine and the human that transcend mere natural activity. Natural decisions create natural habits, graced decisions create graced habits. Sinful habits by contrast presuppose God consciousness, for they contridict in some way the divine will.

The commitment of faith creates a strictly normative frame of reference which purely natural evaluations, decisions, and habits ignore. Those who take responsibility for their faith experience an initial religious conversion. Religious conversion offers, then, a context for relating to God, to one's world, and to oneself, one which transforms and enhances merely natural human responses. As a consequence, religious conversion enjoys the capacity to transvalue natural human experiences.

One may, for example, achieve a measure of self-knowledge simply by reflecting on the way one responds to other persons and things; but that self-understanding takes on new significance once one acknowledges in faith one's call to live as a child of God in the image of Jesus and in the empowering enlightenment of His Breath.

Three forms of conversion—affective, intellectual, and moral—can and sometimes do occur naturally. The pain of neurotic conflict can force one to seek professional help in facing one's disordered affectivity and in the process provoke an affective conversion untouched by the values or realities disclosed to faith. The experience of error and deception can convince one of the importance of monitoring both the truth of one's beliefs and the processes of thought that lead to truth; but such a decision can occur in abstraction from God's self-revelation in Jesus and the Breath. Rage at human dishonesty and injustice may motivate the decision to grow in morally responsible patterns of behavior; but that decision too can be taken only in response to created values.

Because affective, intellectual, and moral conversion can occur naturally, they too can undergo transvaluation in faith. Religious conversion transforms natural affective conversion into graced repentance before God and sound emotional development into Christian hope. We have traditionally called the ongoing healing of emotional disorders in faith the dark night of the senses. It differs from mere therapy in the way that faith healing differs from swallowing a medicine.

Religious conversion transvalues speculative conversion by demanding that growth in critical self-understanding and in an understanding of one's world advance under the guiding illumination both of the Word of God spoken to us in Jesus and of the charismatic anointing of the Holy Breath. When study submits to the light of revelation, it is transformed charismatically into the divine wisdom once prized by the Hebrew wise men.

Religious conversion transvalues moral conversion when revealed realities and values inform the human conscience. Religious conversion ensures that some of the moral absolutes and ultimates that guide ethically responsible decision making are faith derived. By thus conforming the values of the Christian convert to the mind of Christ, Christian conversion transforms charismatically the natural search for virtue into the cultivation of Christian charity.

(4)*Moral conversion helps to orient affective and intellectual conversion practically to realities and values that make absolute and ultimate ethical claims.* Every conversion is fathered by commitment. Every conversion engages evaluative response. Only those realities and values, however, make moral claims which enjoy absoluteness and ultimacy in the sense defined above. One can cultivate emotional health in abstraction from moral considerations. Indeed, many therapists rightly or wrongly fear that the introduction of moral discourse into the therapeutic process only muddies the waters. Nor need the search for truth serve moral ends. The scientific mind can just as easily create wonder drugs as plan a nuclear holocaust.

Nevertheless, the integrally converted individual resists compartmentalization. Conversion seeks integrity; and integrity results from an integrated evaluative response honest to reality. Moral conversion gives practical, decisive orientation to the human search for emotional health and for insight. It demands that the quest for both respect the rights and duties of others and submit to sound moral principles. In the process, it orients affective and intellectual conversion to realities and values that make absolute and ultimate moral claims.

When religious conversion transvalues moral conversion, it discloses new moral claims made by a self-revealing God. By reorienting the morally converted conscience to transcendent realities and values perceived in faith, religious conversion expands the moral criteria that shape decision to include those divinely revealed and re-orients the conscience to God.

(5) *Affective conversion animates intellectual, moral, and religious conversion.* Affective conversion inaugurates the responsible cultivation of healthy emotional development. We first perceive the things we sense affectively. The intellectual, moral, and religious judgments we subsequently make about them lend new conceptupal clarity to these early affective perceptions. The latter, however, endow the search for truth, goodness, and God with zest, enthusiasm, visionary hope, and discerning discrimination.

Affective conversion suffuses intellectual conversion with what Michael Polanyi has called heuristic passion. Most philosophers have by now abandoned the positivistic myth of value-free explanation as an illusory self-deception. We cannot escape the attitudes, assumptions, and beliefs we bring to every inquiry. Our evaluative biases can blind us. When we fear the truth, dislike what we study, or wallow in self-congratulatory complacency over the correctness of our every judgment, we set ourselves up for intellectual humiliation. On the other hand, when we mistrust our fallibility and love what we study enough to want to understand it truly, then passionate involvement with the subject under investigation galvanizes thought, stimulates the imagination, and seeds creative insight.

Similarly, affective conversion suffuses the search for moral integrity with prophetic fervor and wholehearted dedication. Moral decision making engages the heart as much as the head. Clarity concerning moral principles needs to be balanced by a prudential, discerning sense of the fitting; for, while we may argue the pros and cons of any ethical choice, in the concrete the judgment of conscience engages a felt sense of persons and situations.

Finally, as Jonanthan Edwards saw clearly, affections make up a great part of religion. Sorrow, joy, hope, enthusiasm, love suffuse religious piety with transforming fervor. Religion within the bounds of reason alone wins no converts. It generates as much enthusiasm as yesterday's oatmeal. When affective conversion unleashes the wellsprings of religious devotion, it animates religious conversion from within.

(V)

Before we begin to reflect on the methodological implications of the preceding account of the dynamics of conversion, let us summarize the present chapter's argument up to this point. We began by suggesting that the American philosophical tradition points to a different interpretation of experience from Lonergan's. Lonergan equates experience with concrete, "empirical" awareness and suggests that understanding sublates and replaces experience as the mind moves toward judgment and decision. American philosophy suggests a more comprehensive use of the term. John Dewey regarded every evaluative response as a kind of experience. And A.N. Whitehead transformed experience into a transcendental term universally applicable in intent by including in experience not only evaluative responses but the realities evaluated.

Following hints from Dewey and Whitehead, we then offered a construct of experience which portrays it in esthetic, relational terms. We suggested that in every evaluative response we become present in some way to ourselves and to our world. We defined the term conversion and noted that every conversion creates a strictly normative frame of reference. We postulated four kinds of personal conversion: affective, intellectual, and moral conversion each corresponds to identifiable moments in the growth of human experience and can transpire naturally, but religious conversion responds to an historical divine act of self-communication and therefore always transpires graciously.

We noted that our construct for experience invited a specific conception of the dynamics of conversion. Our esthetic, relational model for experience suggested by contrast that the four forms of conversion mutually and simultaneously condition one another. Drawing on insights present in the thought of Jonanthan Edwards, William James, C.S. Peirce, and Michael Polanyi, we were able to identify five normative dynamics within the experience of Christian conversion. First, Christian conversion ought to mediate between affective, religious, and moral conversion. Second, intellectual conversion ought to inform affective, religious, and moral conversion. Third, religious conversion ought to transvalue the other three forms of conversion whenever they transpire naturally. Fourth, moral conversion ought to orient affective and intellectual conversion practically to realities and values that make absolute and ultimate moral claims. Fifth, affective conversion ought to animate intellectual, moral, and religious conversion.

What operational consequences for foundational method flow from these insights? Two problems face us. First, we must explicitate the methodological consequences of redefining the term "experience" in the way that we have and of using it as a transcendental category. Second, we must reflect on the ways in which the dynamics of conversion implied by that redefinition color foundational method.

In *Method in Theology*, Lonergan argues for the need for three nests of foundational categories: transcendentals, general categories, and special categories. We shall further probe the implications of that suggestion in Chapter VI. At present we are concerned only with the operational consequences that flow from using the term "experience" as a transcendental category. We shall once again find that the philosophies of both Whitehead and Peirce help us explicitate those consequences.

Whiteheadian philosophy ambitions a logical, coherent, applicable, and adequate theory of reality. A logical theory suffers from no internal contradiction. A coherent theory uses categories which so imply one another that they cannot be understood in isolation from one another. An applicable theory can interpret some realities. An adequate theory will encounter no realities it cannot interpret (PR, 3–17).

Moreover, as we have seen, in Whiteheadian philosophy every reality is conceived as an instance of experience. Whitehead makes the point most explicitly in the enunciation of his reformed subjectivist principle. The principle states that "apart from experiences of subjects there is nothing, nothing, nothing, bare nothingness" (PR, 167).

Like Whitehead I use the term "experience" transcendentally, although I define it differently from him. The equation of reality and experience invites a rethinking of the traditional transcendental predications: being, one, true, good, and beautiful. Classical philosophy tacitly equates being with the immutable. Since the other transcendentals specify "Being" they must be similarly conceived. In a world of experiences, however, things enjoy reality to the extent that they are in process. Hence, when "Being" is defined as "experience," all the transcendentals must be redefined as instances of becoming. As a result, unity, truth, goodness, and beauty cease to be static metaphysical givens and become instead practical problems, ideals to be achieved and sustained from one moment to the next. In discussing goodness, I must show how experience becomes valuable. In discussing truth, I must show how to validate insights into the developing structure of the real.

The foundational elaboration of a generalized theory of experience ought, moreover, to begin by a descriptive recovery of its many protean transformations; for unless one has retrieved phenomenologically the different facets and transmutations which experience undergoes, one's generalizations about the way it ought to develop risk deficiency. A descriptive elaboration of the term "experience" must answer the question: what generic variables structure experience? Moreover, any descriptive account of experience, ought like Whitehead's to aspire to logical consistency, coherence, applicability, and adequacy.

A phenomenology of an experience of conversion must also deal with a second, related question: When does experience take on a religious character? In other words, in the interests of applicability and adequacy, one needs to elaborate a descriptive account of the kinds of variables that make an experience a religious one.

The transition from descriptive to strictly normative foundational thinking will occur spontaneously when foundational theory attempts to answer a third related question: when does religious experience take on a Christian (Jewish, Hindu, Buddhist, Muslim, etc.) character? Insight into an authenticating religious experience provides the norms for converted religious behavior.

A normative exploration of the dynamics of natural affective, intellectual, and moral conversion would engage the sciences of esthetics, ethics, and logic in Peirce's sense of those terms. In Peirce's division of the sciences, these disciplines flow from phenomenology. The rules set down by the normative sciences for sound affective, moral, and intellectual development would need to be justified pragmatically: by their ability to promote healthy emotional integration, morally responsible decisions, and clear thinking about any topic.

Religious conversion, however, transmutes merely natural conversion. Hence, in addition to offering an account of natural conversion, any adequate foundational theory must also show the practical ways in which religious conversion transmutes and transvalues natural conversion. Moreover, the attempt to deal with the realities encountered within religious conversion, (namely, God, oneself, and the world), inevitably raises metaphysical questions.

In other words, the spontaneous movement of thought in foundational thinking ought to parallel the movement of Peirce's philosophical sciences. Moreover, the entire foundational enterprise can be conceived in the manner of Whitehead as the attempt to elaborate a theory of conversion that enjoys logical consistency, coherence, applicability, and adequacy.

Finally, foundational method would also be well advised to take a methodological page from the work of William Ernest Hocking. Hocking studied under Josiah Royce and team-taught at Harvard with Whitehead. Like Whitehead he believed in the speculative importance of theories of the whole, theories that seek to integrate experience by elaborating categories that seek to interpret any reality whatever. He realized that without such an integrating and integrated vision of the whole, the evaluative shape of experience risks becoming fragmented, eclectic, inconsistent, even self-contradictory. Moreover, like Whitehead he regarded every theory of the whole as no more than a fallible hypothesis; but unlike Whitehead he sought to guard against theoretical oversights in the formulation of such a theory by invoking what he called the principle of alternation. When applied as a speculative principle, alteration demands that thought oscillate between one's idea of the whole and the resolution of more detailed and focused speculative questions.[8] The insights gleaned from more minute investigations ought to provide the conclusions that test the applicability and adequacy of one's theory of

---

[8] William Ernest Hocking, *The Meaning of God in Human Experience* (New Haven: Yale, 1963) 405–527.

the whole; and one's theory of the whole ought to suggest new detailed examinations of this or that aspect of reality.

Whiteheadian method can be said to incorporate Hocking's principle tacitly to the extent that Whitehead's theory of the whole remains open to revision; but Whitehead's theory did not invoke the principle of alternation in its initial elaboration. When implemented within an experiential approach to foundational theory, the principle of alternation would sanction the successive investigation of each of the following questions: How ought the integrally converted individual to understand the human subject of conversion? How ought the integrally converted individual to understand the experience of worship? How ought the integrally converted individual to understand the reality of the God who is encountered in worship? How ought the integrally converted individual to understand the reality of the worshipping community? How ought the integrally converted individual to understand any other reality encountered within conversion? The order of these questions moves from immediate, personal experiences to mediated, more remote ones. As the work of foundational thinking progresses, insights gleaned from the investigation of each question could be used to correct and expand one's theory of experience in general. In other words, one's descriptive account of experience would provide foundational theology with an integrating theory of the whole. Moreover, as each inquiry was completed, it would throw new light on different facets of experience and suggest possible modifications of one's descriptive categories. Those modifications might suggest further detailed foundational explorations of the normative structure of a conversion experience.

(VI)

We have reflected on some of the operational consequences of using "experience" as a transcendental foundational category. A second task remains. We must begin to examine the operational procedures that flow from the dynamics of the conversion experience itself. The dynamics of conversion pose a series of difficult problems for foundational speculation.

The fact that religious conversion mediates between affective and moral conversion demands that foundational theory unmask the inadequacy of any account of the human conscience which fails to invoke religious values; for these values help endow human experience with moral absoluteness and ultimacy. It demands too that foundational theology take into adequate account the best insights of the personality sciences into sound emotional development. Finally, it demands that the foundational theologian elaborate adequate procedures for reaching moral decisions in the light of divine revelation.

The fact that intellectual conversion seeks to inform the other three kinds of conversion demands that all the normative sciences, including foundational theory, submit to sound logical and methodological principles. That fact also calls into question any theory including a theological one which seeks to exempt itself from deductive clarification and inductive verification. The data which tests religious hypotheses is, of course, supplied by the historical events in which God communicates Himself to human beings in faith.

The fact, however, that religious conversion transvalues the other three forms of personal conversion when these transpire naturally demands that foundational theology offer two normative accounts of affective, intellectual, and moral conversion. The first account should discuss how sound emotional, speculative, and moral growth transpires in abstraction from religious values and realities. The second should show how religious conversion transmutes and transvalues those same growth processes by providing them with a context that allows them to advance in faith. More specifically, a foundational theory of religious conversion must explain how one achieves emotional healing and integration in faith, how faith, imagination, and reason mutually condition one another, and how religious ideals enter into the formation of conscience.

The fact that moral conversion orients affective and intellectual conversion to realities and values that make absolute and ultimate moral claims means that no strictly normative account of human affective and intellectual development can claim completeness which abstracts from moral considerations. Not that morality provides the criteria for emotional health or sound speculative procedures. Rather any strictly normative judgment which blinds itself to the moral consequences of therapeutic techniques and specific speculative investigations must be rejected as foundationally inadequate.

The fact that affective conversion animates moral, intellectual, and religious conversion means that any foundational hypothesis must take into account the ways in which feeling and intuition condition thought, decision, and religious belief and practice. In the two chapters which follow we will begin to investigate this enormously complex question for the light it throws on the procedures of foundational theology.[9]

[9] Let me close by comparing and contrasting the approach to personal conversion which I have just suggested with the approach proposed by Walter Conn in his recent book *Christian Conversion* (New York: Paulist, 1986). The two approaches both resemble one another and differ at significant points. Professor Conn and I both recognize four kinds of personal conversion: affective, intellectual (or cognitive), moral and religious. We have both drawn on categories supplied by developmental and clinical psychology in order to amplify insight into the conditions for and consequences of initial conversion in each of these four realms of human experience. Professor Conn, however, acquiesces more systematically than I in the presuppositions of Bernard Lonergan's theory of knowledge. He

therefore tends to find the cognitive stages of human growth described by developmentalists an illustration of Lonergan's "unrestricted desire to know."

My own approach to conversion suggests, however, a second use of the results of experimental and clinical psychology. Drawing on insights from the fallibilistic logic of C.S. Peirce, I have suggested that in addition to using results of experimental and clinical psychology in order to amplify one's understanding of the different forms of conversion, one can also use them to call into question aspects of Lonergan's theory of knowledge, including his belief in the unrestricted desire to know.

In addition, I have invoked an understanding of experience at variance with Lonergan's. Building on this alternative understanding of experience, I have suggested the need not only to explain how each kind of conversion develops but also to explore the dynamics of conversion: viz. the ways in which the different kinds of conversion mutually condition one another. To date Professor Conn has not addressed himself to this question in any systematic way.

CHAPTER III:

CONCEPT AND IMAGE IN FOUNDATIONAL THINKING—I

We began these reflections by recalling the challenge issued to theologians by the second Vatican council to engage in inculturated theological thinking. Faced with the fact that much North American speculative theology, like North American oil, is imported, we cast about for a method that would allow us to create a theology that speaks with a contemporary Yankee idiom. Of all the going theoreticians of theological method, Bernard Lonergan has addressed the problem of theological inculturation most explicitly, for he defines the task of theology as the mediation between a religion and the culture in which that religion roots itself. Accordingly we proposed to test the adequacy of Lonergan's method to foster inculturated theological thinking.

We proposed an experiment. Any method worth its salt will, as John Dewey saw clearly, have the capacity to correct its own presuppositions. We therefore suggested putting Lonergan's theological method into dialogue with North American religious thought in order to see whether that cultural tradition contains insights that might embellish, expand, and correct the presuppositions that shape Lonergan's largely untested program for inculturating theology.

From the thought of James, Peirce, Dewey, Royce, and Whitehead, we derived a construct of experience that challenges Lonergan's own restricted use of this term and which demands that his own construct of conversion be expanded to include an affective moment. We also began to reflect on the ways in which that construct of experience allows one to describe the dynamics of conversion. Having done so, we began to examine some of the methodological consequences that flow from these revisions of Lonergan's epistemology. In the present chapter we will further expand these insights by attempting to answer the question that surfaced at the end of the last chapter: namely, what methodological consequences flow from the fact that within Christian conversion, affective conversion seeks to animate intellectual, moral, and religious conversion?

The argument of the present chapter and of the chapter which follows divides into five segments. For reasons that shall become apparent, we first contrast Lonergan's account of the cognitive grasp of being, of reality, with that proposed by Ralph Waldo Emerson. As we shall see, both espouse contrasting and revisable positions. Second, we will examine the reflections of process theologian Bernard E. Meland on theological method. Those reflections point the way toward reconciling an Emersonian with a Lonerganian theory of the cognitive grasp of being. Third, we will invoke Lonergan's understanding of method in order to expand Meland's position and render it more operationally precise. More specifically we will examine the operations that yield a felt, intuitive grasp of being. Fourth, we will contrast our own account of the role of affective, appreciative forms of knowing with that proposed by Lonergan; and we will argue for the greater adequacy of our own position. Fifth, on the basis of all these reflections we will draw some conclusions concerning the operational procedures of foundational theology. We will thus attempt to answer in a preliminary fashion the question which surfaced at the close of the preceding chapter: namely, what operational consequences for foundational theology flow from the fact that affective conversion ought ideally to animate intellectual, moral, and religious conversion? In the process of attempting to deal with that question we will, as we shall see, be forced to put Lonergan's method into dialogue with a significant contemporary movement in North American theology: namely, with narrative theology.

(I)

Ordinarily one would not think of Bernard Lonergan and Ralph Waldo Emerson as having anything to say to one another; but the systematic application of dialectical method to the interface between a religion and a culture sometimes produces unexpected confrontations. An early and influential spokesman for American Transcendentalism, Emerson elaborated in the course of his career a theory of intuition that contrasts with Lonergan's account of the cognitive grasp of being. How was that challenge issued?

Most critics look upon Emerson as a poet, litterateur, and miscellaneous essayist rather than as a coherent thinker. Nevertheless, Emerson did espouse a fairly consistent philosophical vision of the world. His understanding of religious intuition evolved over the years, but his later insights grew in organic continuity with his early religious beliefs. Moreover, a consistent method structures almost everything he wrote. He described it in one of his sermons and called it "spiritual discernment."

Under the tutelage of his crochety aunt Mary Moody Emerson, Ralph Waldo as a youth read the Enneads of Plotinus. His readings led him to espouse a modified neo-Platonic metaphysics which he never abandoned. In Plotinian metaphysics, the universe results from a series of emanations. From the One, the transcendent source of being, emerges the Intelligence, wherein dwell the eternal forms of things. Emerson called those forms spiritual laws. From the Intelligence emanates the World Soul; from the World Soul, particular souls and matter. Emerson collapsed the One, the Intelligence, and the World Soul into a single divine principle and called the resulting deity "the Over-Soul."[1] Like Plotinus he saw both the human self and the sensible universe as emanations from and participations in that divine reality. Moreover this metaphysical belief sanctioned his method of spiritual discernment.

Emersonian "discernment" uses description to explore human consciousness. Emerson like Plotinus believed that preoccupation with material sensible realities causes the soul to forget its essential unity with the divine but that the soul can through a process of description be led to recall its participation in the Over-Soul. Accordingly, Emersonian discernment begins with some concrete sensible fact and seeks through an elaborate interweaving of descriptive images to lead the reader to recognize intuitively that the fact in question participates in the same eternal, transcendent divine law as does the mind of the reader itself.[2]

Virtually all of Emerson's prose writings follow this descriptive pattern. "The Divinity School Address" illustrates the process. He delivered the address to the graduation class of the Harvard Divinity School on July 15, 1838. It begins with a somewhat florid description of the "refulgent summer" during which the graduation took place. That fact, the beauty and opulence of surrounding nature, then reveals itself through rhetorical expansion to express the eternal laws that rule the cosmos. Those laws are described as not only physical but moral in intent and religion, as their recognition. The sublimity of this universal moral vision is then invoked to criticize the narrowness of sectarian religion. Finally, the graduates of 1838 are invited to become self-reliant prophets of an Emersonian religion of nature rather than the servants of a particular sectarian denomination. Small wonder that the conservative Andrews Norton, a former professor of Harvard Divinity School, lashed out at the Address as "the latest form of infidelity."[3]

In his Unitarian sermons Emerson linked religious insight to the plodding cultivation of moral virtue; but Emerson the Transcendentalist located the human experience of the divine in the creative intuition of beauty. The Transcendental Emerson believed that scientific investigation can reach a true insight into the eternal laws of nature. Like a good Platonist he looked upon those laws rather than material, sensible things

[1] Ralph Waldo Emerson, *Complete Works* (Centenary Edition, 14 vols.; Boston: Houghton, Mifflin & Co., 1903–1904) II, 132–166, 267–291.

[2] Ralph Waldo Emerson, *Sermons*, Houghton (121).

[3] Emerson, *Complete Works*, I, 119–151.

as ultimately real; but he regarded the detached, dispassionate insight of science as cognitively inferior to the knowledge available to the poet and artist. Poets and artists, he insisted, grasp reality simultaneously with both head and heart, as not just true but as beautiful. They do so in a way that taps the creative power of the Over-Soul and that suffuses otherwise valueless, sensible facts with universal, spiritual meaning and significance. In other words the Transcendental Emerson exalted creative artistic and poetic intuition over inferential explanation and looked to the former rather than to the latter to yield a privileged insight into being.[4]

While Emerson's Platonic Transcendentalism cannot be defended as a system, his theory of intuition contrasts with Lonergan's account of the cognitive grasp of being. For Lonergan, the human mind grasps being inferentially. In Lonergan's theory of knowledge, the intellect establishes cognitive contact with reality through judgments. Judgments, as we have seen, grasp the virtually unconditioned. The virtually unconditioned is grasped when the mind encounters some conditioned reality, when its conditions are known, and when its known conditions are fulfilled (I, 280).

Lonergan defines "Being" as "the object of the pure desire to know." It encompasses all that is known and all that remains to be known *through true judgments*. An "all inclusive notion," Being underpins and penetrates all cognitional contents (I, 348–357).

> Experiencing is only the first level of knowing; it presents the matter to be known. Understanding is only the second level of knowing; it defines the matter to be known. Knowing reaches a complete increment only with judgment, only when the merely experienced has been thought and the merely thought has been affirmed. . . . Experience is for inquiring into being. Intelligence is for thinking out being. But by judgment being is known, and in judgment what is known is known as being (I, 357).

In other words "being as such" is grasped only in explanatory judgments, only in an inferential act which comprehends the virtually unconditioned (I, 353).

Lonergan's concern to locate the grasp of the real in an inference, as we shall see, leads him to undervalue imaginative forms of understanding. We shall examine his account of what Emerson calls intuitive insight in the pages which follow. Here it suffices to note that in Lonergan's epistemology intuitive insight never yields a grasp of being as such.

---

[4] *Ibid.*, I, 3–80; *The Early Lectures of Ralph Waldo Emerson*, edited by Robert E. Spiller and Wallace E. Williams (2 vols.; Cambridge, Mass.: Belknap, 1972), II, 22–82.

(II)

Both Lonergan and Emerson offer weighted theories of knowledge. Both ascribe to a particular form of cognition a privileged grasp of being. Emerson decries the cognitive claims of "linear logic" and insists that intuitive, mytho-poetic forms of thinking yield a privileged insight into reality. Lonergan, as we shall discover, dismisses mytho-poetic insights as allegorical and insists rather that we grasp the real finally in inferential judgments.

Experimental studies of human consciousness suggest a way out of this epistemological impasse. C. G. Jung has often been criticized for proposing psychological theories without empirical validation. Nevertheless, the Myers-Briggs test does offer some empirical support for Jungian personality theory. The test gives evidence that the attitudes and functions which Jung describes in his *Psychological Types* do in fact function in human ego development, even though they may function differently at different points in an individual's personal growth.

We need not at this point rehearse all the details of Jung's description of different psychological types. Suffice it to say that Jung discovers within the human psyche both inferential and intuitive thinging as well as two different kinds of judgment: judgments of thought and judgments of feeling. Both of these suggestions enjoy validity; and they throw light on the limitations of both Lonergan's and Emerson's accounts of the cognitive grasp of being. Anyone familiar with the corpus of Emerson's work will recognize that his mind gravitated toward imaginative, intuitive thinking. Many of his essays explicitate through "spiritual discernment" insights reached poetically. His discursive thinking advances rhetorically rather than logically. Because he grasped the real in intuitive judgments of feeling rather than logically, he insisted that Being, reality, is best grasped nonrationally through artistic and poetic insights and judgments.

Lonergan by contrast shows less appreciation for felt, intuitive forms of thinking. The mind, he insists, grasps Being inferentially. Clearly in Lonergan's case we are dealing with a mind biased toward inferential thought rather than to intuition, to reasoned judgments rather than to judgments of feeling.

In fact neither Lonergan's transcendental method nor Emerson's spiritual discernment possesses the wherewithal to overcome the oversights into which a biased, finite ego has betrayed both. Both of their epistemologies eschew any experimental exploration of consciousness beyond the personal thematization of one's own thought processes. Betrayed by the spontaneous egocentrism of the human mind, both thinkers end by over-generalizing personal preferences into theories about the nature of human cognition as such. In the 1830's Emerson like

Lonergan believed the human mind enjoys a kind of virtual infinity, although the mature Emerson eventually confessed the radical finitude of every individual genius. Still, he never quite realized that by endowing intuitive judgments of feeling with privileged access to being he had vested his personal ego bias with totalitarian claims. A similar complaint may be brought against Lonergan's definition of being as the inferential grasp of the virtually unconditioned.

No theory of knowledge that endows a particular ego bias with universal claims can do full justice to the varieties of human cognitive behavior. We need a more balanced account of human knowledge, one which does equal justice to rational and irrational perceptions of reality and to both felt and logical judgments. In the theology of Bernard Meland we find some important hints of ways to strike a balance between an intuitive and a logical grasp of the real.

(III)

As commentators on theological method Bernard E. Meland and Bernard Lonergan might seem at first glance to share nothing in common beyond their first names. Perhaps the most creative American process theologian, Meland speaks critically for the liberal Protestant tradition. A transcendental Thomist, Lonergan speaks for Roman Catholic orthodoxy. Meland approaches theological method retrospectively: he seeks to explicitate the presuppositions that have guided his own theological career. Lonergan approaches theological method programmatically. His method prescribes a largely untested formula for doing theology. Lonergan's method betrays a strong intellectualist bias that places a high premium on abstract, theoretical explanation and downplays artistic, mytho-poetic insight. Meland focuses on what he calls appreciative forms of understanding; his method seeks to restore mytho-poetic thinking to its rightful place within the liberal theological enterprise.

On closer analysis, however, the methods of Lonergan and Meland disclose surprising lines of convergence. Both acknowledge that any theology must establish a critical dialogue between a religion and a culture. Both recognize that the personal faith stance of individuals functions as a mediating principle within that dialogue. Both subordinate theology to faith. Both believe that critical reflection on the operational procedures of theology holds the key to progress in understanding theological method.

These lines of convergence suggest the possibility of a fruitful dialogue between these two theologians of method, a dialogue that could conceivably transform their differences into complementarities. As we shall see, Meland's insights into the dynamics of appreciative thinking do in fact suggest a more fruitful context for interpreting the religious significance of mytho-poetic understanding than Lonergan's derivative discussion of artistic and mythic awareness. At the same time, we shall also see that Lonergan's method contextualizes Meland's insights and can provide Meland with analytic tools which the latter largely ignores.

Several tasks confront us. We must first examine Meland's analysis of the relationship between myth and culture. We shall find that it offers suggestive resources for an expanded insight into the cognitive operations that shape conversion. We will then analyze Meland's discussion of theological method. We will argue that his theory of appreciative consciousness suggests leads for exploring affective conversion, particularly when the latter is viewed in the light of Lonergan's insights into the meaning of method.

Meland believes that we live more deeply than we think. That conviction lies at the heart of his observations on theological method. Meland discovers a mysterious depth dimension to experience in general and to religious experience in particular that eludes and even defies abstract rational analysis.[5] He suggests therefore that theology needs to invoke other kinds of thinking than abstract, analytic thought if it wants to give adequate voice to religious experience. Meland insists that since the Christian myth verbalizes a Christian experience of depth, liberal theology must either legitimate the Christian myth or confess its inability to deal with a fundamental aspect of Christian experience (FFS, 90, 176–182).

Meland's method distinguishes between "mythos," "myth," and "mythology." "Mythos" he describes convolutedly as:

> the pattern of meaning and valuation arising from within the structured experience of a people which has been imaginatively projected through drama or metaphor, expressing the perceptive truths of the historical experience of a people bearing on man's ultimate destiny as these perceptive truths of experience express themselves within culture as psychic energy in the form of hopes, expectations, attitudes of trust or apprehension, or even determination, or in the form of human responses to circumstances, joyous or tragic, promising or threatening and similar historical occurrences affecting the stance in meeting human situations. (FFS, 102).

Put more simply, mythos embodies and expresses any culturally mediated experience of depth. "Myth" for Meland forms an elemental ingredient within mythos, but it remains less durable and pervasive. "Myth" consists of every "spontaneous and innocent" response to what works

---

[5] Bernard Meland, *Fallible Forms and Symbols* (Philadelphia: Fortress Press, 1976), 42–46. Herafter this work will be abbreviated as FFS.

deeply in the life of a people. "Mythology" in contrast to "myth" offers a secondary level of imaginative reflection within the mythic mode and often carries with it specific didactic and speculative intentions. In other words "mythology" begins to transform myth into ideology. "Mythos" then encompasses and transcends both myth and mythology. It yields a broader, pre-cognitive, culturally mediated experience of depth (FFS, 102–103, 108, 112–113).

In Meland's method "logos" complements but never replaces "mythos." "Logos" constructs ontologies inferentially. It implies "the level of rationality implicit in experience which is available through an overt inquiry into conscious experience." "Logos" means "experience as thought." "Mythos" means "experience as lived." Moreover, living constitutes the total act; thinking, only the partial act.

Mythos enjoys less conceptual differentiation than logos. Culture shapes the idiom of the mythos of any given epoch. Mythos however always carries both ontological and cultural judgments about experience (FFS, 103). Within mythos psychic and cultural energies vaguely interweave in complex and subtle ways. As a result, mythos always remains "deeper than, even elusive of" abstract, inferential conceptualization. Nevertheless, logos does explicitate in some measure the ontological judgments implicit within mythos. As a consequence, these two ways of experiencing and interpreting reality complement rather than contradict one another. Mythos expresses "the depth of experience exceeding the conceptual grasp of events." Logos expresses "the occasions of an intelligible grasp of experience accomplished within the limited powers of our structured existence" (FFS, 112).

To deal adequately with mythos, Meland argues, liberal theology needs a method which reverses the demythologizing impulse. He summarizes his program for liberal theology in seven directives.

(1) Liberal theologians must recognize that three "vortices" function in contemporary Christian witness: "The cultus (or church), individual experience, and the culture."

(2) Liberal theology must determine whether the witness of faith is a cultic statement based on a "volitional acceptance" or whether it is available to "everyone within the cultural orbit of meaning who is open to receiving this witness as pointing to a depth of grace and judgment in every man's existence." Meland himself opts for the latter position.

(3) Liberal theology must resist any purely philosophical or psychological account of the depth dimension of experience and must insist instead that depth is a nurturing matrix of the witness of faith.

(4) Liberal theology must recognize that the Judaic-Christian mythos and the cultural forms it embodies historically constitute the nurturing matrix of faith in the West. Liberal theology must elaborate a rational account of experience that illumines the depths of experience

disclosed by the Judaic-Christian mythos. In the process it must endow mythic thinking with contemporary credence.

(5) By legitimizing mythic forms of thought liberal theology must lead the modern mind back to its primal beginnings through a recovery of the Bible as a "primal" document.

(6) That is to say, liberal theology must learn to read scripture in ways that are better attuned to its primal historical form in which kerygma and Christian witness evoked and focused the depth experience embodied in the Christian mythos.

(7) Hence, instead of demythologizing the witness of faith "without remainder," as the early Shubert Ogden originally suggested, liberal theology should opt to "retain mythos as being itself the elemental response to ultimacy appropriate to every man who is sensitive to the limits and depths of his existence, yet concerned to attain what margin of intelligibility is possible under the circumstances of our limitations" (FFS, 148–149).

Meland's seven directives demand in effect that logos allow mythos to teach it modesty. Liberal theology must also accept culture as a fundamental datum of theological thinking. These two consequences imply one another. Those who attempt to formulate religious experience in doctrinal deliverances while ignoring the claims of mythos can all too easily obscure through impoverishment depths of meaning which remain embedded in a religious culture. Meland's directives also demand that the churches remain open to the religious insights present in an allegedly secular culture impregnated by the Judaic-Christian mythos. With Langdon Gilkey Meland hopes that an ongoing dialogue between church and culture will eventually bear fruit in the construction of a Christian humanism which recognizes an increasing openness to the depth of experience coming to expression in "secular" scientific endeavor. All of these cautions, moreover, offer sound corrective to Lonergan's strong intellectual and inferential bias (FFS, 158–161, 165, 167, 171).

Though suggestive, Meland's insights into theological method labor under a certain number of identifiable limitations. In reading him one is often left wondering whether westerners experience the Judaic-Christian mythos as the inescapable fate of Western theologians or whether it can make normative claims in the dialogue with world religions. In portraying the depth dimension of experience as a "given" that is often obscured or ignored by abstract inferential thinking, Meland tends to assume rather than to prove that every experience has a graced dimension. As a consequence, he does not distinguish as sharply as he should between a natural, a gracious, and a sinful experience of depth. Nevertheless, after these qualifications are made, his reflections suggest a possible enrichment of foundational method.

"Foundational theology" in Lonergan's sense of that term attempts, as we have seen, to elaborate a normative account of conversion. In his own theory of conversion, Lonergan originally distinguished three kinds of conversion: intellectual, moral, and religious. He has, as we have also seen, since recognized the need to expand his theory by adding a fourth: affective conversion; but he has rested content to allow other thinkers to develop this facet of foundational theory.

Meland's theology illumines the affective component within conversion. His reflections on method call for the elaboration of operational procedures for exploring experiences mediated by affective perceptions of the religious significance of events. Meland understands more clearly than Lonergan that human affectivity grasps the real as such. His scepticism concerning the limits of abstract, analytic thinking offers a healthy counterbalance to Lonergan's strong intellectual bias. At the same time Meland acknowledges limitations in appreciative forms of knowing. He recognizes that appreciative insight often remains vague, diffuse, rationally undifferentiated. At the same time, because Meland acknowledged that thinking is the partial act and living is the total act, his method demands that theological and doctrinal abstractions be judged by their ability to focus and clarify a lived, appreciative sense of the divine without sublating or replacing it with rational abstractions. As a consequence, his method correctly identifies affectivity as the privileged locus of initial cognitive contact with God.

Meland also offers sound insights into the dynamics of affective forms of knowing. He has seen that we should never characterize human affectivity as merely subjective, but as a way of perceiving a situation. We must feel our way patiently into reality if our abstract generalizations about it are to avoid calloused superficiality. As a consequence, Meland's method enjoins an abiding intellectual humility in approaching an affective, Christian encounter with the divine mystery.

Nevertheless, Lonergan's overall approach to theological method both contextualizes and offers means for developing Meland's germinal insights. More specifically, Lonergan's definition of method and his theory of functional theological specialties provides a broader, interpretative context for understanding and evaluating Meland's work. Meland's *Fallible Forms and Symbols* rests content with speaking of theological method as a single reality. He would have done better with Lonergan to acknowledge that theology embraces a variety of methods, among them foundational method.

Lonergan's method also points the way to extending and embellishing Meland's account of appreciative forms of understanding. I do not suggest that either thinker offers an extensive account of affective perceptions. They do not. Nevertheless, Lonergan's understanding of method does suggest a technique for going about the elaboration of such an account. Lonergan, as we have seen, conceives method in operational terms. He defines "method" as "a normative pattern of recurrent and related operations yielding cumulative and progressive results." (MT, xi)

Lonergan's failure to apply his method systematically to appreciative forms of knowing does not mean that one cannot so apply it, only that the application has yet to be made. Lonergan's method poses then a double question to Meland: can one elaborate a more detailed operational account of appreciative forms of knowing than Meland himself has done heretofore? Moreover, does that operational account throw light on the procedures which ought to structure foundational theological thinking? In the paragraphs which follow we will attempt to answer these two interrelated queries.

(IV)

In this section of the present chapter we abandon dialectical for foundational thinking. Two interrelated tasks face us. First, in conformity withe the methodological postulates set down in the preceding chapters we must explore descriptively the evaluative responses that structure an appreciative grasp of the real. Second, we must examine some of the important ways in which humans seek to bring appreciative insights and judgments to symbolic expression. These two forms of interpretative behavior, appreciative evaluation and symbolic communication, mutually condition one another in ways that define the character and scope of felt intuitive perceptions of the real.

Appreciative insight begins with sensations. We touch, see, hear, taste, and smell the persons and things that inhabit our world. Besides sensing our own bodies externally we also feel our own bodily processes, movements, and orientation in space. Perceptions interpret sensations. Appreciative perceptions consist of feelings and images. They include the positive affections (like pleasure, sympathy, friendship, romantic love, craving, ecstasy) as well as negative feelings (like fear, anger, rage, guilt, sadness, depression, loathing, resentment). Images endow affective perceptions with enhanced differentiation and clarity. Neither positive nor negative perceptions advance rationally. They follow not the laws of logic but those of free association and synchronicity.

Besides perceiving reality affectively and intuitively, we also perceive things abstractly and inferentially. We define terms, systematically describe phenomena, formulate explanatory hypotheses about described data, predict their consequences, verify or falsify predictions, and organize conclusions into finite, rational frames of reference. Rational perceptions advance logically, through controlled definition and sound principles of reasoning.

Sensations present within experience actual events: the interaction of a sensing organism with its impinging environment or the impact of one part of that same organism on another part. Sensations present such events for further interpretation whether through nonrational and appreciative intuitions or through rational and logical descriptions and explanations. Sensations, being affectively tinged, already include a vague and primitive emotive response to reality. Perceptions prolong and develop that inchoate interpretative component within sensation; but perceptions focus attention not so much on events themselves as on their significance, i.e., on the habitual tendencies within experience that generate events.

Positive and negative affections perform a double cognitive function. First, they yield a vague initial interpretation of the kinds of tendencies which are shaping human experience, an interpretation which remembered and imaginative responses clarify intuitively. Second, they pass final judgment both on reality and on one's appreciative responses to the real. Let us reflect briefly on each of these interrelated perceptual functions.

Affective responses whether positive or negative do not, as was once thought, consist of blind impulses whose objects are supplied by powers of cognition like the senses, memory, and imagination. Rather affections function within a continuum of cognitive evaluative responses. They know reality in their own right. More specifically they mediate cognitively between sensory images on the one hand and memory and imagination on the other. When, for example, I see a coiled rattler and start with fear, my fear apprehends the potentially lethal threat in the serpent's venomous jaws. Images render affective perceptions more precise. My fear at the sight of the snake may be accompanied by visions of its striking, by memories of others killed or maimed by rattlers. Such images give shape to my fear. They render the threat my fear perceives more precise.

Nevertheless, affections, both positive and negative do more than perceive reality. They pass judgment upon it. Judgments of feeling differ from abstract and concrete inferential judgments. Abstract rational judgments make general statements about the way entire classes of things ought to be expected to behave. They rest on controlled definitions of the nature of each class and on predefined logical and methodological procedures. Abstract inferential judgments can be expressed in classical or statistical laws. Concrete inferential judgments interpret individual behavior. Close friends who know one another's habits can, for example, usually predict one another's reactions with some accuracy. Both abstract and concrete inferential judgments advance rationally and logically. Judgments of feeling, by contrast, advance nonrationally.

Aesthetic judgments, hunches, and judgments of discernment all exemplify judgments of feeling. The painter who after weeks of creative effort feels that his canvas finally expresses his original artistic intuition does not grasp the virtually unconditioned inferentially. His judgment cannot be analyzed in to an argument. Neither can the irrational hunches that motivate so many human acts. Similarly, judgments of discernment may or may not invoke rational principles; but even if they do, they result finally not from some form of systematic argumentation but from a felt, intuitive sense of the forces operative in persons and situations.

The non-rational character of judgments of feeling does not in and of itself deprive them of accuracy. They labor under fallibility, of course, as do all inferential judgments. They may on occasion express over-reactions rather than sound perceptions; but like logical blunders we can accurately discern over-reactions and correct them. Very often judgments of feeling grasp the real with uncanny precision especially when made by individuals endowed with a developed and healthy affectivity. Images, then, emerge from and clarify a matrix of affective perceptions which also pass judgment on the very images they generate.

Both affections and imaginative perceptions transpire consciously as well as unconsciously. Ego consciousness emerges with the ability to distinguish evaluatively between one's own body and the environment that impinges upon it. Ego consciousness grows through evaluative differentiation and through the inter-relationship of differentiated realities. We become personally conscious of things when we distinguish in some conceptual way between them and when we understand how they interrelate. Because consciousness serves the needs of a developing organism, its finite focus both shifts and flickers as fatigue and interest direct attention from one facet of reality to another. We are most conscious of the persons and things to which we directly attend out of interest or need. We perceive realities on the fringes of conscious attention only vaguely because their details do not concern us immediately. Vague consciousness fades into the unconscious. Unconscious evaluations surface within consciousness as they acquire a felt importance that calls for attentive discrimination.

Images and feeling blend into a complex network of appreciative perceptions. An aura of feeling surrounds every image. Every feeling can evoke an image that clarifies it. The nonrational character of appreciative consciousness reflects the haphazard way in which experience grows. We tend to recall feelings and images in the way in which we originally experienced them. We experience them haphazardly, as we happen to come upon them and they upon us. Mind play and creative fantasy imitate the haphazardness of experience and endow appreciative responses with complexities that go beyond mere memory.

We can distinguish three kinds of personal remembered images: spontaneous, imitative, and reconstructed. Spontaneous memories resemble sensory after images. They reproduce evaluative responses to past events. Spontaneous memories occur; they come to us as events remind us of earlier experiences. Imitative memory reproduces the action of another, as children do when they play follow the leader. We reconstruct memories of forgotten events that for one reason or another have assumed present importance. Reconstructed memories engage self-interest and can invoke self-deception.

Besides personal memories, we share memories with others with whom we have undergone some experience. We also share the memories handed down from generation to generation within a community. Such shared traditional memories must be communicated symbolically and therefore engage more than mere evaluation. We therefore postpone consideration of them until we have examined the communication of appreciative insight.

Memory deals with the past, imagination with the future. Realistic imagination attempts to construct possible futures capable of actual realization. Free fantasy constructs worlds of reverie that never were and never will be. Free fantasy resembles a waking dream and engages the same kinds of fanciful associations as shape dream images.

Archetypal images deserve special attention. While they may have been acquired as experience grows and develops, they introduce something like predictable patterns into the otherwise chaotic flow of images that shape appreciative insight. Archetypal images recur in different individuals, cultures, and epochs. Heavy with affect they draw to themselves other conscious and unconscious images and emotions. As a consequence, they enter conscious experience with unusual power, unleashing a flow of hitherto unconscious affective perceptions. Archetypes organize both positive and negative affections. As a consequence, every archetypal image enjoys both creative and destructive potential. The most psychologically significant archetypes include images of the masculine and of the feminine; images of social relationship; shadow images of the dark, destructive forces in the psyche; and images of integrating or disintegrating wholeness.

Images and affections provide the raw materials of appreciative insight; but language reshapes them into communicated perceptions. Humans give voice to appreciative insights in four significant ways: through the voice of prophecy, through the lyric voice, through the narrative voice, and through the voice of discernment. Let us examine the methods of communication characteristic of each of these voices. They differ, as we shall see, in their authority, intent, and principal symbolic techniques.

The voice of prophecy claims divine authority. The term "prophecy" can be taken broadly to include any human attempt to speak for God. In this broad sense prophecy includes any divinely inspired teaching. In the narrow sense of the term, however, prophecy voices an appreciative insight into God's actions and intentions within history. To the extent that prophets state beliefs about the persons and events they address, they may also engage in abductive, or hypothetical, inference; but if we take biblical prophecy as a norm for prophetic discourse; prophecy gravitates to poetic forms of diction. The prophet can also on occasion employ narrative discourse: parables and myths which startle listeners into a new understanding of themselves and of their situation. By and large, however, prophecy prefers lyricism to narration.

The prophet intends to bring about a conversion, a change of heart in those addressed. The prophetic voice summons one to deal consciously with hitherto neglected and potentially destructive unconscious drives. As a consequence, the prophetic voice uses image and narrative to shatter religious, moral, intellectual, and emotional complacency while simultaneously holding up a vision of a heart and world transformed through repentant obedience, love of the divine will, and faith and hope in God. To the sinful hypocrite prophets speak a word of repentance and recommitment; to the despairing, they speak a word of comfort and of hope. Both forms of prophetic discourse deal with repressed negative feelings, whether of fear and violence or of guilt and despair. The visionary and predominantly lyric character of prophetic discourse situates it solidly in the realm of appreciative understanding.

Prophets need discernment as well in order to identify both the divine impulse to speak for God and the character of those forces in individuals and in situations in need of repentant confrontation. Prophetic discernment also links the voice of prophecy to appreciative insight. Moreover, as we shall see, the voice of discernment like the prophetic voice can on occasion lay claim to divine authority.

The mere lyricist makes no claim to divine inspiration. The authority of the nonprophetic lyric, voice rests on the truth of its perceptions.

Although lyricists like prophets may when it suits their purpose use narrative, still the lyricist sets out not to tell a story but to explore through language and symbol the whole gamut of human affectivity. The lyric impulse, therefore, includes more than the literary lyric. It encompasses music, abstract painting and sculpture, dance that makes no attempt to tell a story, indeed any non-narrative symbolic excursion into human affectivity.

Lyricists employ metaphor (and simile) as a primary symbolic technique. A metaphor may be painted, sculpted, danced, or spoken. Metaphor yields an appreciative grasp of analogy. Analogies express an awareness of simultaneous likeness and difference among persons and things. In nonlinguistic metaphors the primary analogy obtains between the attitudes and feelings being expressed and the art object which expresses them. "What I feel," the nonlinguistic artist equivalently says, "resembles this leap, this abstract design, this abstract shape, although as we both know the feeling is not just a leap, a shape, a design." Linguistic metaphors break realistic speech patterns in order to identify two realities that can never in the real order be literally identical. Similes call attention to the fact that comparison should not be taken literally.[6]

Abstract rational thinking also grasps analogy; but unlike appreciative insight it attempts to specify precise points of similarity and difference. The metaphorical grasp of analogy eschews such rational precision, because it ambitions an irrational insight into the analogous structure of experience. Metaphors trust the felt connotations of images and symbols to convey their meaning.

Those accustomed to the linguistic precision of rational thought often complain of the vagueness and undifferentiated character of metaphorical analogies. Only a confused mind, however, would apply standards of inferential clarity to non-rational thinking. True, one cannot translate metaphors exhaustively into the abstract rational concepts. Still when judged by intuitive rather than rational standards, images can convey insight with remarkable precision. Indeed, every artist searches for the one untranslatable, irreducible image that conveys precisely a specific intuitive perception of the forces that shape experience. Georgia O'Keefe once remarked that she preferred painting as a means of communication because colors express intent much more precisely than words.

Indeed, metaphorical discourse attempts to convey a felt sense of relationship that transcends anything that controlled, carefully defined, rational discourse can convey. The way one thinks of the metaphorical grasp of relationship through analogy depends then in part on the way one thinks of the inferential grasp of relationship itself.

Classical philosophy reified essences, transforming them into principles of being. This speculative blunder led to another: it endowed rational thinking with misleading totalitarian claims. The controlled definitions of rational thought were believed to render precisely the essences that structure the real. In classical thought metaphors were as a consequence degraded into mere persuasive tropes, that is, into rhetorical illustrations of truths more properly grasped by reason.

Essences, however, function within experience not as principles of being but as fallible modes of sensation and perception. As a con-

---

[6]Andrew Burgess, "Irreducible Religious Metaphors," *Religious Studies* (December, 1972) 8:355–366; James D. G. Dunn, *The Way of all the Earth: Experiments in Truth and Religion* (New York: Macmillan, 1972); Paul Ricoeur, *Interpretation Theory: Discourse and the Surplus of Meaning* (Fort Worth, Texas: Texas Christian University Press, 1976); Sallie TeSelle, *Speaking in Parables: A Study in Metaphor and Theology* (Philadelphia: Fortress, 1975); Amos Nevin Wilder, *Theopoetic* (Philadelphia: Fortress, 1973).

sequence, rational, logical thinking can claim no privileged metaphysical status. Moreover, fallibilism demotes inferential thought to one way among many of perceiving the real; but we perceive reality in other ways than inferentially, namely, through intuitive and mystical insights.

What inferential thinking gains in precision through controlled definition and prescribed operational procedures, it forfeits in scope and depth. Inferential abstractions omit finally more reality than they disclose. Metaphor breaks the pattern of controlled inferential discourse by asserting an identity between two images that can never be reified as such. In the process metaphorical thinking invites an openness to what Bernard Meland has called an experience of depth, to a felt sense of the complexities of experienced relationship.

Among the relationships metaphor grasps we must include causal relations, as the following poem by Langston Hughes illustrates:

> I've known rivers;
> I've known rivers ancient as the world and older than the flow of human blood in human veins.
>
> My soul has grown deep like the rivers.
> I bathed in the Euphrates when dawns were young.
> I built my hut near the Congo and it lulled me to sleep.
> I looked upon the Nile and raised the pyramids above it.
> I heard the singing of the Mississippi when Abe Lincoln went down to New Orleans, and I've seen its muddy bosom turn all golden in the sunset.
>
> I've known rivers:
> Ancient, dusky rivers.
> My soul has grown deep like the rivers.

The identification of the soul of black people with a river provides the controlling, unifying metaphor in Hughes' poem. As the image of the river acquires rhetorical embellishment, it evokes a felt sense of the historical identity of the American black with all blacks. Black perceptions, the metaphor asserts, express the whole history of black people. Hughes evokes the scope of that history with images of ancient grandeur, of primitive closeness to nature, and of slavery and liberation. The metaphor grasps an historical truth, a causal relationship, not rationally, but intuitively, not by cataloguing facts or identifying the controlling events of black history but by evoking its grandeur, mystery, and poignancy. It leaves one with a felt sense of the complexities and implications of that history for contemporary, American black experience which no scholarly history of American blacks could convey in the same way.

The poem also dramatizes the illegitimacy of another rationalistic complaint against metaphorical insight. Rationalists sometimes attempt to arrogate to logical thinking the grasp of the universal as such. They decry imagistic thinking as concrete and sense-bound. In point of fact, of course, abstract concepts enjoy as much particularity as images. Indeed qualitative particularity characterizes every human evaluation from sensations to logical inference. Both images and logical concepts acquire universality through use, by being extended in intent to all the members of a given class. Hughes' poem makes a metaphorical statement about the character of every black person. Its images enjoy as much universality as any rational, historical generalization.

Metaphor does not, of course, exhaust the lyricist's panoply of symbolic techniques. Rhetorical surprise, repetition, evocative description, the use of terms rich in affective connotation, indeed any emotive use of language and symbol serves the lyricist's purpose.

Lyric discernment gives rise to esthetic judgment. Esthetic judgments terminate a process of creative interaction with some symbolic medium. They pronounce the lyric complete, an adequate expression of the intuitive perceptions which the lyricist sought to convey.

The lyric voice speaks in soliloquies that are either addressed directly to an audience or intended to be overheard by one. The narrative voice also explores the realms of appreciative insight; but it does so by telling a story. Stories occur in three cultural contexts. Professional literateurs enrich elite culture with carefully crafted tales. Popular culture tolerates much lower standards of narrative craftsmanship. Folklore creates an oral narrative culture.

A relatively new and somewhat diffuse speculative movement in the North American church, narrative theology has attempted to vindicate the importance and irreplaceable role of the narrative voice within both Christian revelation and the theological enterprise as a whole. Narrative theologians correctly call attention to the narrative structure of large segments of both the Old and the New Testaments. Suspicious of any attempt to reduce the message of Christianity to a set of doctrines or theological abstractions, they celebrate the narrative structure of experience itself. They point out the capacity of narrative thinking to explore a religious experience of mystery and of depth. Some link the very survival of religion to story and narrative: no stories, no religion.[7]

---

[7] R. B. Braithewaite, *Am Empiricist View of the Nature of Religious Belief* (Cambridge: Cambridge University Press, 1955); James H. Cone, "The Story Context of Black Theology," *Theology Today* (July, 1975) 22: 144–150; Harvey Cox, *The Seduction of the Spirit* (New York: Simon & Schuster, 1973); John S. Dunne, *A Search for God in Time and Memory* (London: Macmillan, 1967); Ted L. Este, "The Innarrable Contraption: Reflections on the Metaphor of Story," *Journal of the American Academy of Religion* (September, 1974) 42: 415–435; Langdon Gilkey, *Naming the Whirlwind: The Renewal of God Language* (New York: Bobbs-Merrill, 1969); Stanley Hauerwas (with Richard Bondi and David B. Burrell), *Truthfulness and Tragedy: Further Investigations in Christian Ethics* (Notre Dame: University of

Despite its suspicion of philosophical and theological abstractionism, narrative theology roots itself in and draws sustenance from the North American speculative tradition. Narrative theologians tend to conceive the human person in ways that reflect the thought of Josiah Royce, George Herbert Mead, H. Richard Niebuhr, and contemporary process philosophy and theology. They portray the human person in relational, social terms reminiscent of Niebuhr's "responsible self." With Mead they conceive each self as an historical event. With Royce they speak of the human person as a self-defining process accountable not only to others for the consequences of personal choices but also to God for the kind of person each individual chooses to become. With process theology they imagine the reality of persons as the sum total of their individual and collective histories. Moreover, narrative theology approaches religion experientially; and, like other North American thinkers since Jonathan Edwards, it concerns itself especially with the affective and intuitive dimensions of religious experience.

The construct of experience elaborated in this chapter and in chapters II and V sanctions the attempt of many narrative theologians to portray the dynamic structure of experience as fundamentally "narrative" in character, if by narrative one means narrable. Our construct of experience conceives all created reality as spatio-temporal, relational, social, and developmental. In a world constructed of experiences we must conceive reality itself as social process. Things derive their essences, what they are, not from some fixed and immutable metaphysical form crystallizable into an unchanging abstraction but from their respective histories. The character of each history and of the self which emerges from it results from the encounters, impulses, evaluations, interpretations, and decisions which have shaped it. Moreover in a world of experiences, individuals exist not in themselves only but in one an-

Notre Dame Press, 1977); *Vision and Virtue* (Notre Dame: Fides/ Claretian, 1974); Frank Kermode, *The Genesis of Secrecy: On the Interpretation of Narrative* (Cambridge: Harvard, 1979); Wesley A. Kort, *Narrative Elements in Religious Meaning* (Philadelphia: Fortress, 1975); Robert McAfee Brown, "'My Story and 'The Story,'" *Theology Today* (July, 1975) 22: 166–173; James William McClendon, Jr., *Biography as Theology: How Life Stories Can Remake Today's Theology* (Nashville: Abingdon, 1974); Johannes Baptist Metz and Jean Pierre Jossua, *The Crisis of Religious Language* (New York: Herder & Herder, 1973); H. Richard Niebuhr, *The Responsible Self* (New York: Harper and Row, 1963), *The Meaning of Revelation* (New York: Macmillan, 1953); Michael Novak, *Ascent of the Mountain, Flight of the Dove: An Invitation to Religious Study* (New York: Harper and Row, 1971); Robert P. Roth, *Story and Reality: An Essay on Truth* (Grand Rapids, Michigan: Eerdmans, 1973); John Shea, *Stories of God: An Unauthorized Biography* (Chicago: Thomas More Press, 1978); George W. Stroup, *The Promise of Narrative Theology* (Atlanta: John Knox Press, 1981), "A Bibliographical Critique," *Theology Today* (July, 1975) 22: 133–143; Brian Wicker, *The Story-Shaped World: Fiction and Metaphysics, Some Variations on a Theme* (Notre Dame: University of Notre Dame Press, 1975); James B. Wiggins, ed., *Religion as Story* (San Francisco: Harper & Row, 1975).

other. As a consequence personal experience can never be separated from shared social experience. The character of communities like that of individuals results from their histories; for communities like persons happen and acquire their character from the totality of events, selves, evaluations, and decisions that make them up.[8]

The narrable structure of a world constituted of experiences means that not only theology but any human attempt to grapple with the real can never succeed if it ignores or misprises narrative forms of understanding. The stories and histories of persons, communities, and things tell us more about their specific character than any rational abstraction; for abstractions omit more than they disclose.

Unfortunately, however, the polemic tone of some narrative theologians causes them to speak in ways that suggest that story alone enjoys the capacity to explore the narrable structure of experience. In the process they overlook the fact that logical inference too is shaped by and seeks in its own way to deal with the narrable structure of the real. It does so not through stories as such but through the attempt to predict behavior accurately.

Indeed, the three forms of inference can endow the very perception of time and space with an enhanced clarity and precision. Through the precise clarification of abductive inference we become more vividly present to ourselves and to the world with which we interact. When, for example, through diagnosis I learn that the vague burning feeling in my stomach results from an ulcer, I become present to my body in a new way. In other words precise classification enhances one's sense of the present moment and of the realities that shape it. Moreover when we predict deductively the behavior of realities we have abductively classified, the enhanced sense of the present effected by that intial classification begins to become a clarified future. When we verify or falsify deductive predictions about behavior, a deductively anticipated future becomes a present experience. In other words because inference always involves a transaction between human selves and their world and because evaluation grounds our experience of the present moment, inference itself helps endow experience with its narrable, spatiotemporal structure by endowing time perception with rational precision and clarity. As a consequence we can both narrate the development of thought and construct theories about why narrable events advance in the ways that they do. Narrative and rational inference offer therefore complementary and not contradictory ways of perceiving the narrable real.

Not only do we explore the narrative structure of experience both

---

[8] Stephen Crites, "The Narrative Quality of Experience," *Journal of the American Academy of Religion* (September, 1971) 39: 291–311.

through logical inference and through story, but some forms of narrative attempt to provide a rational account of events. We call rationally controlled narrative history.[9]

Some positivists question the scientific character of history, because the facts history studies no longer exist in the way that experiential facts studied by positive science do; but positivists overstate their position. The fact that history studies the past does not mean that historical hypotheses lack all factual verifiability. Historical arguments, of course, qualify more as scholarly rather than scientific, if by "science" one means an investigation that employs precise mathematical measurements. Nevertheless, historical hypotheses need to be measured against two sets of facts: one set given, the other reconstructed. The first set consists of the existing residue of past events that provides history with its most basic data: the places where events transpired, monuments, chronicles, autobiographies, biographies, and previous historical interpretations of the past. From this existing data the historian must reconstruct as accurate a scholarly chronicle of events as possible. Chronicles set forth the order of past events without presuming to generalize about their causes. They order historical facts more or less accurately. Scholarly chronicles attempt to deal with conflicting accounts of the order of past events and to formulate the most plausible chronicle of what actually transpired.

Historical hypotheses attempt to explain why chronicled events transpired in the way they did. They seek to identify the causes that changed the direction of events. The bombing of Pearl Harbor, for example, certainly ranks as the decisive cause of the entry of the United States into the Second World War. An adequate historical explanation of that epic event must, however, also deal with its less decisive contributing causes. Hypotheses concerning decisive and lesser contributing causes require deductive clarification. Their consequences must be tested against the most accurate and completest scholarly chronicle of events available under the circumstances. Since new primary historical data can at any time be uncovered which may require the revision of scholarly chronicles and their causal explanations, historical hypotheses enjoy the same fallibility as all human hypotheses.

The emergence of more demonstrably adequate frames of reference for interpreting historical chronicles may also force the revision of causal explanations of historical events; for a historian's frame of reference conditions the discrimination of decisive and contributing causes. A

---

[9] Langdon Gilkey, *Reaping the Whirlwind: A Christian Interpretation of History* (New York: Seabury, 1981); James B. Wiggins, "Re-imagining Psychohistory," *Theology Today* (July, 1975) 22: 151–158; Morton White, *Foundations of Historical Knowledge* (New York: Harper & Row, 1965).

church historian and a political historian will, for example, offer different and finally complementary accounts of the causes of the Protestant Reformation.

Scholarly history will always aspire both to the most accurate and thorough chronicle of the past possible under the circumstances and to the accurate identification of the decisive and merely contributory causes of those events. We can distinguish two kinds of historical explanations: those which explain why specific things occurred and concrete decisions were taken and those which explain why individuals reacted evaluatively to events in the ways in which they did. We sometimes call the latter the history of ideas.

Sacred history ambitions a scholarly account of the action of God in human history. That divine activity may take two forms: miraculous occurrences which suggest some direct divine intervention or deeds of faith in which creature and creator collaborate to direct the course of history. When undertaken as a rational, scholarly enterprise, sacred history employs fundamentally the same techniques as secular history, although sacred history interprets religiously significant data, whether existing or reconstructed, as religious. Moreover, in sacred history religiously significant events occupy center stage. One may then anticipate that secular history will handle the same data differently. An economic history of a people may, for instance, legitimately concern itself with its religious beliefs, not as religious, but as affecting trade, commerce, and technological development.

History whether sacred or secular does not, however, exhaust the narrative voice. Indeed, many stories, perhaps most, offer not a rationally ordered inferential explanation of events, but some kind of appreciative perception of the real. In order to compare historical and non-historical forms of narrative, we must distinguish the fundamental elements of narrative, the authority of narrative, the kinds of narrative, and the meaning of narrative.

The elements of narrative include a story-teller, an audience, and a tale. All three shape the character of a narrative.[10]

In telling a tale the narrator communicates personal beliefs, attitudes, and a vision of the world; for every narrative attempts to imitate life, though not all narratives reproduce it slavishly. In more sophisticated forms of narrative, one must deal with two kinds of narrators: the actual author of the story and characters within the tale that narrate either the entire story or some significant portion of it. When an author speaks through a character, a sound interpretation of the meaning of the

---

[10] John Dominic Crossan, *The Dark Interval: Towards a Theology of Story* (Niles, Illinois: Argus, 1975); Robert Scholes and Robert Kellog, *The Nature of Narrative* (New York: Oxford, 1966).

narrative must rest on a determination of the extent to which the narrator in the story speaks for the author. A well told tale will be constructed in such a way that the fate of the characters will reveal which ones speak for the author and which do not.

The audience addressed by a tale also shapes the story in significant ways. Stories seek to communicate; and one communicates different things differently to different kinds of people. One writes differently for children and for adults. Sacred narrative presupposes and seeks to evoke a response of religious faith. One satirizes a corrupt audience or challenges their world through parables. The sound interpretation of a story demands therefore that one understand how the world created by the story relates to the world of the audience to whom it is told.

Stories narrate events. Events happen in a time and place. They are organized into a plot by the story teller. As the plot unfolds characters help give shape to narrated events by their words and deeds, by affective, inferred, and symbolic responses.

All these narrative elements give a story its meaning. In interpreting the story one must understand how narrated time and place relate to the time and place of the author and audience; for that relationship will disclose the story teller's attitudes toward the actual world. The forces with which the characters deal will assert something more or less explicit about the forces that shape real life. The way in which the characters respond to events will make some sort of assertion about human beings and the way they live.

In oral narratives the narrator communicates face to face with an audience. As a consequence both narrator and audience share the same actual world. Narratives written for a specific audience can by contrast become detached from both author and audience and over a period of time enter worlds very different from the one for which they were written. Then the task of interpretation takes on new complexities. Written classics continue to speak to worlds other than those for which they were written by addressing perennial human problems, experiences, and needs. Nevertheless, the full interpretation of an historically displaced narrative requires the scholarly reconstruction of the world that produced it. Insight into the analogies between that world and the one in which it is being read will then yield more accurate understanding of its meaning for its actual audience.[11]

Characters divide into the good, the evil, and those of mixed or ambiguous moral responses. The kinds of persons portrayed as good or evil will reveal which values and attitudes the story teller endorses or

---

[11] In this context I find David Tracy's analysis of the classic piece of literature clarifying and suggestive. Cf. David Tracy *The Analogical Imagination* (New York: Crossroad, 1981) 99–229.

considers important. The fate of characters also reveals the author's beliefs and attitudes. Comedy and tragedy, for example, make different kinds of statements about the meaning of life, each valid in its own way.

Stories which claim divine inspiration attempt to speak with prophetic authority. Those that claim no such authority, like the ordinary lyric, stand or fall on the truth and adequacy of the perception of reality they enunciate.

Narratives may be classified in a variety of ways. Among the principal ways we should include classification by the mode of communication, classification on the basis of the way the world of the narrative and the real world interface, and classification on the basis of the realm of meaning the narrative seeks to explore.

Stories can be communicated in a variety of manners. In pre-literate cultures they are handed on orally. Epics, fables, fairy tales, sagas, myths, parables, ballads take shape initially within a living oral tradition but can with the transition to literate culture come to be written down. As soon as the written story emerges, it attracts better narrators whose work quickly eclipses in complexity and variety that of the oral artist. Eventually, written narrative divides into popular and literary narrative. Stories both written and oral can be communicated in either poetry or prose.

The epic and the ballad constitute the two principal forms of verse narrative. Some narratives like myths, fables, folk tales, sagas, and chronicles can be rendered in either poetry or prose. Other forms of narrative are ordinarily rendered in prose.

All narratives present a world in some fashion; but not all narratives relate to the world they present in the same way. Myths create a world. They describe its origin and consummation and enunciate its basic presuppositions. Despite a commonly expressed misconception to the contrary, not all myths qualify as sacred. The myth of Yoknapatapha County, for example, creates the world in which the fictional characters of William Faulkner lived, struggled, and died. Religious myths arise in communities of faith and usually shape shared ritual worship. Religious myths deal with ultimate realities and values. As a consequence, they frequently make universal claims by describing the way all people ought to relate to God and to the world in which they live.[12]

Apologies defend a world. They seek to correct misunderstandings about it and its values. Though apologies can be argued rationally, they

[12] Ian G. Barbour, *Myths, Models, and Paradigms* (New York: Harper & Row, 1974); John S. Dunne, *Time and Myth* (New York: Doubleday, 1973); Lee W. Gibbs and W. Taylor Stevenson, *Myth and the Crisis of Historical Consciousness* (Missoula, Montana: Scholars Press, 1975); Morton P. Kelsey, *Myth, History, and Faith: The Remythologizing of Christianity* (New York: Paulist, 1974); Alan M. Olsen, ed., *Myth, Symbol, and Reality* (Notre Dame: University of Notre Dame Press, 1980); Tony Stonebrunner, ed., *Parable, Myth, and Language* (Cambridge, Mass.: The Society, 1968).

also assume narrative shape. Even narrated apologies seek to persuade and to that extent resemble reasoned defenses. In narrated apologies some of the characters may offer rational arguments in defense of the world under siege by critics; but narrated apologies persuade primarily through the attractiveness with which they portray the characters who speak for the world they defend or through the very attractiveness with which that world itself is portrayed.

Comedy engages the negative affections and attacks a world either affectionately or bitterly. Embittered attacks satirize. Tragedies deal differently with suffering and evil. They engage the sympathetic emotions and seek to evoke empathy and compassion for human suffering, failure, and defeat.

Parables subvert a world. The parable begins by representing a world familiar to its auditors or readers but ends by calling into question some of their most cherished commitments, values, and presuppositions.

Other forms of narrative merely describe a world. They do so either realistically or unrealistically. Realistic narrative divides into representational and fictional. Representational narrative speaks of actual persons, realities, and events; it includes autobiography, eye witness chronicles, diaries, biography, and history.

Realistic fiction attempts to describe a non-existent world that could conceivably exist. This narrative impulse finds its purest expression in slice-of-life stories in which the concern for a well constructed plot gives way to an attempt to reproduce imaginatively the randomness and occasional chaos of day-to-day existence.

Unrealistic narrative divides into romance and didactic stories. Romance creates imagined worlds which make no pretence at reproducing the actual world in which we live but which enjoy self-consistency and enough interest and attractiveness to persuade an audience to acquiesce in their reality. As a consequence even romantic stories must engage the actual world of the audience in some way: either by offering an escape from its drabness or by commenting metaphorically on it in some way.

Didactic stories divide into fables and allegories. Fables ordinarily seek to educate one to sound attitudes and moral values. Allegories too can teach moral values, but they can also inculcate broader and more theoretical beliefs about what is real and important.

Because narrative thinking engages appreciative understanding, all of the nonrealistic narrative impulses we have just named and briefly described blend and interweave with intuitive spontaneity. That spontaneity explains the richness and variety of narrative thought and constantly frustrates the attempts of the rational mind to produce exhaustive categorizations of narrative.

Nevertheless, while narrative thought advances irrationally, it explores every realm of meaning from the most concrete to the most abstract. Representational narratives offer accounts of actual events and their causes. Realistic fiction deals with concrete actuality indirectly by describing how events might in fact transpire. In both realistic and unrealistic fiction specific characters can begin to assume universal symbolic significance. They may make a statement about a whole class of persons, like Moliere's *Bourgeois Gentilhomme;* or like Luke Skywalker in *Star Wars* they may speak a universal message by imaginatively incarnating an archetype. Other narratives like myths, fables, and allegories make abstract and universal statements about the nature of things and the way people ought to behave.

We have described three voices that express appreciative perceptions of reality. A fourth remains: the voice of discernment. Discernment divides into natural discernment and the charismatic discernment of spirits. Both forms of discernment draw on an appreciative insight into reality in order to make judgments about how to deal with it practically. The charismatic discernment of spirits claims divine inspiration. As we have seen, it helps give judgmental shape to all forms of prophetic discourse.

Natural discernment divides into prudence and esthetic judgment. Prudential judgments concern themselves with both pragmatic and moral considerations. Pragmatic decisions seek to deal realistically and successfully with one's world, but they prescind from values and realities that make absolute and ultimate claims. Moral judgments of prudence plot courses of action that submit to realities and values that do make absolute and ultimate ethical claims. Charismatic discernment does so as well but derives some of the absolutes and ultimates that judge and direct human behavior from some historical self-communication of God. Though they may invoke rational principles, authentic prudential judgments express a felt sense of the fitting rather than a logical conclusion.

Aesthetic judgments of feeling function both in the creation and critical evaluation of human arts and letters. Artists and writers must judge affectively when a work accurately says what they intend it to say. Artistic and literary critics judge affectively the accuracy of the esthetic judgments artists and writers make concerning their own work. Artistic and literary criticism may invoke general principles; but once again the concrete judgment of specific art objects rests finally on an appreciative grasp of their meaning and significance.

We began this chapter by contrasting two accounts of how the human mind grasps reality. Emerson claimed that intuition yields a privileged grasp of being; Lonergan claimed the same privilege for inferential judgments. We found in the thought of Bernard Meland hints of how these conflicting epistemologies might be reconciled. We then invoked Lonergan's operational definition of method to expand descriptively Meland's account of how appreciative insight advances. We examined two interpenetrating sets of operations: the evaluative responses that structure an appreciative perception of the real and the symbolic acts that attempt to communicate those perceptions: prophecy, lyricism, narrative, and discernment.

Three final tasks face us. First, we need to reflect on Lonergan's own account of the cognitive status of feeling and intuition. We shall examine the relationships in Lonergan's thought between feeling and judgments of value, his account of artistic insight, his description of the difference between symbols and language, and his understanding of mythic thinking. Second, we need to compare and contrast his position with our own account of appreciative thinking. Third, we need on the basis of all these insights to hazard a preliminary response to the question that surfaced at the end of the last chapter: namely, what operational consequences for foundational theology flow from the fact that affective conversion seeks to animate the other forms of conversion? To these three considerations we turn in the chapter which follows.

CHAPTER IV:

CONCEPT AND IMAGE IN FOUNDATIONAL THINKING—II

The present chapter concludes the argument of the preceding one. In both we are attempting to answer the question: what operational consequences for the conduct of foundational theology flow from the fact that affective conversion seeks to animate the other forms of conversion?

The argument of the present chapter falls into three parts. In the first we shall examine Lonergan's account of feeling and intuition. In the second part of the argument, we will compare and contrast that account with the position developed in the preceding chapter. In the third part of this chapter we will attempt to answer the question with which it and the previous one deal.

(I)

The Lonergan of *Insight* all but ignores the role of feeling in human perceptions of the real. When he does take account of it, he contents himself with insisting on their irrelevance to intellectual judgments about order and value. He asserts:

> . . . . emphatically that the identification of being and the good bypasses human feeling and sentiments to take its stand exclusively upon intelligible order and rational value.
>
> Feelings and sentiments are bypassed for, though one begins from objects of desire, one finds potential good not in them alone but in the total manifold of the universe (I, 606).

Until one grasps the good intellectually one must rest content with noting only the multiplicity of potential goods; for only the intellect can order and judge the value and the true desirability of the potential objects of desire (I, 604–606). The ethical sphere stands to the aesthetic as position to counterposition, even though humor and satire pose an effective practical challenge to moral selfishness (I, 624–626).

The Lonergan of *Method*, however, manifests a slightly more nuanced sense of the role of feelings in human evaluative responses. He distinguishes non-intentional feelings, like irritability, bad humor, and anxiety from intentional trends and urges like hunger, thirst, and sexual discomfort. Non-intentional feelings have causes but no goals. Intentional feelings seek goals, objects. Feelings orient us "massively and dynamically" in a world mediated by meaning (MT, 30–31).

Intentional feelings seek two main classes of objects: the agreeable or disagreeable, the satisfying or dissatisfying, on the one hand, and values, on the other. Values orient the self to self-transcendence and disclose the "true good." We grasp value through judgments. True value may or may not coincide with the agreeable and satisfying. True values can be arranged hierarchically beginning with religious values and descending then to personal, cultural, social, and vital values (MT, 31–32).

Feelings develop like skills. Some feelings come and go; some repressed feelings orient the subject unconsciously. Feelings channel attention and direct one's life. Feelings embody fairly permanent attitudes, like being in love. Some feelings develop into aberrations that attack and belittle true and authentic value. The possibility of developing aberrant feelings imposes the need for self-knowledge at the level of affectivity (MT, 32–34).

Even for the mature Lonergan, however, one never grasps the "true good" with feelings as such. The "true good" can be grasped only in inferential judgments of value. The Lonergan of *Insight* identifies the grasp of the good with the judgmental grasp of being. (I, 60) The Lonergan of *Method* nuances this earlier position and holds that judgments of value differ in content but not in structure from judgments of fact. Judgments of fact, presumably, assert concrete realities as existing. Judgments of value either assert "that some X is truly or only apparently good or compare the relative importance and urgency of different goods." Judgments of value differ from judgments of fact in content because "one can approve of what does not exist, and one can disapprove of what does." The two kinds of judgments resemble one another structurally because both distinguish between the self-transcendence of the subject and the meaning of the judgment which is or claims to be independent of the subject. Subjects reach the fullness of moral self-transcendence when they not only know but do what is right (MT, 36–37).

Apprehensions of value differ both from judgments of value and from feelings. Lonergan as we have seen distinguishes intentional from non-intentional feelings. Both differ from apprehensions of value. Non-intentional feelings have causes but no objects; apprehensions of value, however, by contrast exemplify intentional states and have objects. Intentional feelings do have objects but may or may not prove morally good. Apprehensions of value glimpse as yet unrealized possibilities of moral self-transcendence. Judgments of value begin then in a knowledge of reality, but they emerge from a more or less differentiated apprehension of human ethical potential (MT, 37–39).

The Lonergan of *Method* displays an enhanced sensitivity not only to feeling but to the distinction between judgments of fact and value. He also attends more explicitly to the intentional structure of artistic and symbolic forms of knowing. Following Suzanne Langer he defines art as "the objectification of a purely experiential pattern." Art objectifies both abstract and concrete terms. The artist selects among possible patterns including some, excluding others. Lonergan insists on the purely experiential character of artistic judgments. Artistic patterns structure elemental forms of consciousness which, nevertheless, transform experience. We are transported by a painting, for example, from the world in which we live into the world envisaged by the artist. Artistic objectifications give psychic distance from feelings by recollecting emotions in tranquility. They invite us to see and experience for ourselves but offer no "conceptual clarification or judicial weighing of conceptualized evidence" (MT, 61–64).

Symbols structure experience intentionally. Lonergan defines a symbol as "an image of a real or imaginary object that evokes a feeling or is evoked by a feeling" (MT, 64). Feelings link subjects to objects. Some feelings reinforce one another, others conflict. The same symbol can evoke different felt responses from different subjects. Symbols lack affective differentiation but can be combined in ways that enhance their felt intensity and reduce their ambiguity. Symbols obey, not the laws of logic, but those of feeling and image. Symbols express "what logical discourse abhors: the existence of internal tensions, incompatibilities, conflicts, struggles, destructions." They allow mind, heart, and body to commune. They express an elemental union not yet conceptually objectified. Psychoanalytic theories offer conceptual objectifications of symbol systems that go beyond the symbols themselves.

Language creates a realm of meaning beyond symbol. Linguistic meaning leans toward univocity. Its truth may contrast with either deliberate mendacity or mere falsehood. It distinguishes different realms of intentionality. It objectifies what it interprets (MT, 60). It employs an indefinitely multipliable set of signs. Language shapes conscious intentionality in the world in which subjects attempt to communicate. Ordinary language facilitates day-to-day transactions. It expresses common sense insights as viewed by a particular individual. Literary language compensates for the elliptical character of ordinary language by trying to create a common bond of understanding and feeling between the literary artist and his or her audience. Literary language follows the laws of image and affect rather than those of logic (MT, 70–73).

In both *Insight* and *Method* Lonergan displays little sympathy for mythic forms of thought. The Lonergan of *Insight* describes mythic consciousness as devoid of self-knowledge. Myth results from "an un-tutored desire to formulate and understand the nature of things." It must be overcome by metaphysics (I, 542–543). Mythic consciousness is "identified . . . with the counterpositions, with the inability or refusal to go beyond description to explanation, and with the lack or neglect of effective criteria for passing judgments on anticipations and acts of understanding" (I, 544). Mythic thinking does lead the mind to search for meanings that transcend the sensibly perceivable. Nevertheless, my-thic expression contrasts with the language of "developed expression," that is, with the language of inferential explanation. As a consequence, mythic thinking marks only a stage on the way to insight and judgment. The creation of new myths effects linguistic breakthroughs only. Such breakthroughs solve problems of expression and are attempts of the mind to free itself from the fetters of untutored thought; but their meaning remains merely allegorical rather than explanatory (I, 545–547).

The Lonergan of *Method* looks on myth somewhat more benev-olently; but he continues to speak of mythic thinking as only a confused form of cognition which should be transcended through explanatory insight. He suggests that myth marks the mind's transition from the world of immediacy to the world of mediated meaning; but at the level of mythic consciousness the mediation of meaning falls short of pure cognition. The mind reifies mythic structures of understanding un-critically. Although myths allow or even facilitate the practical ordering of life, mythic thinking falls short of explanation (MT, 88–90). It fails to distinguish between mere representation and real perception (MT, 92).

The Lonergan of *Method* also characterizes fallacious epistemological counterpositions as mythic (MT, 212–213, 128–129). He links mythic thinking to idolatry and magic (MT, 111). The human mind abandons myths only slowly and reluctantly for grammar, logic, method. Myths rank only as pre-philosophic, pre-scientific thinking. Myths, therefore, should not be characterized as untrue because mythic thinking precedes a struct judgmental concern with truth (MT, 122–206).

The logic of Lonergan's position would seem to point to the con-clusion that mythic forms of cognition offer only an inverse insight into reality, that feeling, dream, and myth cannot finally grasp the real as such and must be superceded by grammar, logic, and method.

(II)

What can be said of Lonergan's account of appreciative forms of knowing? Clearly Lonergan understands that not all thinking advances rationally. He also sees that emotions develop in healthy or unhealthy ways, can perdure to different degrees, and function both consciously and unconsciously. He recognizes, too, that language shapes human perceptions. He acknowledges the difference between ordinary, literary, and technical language, and he correctly distinguishes between apprehensions and judgments of value on the one hand and between true and false values on the other. He accurately describes some of the ways that symbols structure appreciative insight. Other aspects of his account of appreciative forms of knowing, however, need qualification.

One may, for example, question whether Lonergan's definition of being as that which is grasped by the totality of true inferential judgments enjoys the all-inclusiveness he claims for it. It certainly fails to take into adequate account both the grasp of reality through intuitive judgments of feeling and the experience of Christian mystics. Even if we could formulate an exhaustive inferential explanation of the whole of reality (an eventuality which Lonergan himself discounts), we would not yet understand it fully. For we would grasp it with our heads only but not with our hearts. The heart, however, knows in ways that the head does not. It also grasps realities that transcend rational insight. Here Christian mysticism offers a healthy corrective to the totalitarian claims of philosophical intellectualism, as William James correctly saw generations ago. In the experience of infused contemplation mystics know realities which, they insist, can never be expressed in concept or image.

Lonergan's conviction that reality is grasped finally in inferential judgments also prevents him from doing justice to the way human beings understand values. His distinction between judgments of fact and judgments of value implies that some cognitive acts are evaluative and others are not, whereas if truth be told, every cognitive response from sensation to feeling to intuition to inference engages evaluation. Instead of opposing judgments of fact to judgments of value we should rather speak of different kinds of evaluative responses to events: sensate, appreciative, speculative, moral, religious.

More directly to the point, however, we grasp moral and religious values in other ways than inferentially. We also grasp them appreciatively: intuitively and in judgments of feeling. Indeed the prudent person should mistrust inferences about values which intuitive judgments of prudence and discernment fail to corroborate, just as one should mistrust felt, intuitive judgments which contradict truths that we know through inference.

Lonergan's reluctance to allow the grasp of reality as such within the realm of what he calls experience also clouds his understanding the way intuitive insights advance. It causes him to disparage allegorical insights and to ignore the way in which mythic perceptions grasp the real. The human mind can, of course, naively reify mythic perceptions in the way that Lonergan suggests, just as it can naively reify its inferences. Nevertheless, the mind can legitimately formulate world hypotheses that actually interpret experience, and it can create imaginative worlds through mythic narratives which enunciate profound insights into the world in which we live. Similarly, allegories like *Pilgrim's Progress* or *Everyman* function within narrative thought in ways that explanation functions in rational thinking: both offer generalizations about the nature of things. Allegories express dramatically abstract truths that reasoning grasps inferentially.

Similarly, one must question the adequacy of any account of art which reduces it to the mere schematization of patterns of "empirical consciousness" and which implicitly deprives it of the ability to grasp reality as such. True artistic insight does not grasp the real through precise definition and the weighing of evidence. It does so affectively and intuitively but no less precisely and accurately. In *Art as Experience* John Dewey correctly argues that any theory of knowledge which cannot adequately account for the ways in which artistic insight grasps the real in judgments of feeling fails to answer the challenge which art poses to philosophy. Alas, I fear, under such a censure Lonergan's epistemology lies.

Moreover, no one who understands the workings of the intuitive mind would oppose the grasp of value to feelings. Instead they would concede that value can be grasped either inferentially or in judgments of feeling. Moreover, one may legitimately question whether any emotive responses should be characterized as non-intentional. Some affections may be vaguer than others; but all yield perceptions of the tendencies, the laws, that lend dynamic structure to experience.

A similar artificiality attends Lonergan's attempt to contrast language and symbol; for literary language uses symbols in order to communicate an appreciative insight into reality. Nor does all language objectify. Even rational language systems can do justice to the relational character of experience.

The preceding observations illustrate that the shift from Lonergan's understanding of experience to the one suggested in chapter II involves more than the substitution of one term for another. An experience endowed with presentational immediacy grasps reality in two ways: through inference or through judgments of feeling. Lonergan's epistemology, by contrast, allows finally only for the inferential grasp of Being.

The construct of experience which we have suggested also requires the coordination of intuitive and inferential perceptions of reality; for when we perceive reality one way with our heads and another with our hearts we court neurosis or even psychosis.[1]

---

[1] For a symptomology of stages in psychic deterioration, see: Karl Menninger, Martin Mayman, and Paul Pruyser, *The Vital Balance: The Life Process in Mental Health and Illness* (New York: Viking, 1963).

The need to coordinate intuitive and inferential perceptions of reality forces the coordination as well of the symbols we use to communicate them to one another. Sound coordination respects the autonomy of both kinds of thinking. One can no more force mytho-poetic insight to submit to the constraints of logic than one can argue both logically and nonrationally. Not that every form of inference follows strict logical rules. Only deduction and induction do; for we have no rules for coming up with the correct hypothesis. Hypotheses result from mind play, from toying with the evidence. Once formulated, hypotheses can be measured against logical criteria; but the most rigorous argument begins in fantasy. Abduction bridges appreciative and logical thinking.

Models mediate between intuitive and inferential thinking. We need to distinguish disclosive models, mathematical models, and analogical models. Disclosive models represent things not directly observable. The model's structure must correspond to the reality it represents, though the model need not reproduce reality slavishly. Architectural models, for example, represent on a smaller scale the way a building will look upon completion. The figures of plane and solid geometry illustrate mathematical models. Analogical models extend metaphors. In the early days of atomic physics, for example, scientists imagined that the structure of the atom resembled the solar system, and from that model they derived hypotheses about atomic activity.

Models organize data in preliminary ways that allow us to begin thinking about them. The inferences we make fall, as we have seen, into three different categories. Abductive inferences classify data in a preliminary fashion on the basis of a principle assumed to be true. Deductive inferences predict that facts not presently in evidence but logically implied by a particular hypothesis will materialize. An induction argues that the general principle assumed by a hypothesis obtains in reality when the predicted evidence materializes. An induction argues the opposite when the evidence fails to materialize or that the principle holds valid only within a certain percentage of instances. Abduction in other words concludes to a class, deduction to a fact, induction to a law, although facts, rules and classifications function in all three forms of inference.

To cite a homely and somewhat grisly example, I may come across a bottle with a skull and crossbones on its label. I infer abductively that it contains poison on the assumption that humans habitually put such a symbol on a bottle with toxic contents. Having classified the contents of the bottle abductively, I can predict that, if I feed it to my neighbor's cat in sufficiently large doses, either harmful or lethal consequences will follow. Having mixed the substance in with kitty's Meow Mix I subsequently observe that the beast goes into a catatonic fit and dies. I therefore infer inductively that true to form some kind soul put the skull and crossbones on the bottle to warn about its toxic contents.

We express inferences linguistically in propositions; and we organize propositions logically into different frames of reference. We may, therefore, distinguish two kinds of hypotheses: focused hypotheses and world hypotheses. Focused hypotheses attempt to explain specific events. World hypotheses conceive the whole of reality analogously by referring everything to some organizing root metaphor. For example, thinkers tend to imagine that the structure of reality resembles ideas (Platonism, Aristotelianism), machines (mechanism), events (contextualism), or organisms (organicism).[2]

As particular ways of thinking rationally about reality acquire social acceptability they are transformed into paradigms. Paradigms normally fail to explain all the data relevant to a particular problem or set of problems; but they offer a way of handling the data and ambition exhaustive explanation eventually. The practitioners of ordinary science adust paradigms to accommodate discordant data; but the multiplication of recognized and important anomalous facts may force a paradigm to shift. New explanations or techniques of investigation emerge, find supporters, and if more successful at explaining anomalies than the old paradigm eventually replace it. As the new approach acquires fairly universal support, it is transformed into the accepted paradigm.

The shift from Ptolemaic to a Copernican universe illustrates the emergence of a new scientific paradigm. Just before Copernicus proposed his new model of the universe, Ptolemaic astronomy found itself plagued with a mounting number of observed anomalies in the movement of the heavenly bodies which it could not explain. Copernicus offered a new way of thinking about the stars that made sense out of many of these anomalies. Despite initial resistance in the scientific community, the new astronomy found a handful of vocal defenders and eventually won general acceptance.[3]

All these rational structures of interpretation have intuitive, appreciative analogues. World hypotheses create universes rationally; myths do so through narrative. Inferences express abstract or concrete beliefs that make either particular or universal claims, but such beliefs can be expressed either lyrically or in narrative. Inferences offer causal explanations; but both narrative and lyricism also deal with causal relationships. Finally, the paradigm shifts which occur in science are paralleled by shifts in esthetic modes of perception. Luminism, cubism, pointillism, and impressionism, for example, all created new artistic paradigms for perceiving the world. Moreover, the finitude and inertia of the human ego give rise to behavior among artists and literati analo-

[2] Stephen C. Pepper, *World Hypotheses: A Study in Evidences* (Berkeley: University of California Press, 1942).

[3] Ian G. Barbour, *Myths, Models, and Paradigms: A Comparative Study in Science and Religion* (New York: Harper & Row, 1974).

gous to the behavior of scientists. Radically new ways of perceiving reality intuitively tend to be derided initially by the old guard in the artistic or literary community, but the new paradigm eventually finds more supporters and eventually becomes an accepted way of expressing oneself either literarily or artistically.

The preceding account of the relationship between intuitive and inferential thinking provides, I would suggest, a sound basis for understanding the way rational concepts and intuitive images function interpretatively within foundational thinking. To this problem we now turn in the section which follows.

(III)

An important question surfaced at the end of Chapter II: what operational consequences for foundational theology flow from the fact that affective conversion seeks to animate intellectual, moral, and religious conversion? In the present section we will attempt to answer this question in a preliminary fashion. We shall discuss three interrelated tasks facing the foundational theologian. First, foundational theology must identify and develop sound criteria for distinguishing true from false hopes. Second, foundational theology must resolve dialectical conflicts among appreciative perceptions of the real. Third, foundational theology must resolve dialectical conflicts between appreciative perceptions of reality on the one hand and inferential perceptions on the other.

One can, as we have also seen, speak of two different ways of perceiving the reality within ego-consciousness: one can do so either affectively or inferentially. One can also perceive the reality of God in both of these ways. One can both savor appreciatively and reflect rationally on the movements of divine grace; one can feel as well as understand the breathing of God. Moreover, an experiential construct of human nature together with the Christian mystical tradition links the birth of hope not to the spiritual faculty of the will, but to a repentant confrontation with unconscious negative affections and to the healing of memories. Repentance ordinarily engages both intuitive and inferential insight. When we confront unconscious rage, fear, guilt, and envy instead of repressing them, we can begin to integrate them in positive life-giving ways into our affective perceptions of reality. After all, some things should make us angry; nor does every fear spring from neurosis. Guilt can be healed through forgiveness, and envy through gratitude. Through repentance, the sympathetic emotions acquire greater freedom of scope. We become increasingly sensitized to beauty as the heart expands to attractive visions of a world transformed and renewed. In other words, hope is born.

The child of affective conversion, hope, then, results from emotional integration and frees the imagination to see visions and dream dreams. Hope also nurtures all other forms of human development. Before we can grow speculatively, we need to see learning as an attractive and interesting possibility. We must glimpse the beauty and wonder of understanding anything: our God, our world, ourselves; and we must allow that beauty to captivate our hearts. If we expect to grow morally we must first be drawn by the beauty incarnate in courageous, generous and heroic people and want to become like them. Political activists must first dream of justice and peace and believe that they are worth living and dying for. Religious conversion, as we have seen, demands the trans-valuation of human hope and faith; but faith does not abolish the psychodynamics of natural hope. It merely provides human affectivity with a new scope to expand and with a new context in which to develop, as the leaping heart begins to glimpse undreamed of possibilities in a future prepared and promised by God.

Foundational theology must then learn to differentiate true from false hopes and adequate from inadequate ones. Inferential perceptions enjoy no ex-clusive corner on truth and adequacy. We can fix our beliefs rationally and adopt logical frames of reference; but we can, as we have seen, also judge reality nonrationally and adopt intuitive frames of reference. Our hopes for ourselves and for others spring from imaginative visions of attractive possibilities and from judgments of feeling about their prac-ticability.

False and inadequate hopes spring alike from ego inflation and from ego deflation. The inflated human ego has lost touch with its own unconscious motives for acting. Cocksure and arrogant, it allows nar-rowly egotistical feelings of self-importance to cause it to overreach itself. Inflated hopes underestimate the difficulty that attends the realization of cherished dreams and overestimate the prospects of success. Such hopes blind one to the destructive consequences of personal choices and to one's personal accountability for one's own actions. The vicious inflated ego dreams dreams of malice. Similarly, ego deflation stifles hope. In moments of deflation, we confront the dark, destructive and conflicted side of our personalities. Our enthusiasm for life evaporates, and hope gives way to timidity, discouragement, and despair. In such moments of darkness our hopes will more likely suffer from inadequacy than from mere falsehood, though they can suffer from both.

We can deal with false and inadequate hopes therapeutically or prophetically. The two approaches complement one another. Both re-quire natural prudence and charismatic discernment. Foundational the-ology should supply the discerning heart with sound psychological, moral, and theological principles for dealing with false and inadequate hopes. It should also formulate psychological and theological principles for fostering the kind of ego integration in faith that nurtures true and adequate hopes.

For example, foundational theology should explore the ways that authentic spirituality and the personality sciences both illumine and correct one another's insights. More specifically, Christian spirituality insists that the healing of disordered affections in faith ought to follow upon integral conversion. Contemporary psychology advances beyond the descriptive accounts that spiritual writers offer of affective disorder by providing a detailed symptomology of emotional pathology. At the same time Christian spirituality corrects any psychological approach to healing which discounts the healing power of God and looks to human contrivances alone in order to effect healing and integration.

True hopes respect reality. They express an accurate understanding of oneself and one's world, as they advance toward a realizable future that incarnates sound moral, speculative, and religious ideals. As we have seen, not every world constructed by the lyric or narrative imagination necessarily enjoys a direct relationship to practical living. We can imagine worlds just for the fun of it. Nevertheless, since every exercise of the imagination expresses either healthy or unhealthy attitudes that orient us in some way toward reality, the prophetic, lyric, and narrative voices should seek to educate human affectivity cooperatively to the kind of emotional integration that fosters true and adequate hopes. Foundational theology will, therefore, also need to provide sound psychological, speculative, moral, and theological principles for discerning the health, the truth, and the adequacy of the intuitive perceptions voiced by a given culture.

We have been reflecting on the first of three interrelated foundational tasks, namely, on the need for foundational theology to develop criteria for distinguishing true and false hopes. We now turn to the second task. *Foundational theology must also resolve dialectical conflicts among appreciative perceptions of the real.*

As we have seen, we grasp the real either in inferential judgments or intuitive judgments of feeling. We give voice to our intuitive judgments lyrically, prophetically, dramatically. We also do so practically in artistic judgements, naturally prudential judgements, or charismatic judgments of discernment.

Not all judgments of feeling automatically agree either in their account of reality or in their assessment of the way in which we ought to respond to reality practically. The conflict among judgments of feeling poses a problem for dialectical theology distinct from the conflict among logical, inferential interpretations of the real. The latter conflict forces a dialectical analysis of true and false beliefs. The conflict among judgments of feeling, however, demands that dialectics deal as well with true and false hopes. Christian theology needs not only to identify true and false hopes, it must understand their motives by identifying true and adequate hopes on the one hand and false and inadequate ones on the other. The fathers of the Church saw this truth clearly in their confrontation with Gnosticism. They saw that Gnostic myths not only denied Christian belief in a benign creator but betrayed Christian hope in the resurrection.

Dialecticians will, however, employ similar techniques in dealing with both rational and irrational conflicts of judgment. The dialectician must first assemble the data relevant to understanding the terms of a conflict and then decide the relative importance of different kinds of data. Areas of apparent conflict need to be identified and the motives behind conflicting judgments of feeling examined. The dialectician must then decide between real and merely apparent conflicts. Then the terms of real conflicts must be clarified.

Foundational theology ambitions a strictly normative insight into the experience of conversion which will provide criteria for selecting between conflicting judgments, whether logical or intuitive. Both kinds of judgment attempt to interpret reality. The normative claims of both must, then, be measured by the realities of which they give an account. False judgments must be set aside as misleading. Moreover the reality that judges the truth and falsity of both logical and intuitive judgments includes the reality of God's historical self-revelation and self-communication in Jesus and the Holy Breath.

While inferential judgments must conform to sound logic, judgments of feeling lie under no such constraint; for they are not reached logically. They can, however, be judged by sound literary, artistic, psychological, moral, and religious norms. Literary and artistic norms assess the success or failure of a particular judgment of feeling to communicate what it intended. Psychological norms assess the extent to which particular judgments of feeling express and foster healthy affective integration and human aspiration. Ethical norms measure the spontaneous aspirations of the heart against realities and values affirmed with moral ultimacy and absoluteness. Religious norms assess the extent to which particular judgments of feeling give authentic voice to Christian hope.

In resolving conflicts among judgments of feeling, foundational theology will find help in artistic and literary criticism, but it cannot rest content with esthetic criteria alone in judging the authenticity of human hopes. This or that artistic or literary genius can express with polished elegance misleading, perverted, malicious, unjust, or blasphemous visions of human life and reality. We should, of course, prefer the plain spoken truth to an elegant lie. Nevertheless, esthetic criteria do function in judging the authenticity of appreciative perceptions, for we should also prefer elegant expressions of sound appreciative judgments to artistically or literarily mediocre expressions of the same insight. Elegance of style sensitizes the heart more effectively to the perception of beauty, while tawdry artistic or literary expressions even of true insights cheapen the truth they express. Think, for example, of tasteless religious art.

Besides judging the truth and falsity of particular judgments of feeling, dialectical and foundational theology must also judge the relative adequacy of appreciative frames of reference. Paul Ricoeur's *Symbolism of Evil* exemplifies the kind of foundational judgment I mean. After comparing cosmogonic myths, tragic myths, and the adamic myth, Ricoeur argues persuasively that the adamic myth offers a more adequate account of the origin of evil than either of the other two mythic systems. A similar comparison could be made between Gnostic and Christian mythic systems and an argument made for the greater comprehensiveness of the Christian perception of life. In our own day, contemporary feminist critiques of Christian appreciative perceptions of the world are forcing the reevaluation of some of the spontaneous intuitions that shape Christian behavior.

Foundational theology cannot, however, rest content with fostering the ongoing integration of intuitive perceptions of reality among themselves, though let no one gainsay the importance of that task. For *yet a third challenge confronts foundational thinking. It must attempt to coordinate intuitive with inferential perceptions of reality.* Otherwise a psychologically unhealthy rift begins to open between the heart and the head, between appreciation and reason. That rift fosters neurosis and inevitably insinuates fragmenting inauthenticities into the religious experience of converted Christians.

The history of Christian pneumatology illustrates the evils that flow from such fragmentation. The Old and New Testaments articulate narrative, prophetic, and intuitive insights into the activity and reality of the Holy Breath. These appreciative insights into Her reality portray Her as a transcendent feminine source of divine wisdom and as the principle of all gracious enlightenment. In the New Testament She is portrayed as the mind of God and of Christ. By the third century of the Christian era, however, theologians like Clement and Origen of Alexandria had for rational and philosophical rather than for intuitive reasons identified the second person of the Trinity, the Logos, as the source within the triune God of both rational and gracious enlightenment. As a consequence, Christians ceased to hope in the Holy Breath in the way in which the first converts to Christianity had. Her role within the process of salvation became obscured, and eventually She was degraded to the role of a mere creature in the teachings of Arius.

Other splits between heart and head have occurred in the development of Christian pneumatology. By the high Middle Ages Christian theologians had agreed that the three members of the divine triad should be conceived as persons, even though they did not all agree on how "person" should be defined. Medieval Christians, however, lacked a personal image of the third member of the trinity, and the cult of the Virgin eclipsed living hope in the Holy Breath in popular Christian piety.

Foundational theology will succeed in correcting appreciative and inferential perceptions of reality only if it can successfully resolve dialectical conflicts between felt, intuitive judgments and rational, inferential ones concerning one and the same reality. We must, of course, preserve the autonomy of both modes of perceiving and judging. We should not force prophets, poets, artists, and story tellers into rational straight jackets, nor should we expect rational perceptions to stir the heart the way intuitive perceptions do.

The foregoing analysis of the dynamics of appreciative and rational consciousness suggests multiple areas of needed coordination between intuitive and inferential perceptions of the real. We must coordinate myths with world hypotheses; rational and biblical narratives with theoretical and practical inferences; imaginative narratives and inferential perceptions; prophetic and lyric visions with logical accounts of the world; and judgments of prudence and of discernment with rationally argued beliefs. Let us reflect briefly on the problems posed by each of these tasks of correlation.

Myths create worlds. Not every myth interprets the world in which we live directly. A literary myth like J.R.R. Tolkien's *Silmarillion*, for example, creates a world of fantasy one step removed from the real world we inhabit. The events that transpire in Middle Earth and the myths which orchestrate them do make some important statements about the real world; but they do so indirectly. Middle Earth never existed, but it functions in Tolkien's stories as a metaphor for the world in which we live. Literary myths like the *Silmarillion* belong in a different category from myths which interpret directly the origin and destiny of nations, religious communities, and the human race to which we belong. The latter pass direct judgment on the very world in which we live. They interpret that world, its presuppositions, purpose, and the way living persons ought to behave. They are often linked to cult, and they communicate felt, intuitive judgments about the nature of reality itself.

World hypotheses, as we have seen, enunciate rational judgments about the nature of reality in general. Like myths they make broad and sweeping generalizations through the systematic, logical elaboration of an organizing root metaphor.

For foundational theology to foster integration of heart and head within conversion, it must make sure that personally appropriated mythic interpretations of the nature of reality do not contradict personally espoused world hypotheses and vice-versa. Such contradictions can and do occur. The adamic myth, for example, asserts that the human race has by its own free choice deviated from the will of a benevolent creator. Mechanistic world hypotheses, however, foster the belief that all events, including human choices, occur with mathematical necessity. In other words, the intuitive account of the origin of evil formulated in the adamic myth contradicts an important facet of many mechanistic philosophies.

Myth-makers do not think logically, but we can legitimately demand that they offer a coherent account of the real. Within the myth itself felt intuitive judgments about the nature of reality must not contradict one another. In addition we need to judge mythic accounts of the real by their applicability and adequacy. Since realistic myths generalize about the origin and destiny of specific communities or of the human race in general, mythic systems must be judged by their ability to interpret every facet of the realities they describe.

World hypotheses are formulated logically. They must therefore be judged not only for their logical coherence but for their logical rigor as well. Logically coherent hypotheses employ a unifying set of categories so defined as to remain unintelligible apart from one another. Rigorous world hypotheses obey sound principles of logic and of method. Like realistic myths world hypotheses need to be evaluated for their applicability and adequacy.

Mythic perceptions which shed light on realities unthinkable by a particular world hypothesis demand the latter's appropriate revision or replacement by a better hypothesis. Similarly, world hypotheses which explain realities unimaginable in a particular mythic context demand the appropriate modification of the myth or its replacement by another more adequate myth. Thus, the sound insight into the experience of human freedom expressed in the adamic myth demands that a mechanistic account about the nature of reality either be modified to make place for human freedom or discarded. Similarly, a rational demonstration of the immorality of sexism or racism demands either the appropriate modification of patriarchal and racist myths or their replacement by some other account of the real. In other words, foundational theology coordinates mythic perceptions of reality with world hypotheses by making sure that mythic judgments of feeling agree with the rational judgments which a particular world hypothesis sanctions, and vice versa.

An even tighter coordination of these two modes of perception will be achieved if the images which structure mythic perceptions of reality connote the root metaphors that structure world hypotheses. A philosophy of organism, for example, offers a better rational frame of reference than mechanism for interpreting Paul the apostle's intuitive portrayal of the risen Christ as the head of his mystical body, for in a philosophy of organism all reality is understood by an appeal to the root metaphor of a living organism.

Scholarly history reconstructs the past systematically and offers rational explanations of why things happened the way they did. Lonergan's theory of functional specialties offers a very practical way of coordinating historical narrative and personal belief. The specialties that structure mediating theology—research, interpretation, history, and dialectics—collectively reappropriate the common history of religious communities and of the cultures in which they thrive. Mediated theology—foundations, doctrines, systematics, and communications—reformulate the shared beliefs of religious communities and orient those communities toward a common future. Both processes foster communal self-awareness. Communities reach a shared sense of identity by reappropriating their stories; for communities result from the living product of the events that produce them and shape their shared attitudes, beliefs, and practices. Consensus about the significance of a community's originating event and its subsequent history unifies a community by giving it an integrated perception of its identity. Dissent concerning those same events fragments a community. Think of the tragic dissolution of the Christian community produced at the time of the Reformation through conflicting accounts of Christian origins. The sense of common identity allows a community to project a common future based on shared self-understanding. Communities, however, need more than shared hopes to achieve full shared awareness. They need also to orchestrate the gifts of their members to realize the future to which they aspire. The shared labor involved in realizing shared goals also heightens communal self-awareness.

If, then, religious communities hope to achieve shared consciousness, they must resolve the conflicts that divide them and agree on a practical vision of their future. Lonergan's method assigns to dialectical and foundational thinking the task of laying the groundwork for achieving the needed consensus. Dialectics does so by distinguishing real from apparent conflicts and by clarifying the terms of real disagreement. Foundational theology provides the criteria needed both to evaluate the motives that divide members of religious communities from one another and to distinguish sound from unsound hopes, beliefs, and practices. Collectively the eight functional specialties systematically coordinate historical self-understanding with living faith and practice.

Communities need to appropriate their past not only rationally but also appreciatively. The myths, legends, songs, tales, literature, and art of a community also shape its self-understanding and hopes for the future. As a consequence, communities and the individuals who comprise them also need to identify those intuitive voices which authentically interpret shared hopes, beliefs, and practices. Here too dialectical and foundational thinking offer a practical method for distinguishing true from false intuitive perceptions and for coordinating them with rational beliefs.

Moreover, in striving for an appreciative and rational appropriation of its history and heritage, the Christian community needs to respect the unique character and normative claims of biblical narrative. The Bible tells many kinds of stories, but we may distinguish four principal genres: myths, the sacred history of the Old Testament, the gospels, and apocalyptic. We have already reflected on the coordination of mythic and rational perceptions of the real. Both Jewish sacred history and the Christian gospels stand somewhere between scholarly history and imaginative story-telling. The sacred historians of the Hebrews show somewhat more concern than the authors of the Christian gospels to reconstruct a scholarly chronicle of events. The gospel writers for the most part order both their stories about Jesus and their summary of his teachings with a regard for the pastoral needs of specific communities, although all four gospels respect the schematic chronicle of Jesus' life and ministry preserved in the Niceno-Constantinopolitan creed. Nevertheless, both Jewish sacred history and the gospels offer interpretations of the events they narrate. Those events are understood to reveal the reality of God not only in His miraculous interventions in human history but also and especially in the careers of people of faith who either submit to the commissioning Word and Breath of God or defy both. The destiny of both kinds of persons discloses and interprets progressively God's saving intentions.

The Christian gospels differ from Jewish sacred history by sharing the parabolic flavor of the teachings of the figure who dominates their pages, Jesus of Nazareth. Parables, as we have seen, seek to subvert a world. They begin by describing familiar persons and events but end by startling those who hear them into a critical re-assessment of cherished presuppositions. The four evangelists transform the story of the ministry, death, and resurrection of Jesus into the ultimate parable that subverts human egocentrism with all its works and pomps and demands a new understanding of God, of human life and destiny, and of the relationship between the world and God.

The composition of both the gospels and Jewish sacred history required some basic scholarly skills, but one finds in both more than just a rationally ordered account of religiously significant events. Both forms of narrative offer an intuitive perception of the religious significance of the events they record, for their authors believed that only a heart transformed through repentant self-dedication to God can perceive the saving religious significance of historical events or grasp the way that God has chosen to deal with His creatures. The intuitive character of biblical interpretations of the religious significance of events sets it apart from contemporary scholarly history and limits as well the application to biblical narratives of purely rational methods of interpretation. Anyone who reads either the gospels or Hebrew sacred history in the hope that reason alone will explain their meaning will almost certainly miss their point. Their significance must be grasped first with the heart before it can be transformed into rational, inferential propositions. Failure to respect this basic hermeneutical principle has led more than one contemporary exegete to offer shallow, rationally reductionist interpretations of sacred narratives.[4]

In its attempt to coordinate historical narrative with rationally justified beliefs, both dialectical and foundational theology must respect not only the literary distinctiveness of biblical history but also the normative claims it makes on Christian belief and practice. The converted Christian lives in the end time in which God has come to definitive revelation in Jesus and in the Breath that flows from Him in eschatological plentitude. The Bible narrates those events which prepared and embodied that normative, eschatological self-disclosure of the Godhead in human history.

The literary uniqueness and normative character of biblical narrative pose special problems for any theological attempt to coordinate historical narrative on the one hand and personal religious beliefs and practice on the other. First of all, historians need to coordinate biblical and scholarly accounts of religious history. In the interface between these two narrative accounts of the origins of the Christian community, each can make normative claims on the other. Scholarly history can complete and on occasion can correct biblical narrative in what concerns both the chronicle of events recounted in the Bible and their rational explanation. For the believing Christian, however, the Bible makes normative claims upon scholarly history in interpreting the religious significance of those events.

The two apocalyptic narratives accepted into the biblical canon both differ notably from later Jewish apocalyptic. The book of Daniel adopts the standard apocalyptic literary technique of interpreting events that have already occurred by having them foreseen by some prophetic figure (in this case Daniel) who antedated those same events and who speaks in oracular terms of their coming and significance. The author of the book of Daniel seems not to have succumbed to the extreme pessi-

[4] William A. Beardslee, *Literary Criticism of the New Testament* (Philadelphia: Fortress, 1970); Robert W. Jenson, *Story and Promise: A Brief Theology of the Gospel About Jesus* (Philadelphia: Fortress, 1973); Norman Perrin, *What is Redaction Criticism?* (Philadelphia: Fortress, 1969); Amos Wilder, *Early Christian Rhetoric: The Language of the Gospel* (New York: Harper & Row, 1964), *The New Voice: Religion, Literature, Hermeneutics* (New York: Herder & Herder, 1969).

mism and disillusionment which characterize later Jewish apocalyptic. Later Jewish apocalyptic piety succumbed to a self-righteous elitism, to a belief in the irreformable corruption of human society, and to a despair of God's immediate intervention in human history. Instead it postponed that intervention until the messianic inauguration of an end time in which the righteous would be exalted and their enemies be given their just deserts.[5]

In this respect Christian apocalyptic both corrects later Jewish apocalyptic and fulfills the book of Daniel in ways analogous to the way in which the gospels fulfill Jewish sacred history. The book of Revelation announces that the end time has already begun in Jesus and looks forward to its consummation in the second coming. Moreover, just as the gospels make normative religious claims on both scholarly history and Christian faith and practice, soo too the book of Revelation through its inclusion in the biblical canon makes normative claims on Christian hope.

Because we perceive reality both appreciatively and inferentially, we need to coordinate intuitive judgments of discernment with rational moral insights into the direction of Christian conduct. The dynamic, dialogic, charismatic structure of the Christian conscience seeks to effect that coordination. The dynamic structure of the conscience demands that felt, intuitive judgments of prudence and discernment confirm the conclusions of moral argumentation and vice versa. The finitude and fallibility of the human mind demands that moral reasoning, like speculative, advance dialogically. Those in the Christian community specially gifted with prudential insight and with the charismatic discernment of spirits need to confirm and apply the ethical arguments and conclusions of academic moralists. At the same time, intuitive moral judgments need to submit to sound inferential insights into reality and human conduct.

A final task of coordination faces the foundational theologian concerned to integrate the converted heart with the converted head. Not only must foundational theology coordinate felt intuitive judgments with logical inferential judgments about religious realities, but it must also achieve the same integration of imagination and inference in its understanding of the secular forces that contextualize and condition Christian conversion. American Catholics, for example, need to reappropriate the story of the American Catholic Church and understand its place in the story of the Church universal. They need also to appropriate their story as Americans and come to terms with the issues, challenges, and opportunities which the American secular tradition offers. As Bernard Meland has correctly suggested, American secular culture has been shaped in

---

[5] Walter Smithals, *The Apocalyptic Movement: Introduction and Interpretation* (New York: Abingdon, 1975) 10–19, 31–35.

part by the Judaeo-Christian tradition; but it is also marred by racism, commercialism, materialism, chauvinism, nationalism, sexism, militarism, neocolonialism, and other human sins and aberrations irreconcilable with an integral fourfold conversion. The secular myths, stories, lyric flights, and rational beliefs that inform life in this country need to be analysed dialectically and assessed foundationally in an attempt to unify mind and heart in ways that blend the best secular and religious perceptions our tradition offers while simultaneously excluding inauthentic and erroneous ones.

IV

In Chapter I we suggested that Lonergan's failure to deal adequately with intuitive, mytho-poetic knowledge called into question the ability of his method to deal with the problems and issues raised by cultures that grasp reality lyrically, dramatically, and mythically rather than through controlled inferential processes. In the last two chapters we have attempted to overcome that deficiency. We have explored descriptively the felt intuitive perceptions that shape appreciative consciousness. That exploration disclosed an irrational principle of judgment quite distinct from the inferential judgments Lonergan describes but capable nonetheless of grasping the real in its own right. We argued that the redefinition of experience suggested in Chapter II entails more than the substitution of one linguistic convention for another. We have reflected on the prophetic, lyric, dramatic, and discerning voices that express an appreciative grasp of the real. We have also identified operational procedures for coordinating intuitive and inferential judgments within an experience of integral fourfold conversion. In the course of our argument we have drawn on the insights of narrative theology and on Lonergan's theory of method in order to render more operationally precise and practical the methodological insights of Bernard Meland, whose approach to theological method points a way beyond the epistemological impasse with which the preceding chapter opened.

If the insights we have reached in the course of our reflections enjoy validity, then we must also expand the basic postulates of Lonergan's method. That method enjoins that in approaching any question speculatively, one should be attentive, intelligent, reasonable, responsible, and loving. Our own insights into the dynamics of intuitive perceptions and judgments demand in addition that before ever we attend to the data relevant to the formulation of speculative questions, we need to approach the realities we desire to understand with repentant appreciation. Authentic appreciation includes a repentant moment because before we can grasp intuitively any reality let alone explain it logically, we must deal with any personal fears, resentments, and self-doubts that prevent us from appreciating the reality that confronts us. Moreover, until we reach a positive, intuitive appreciation of the complexities of any reality, we are in no position to deal with it rationally. In the absence of a true appreciation of what we are dealing with, we are prone to overlook or undervalue what is most important about it. To the operational postulates: be attentive, be intelligent, be reasonable, be responsible, be loving, we must then add a sixth: namely, be repentantly appreciative.

Repentant appreciation takes into account the perceptive character of human affections. As we have just seen, however, appreciative thinking also understands reality imaginatively and expresses that understanding in narrative, lyric, and prophecy. The postulate "Be repentantly appreciative" needs then to be followed by yet another postulate that envisages irrational, intuitive acts of understanding: namely, be imaginative.

Human affections not only perceive reality but judge it as well aesthetically, prudentially, and charismatically. A third postulate, then, governs appreciative thinking. It corresponds to the inferential postulate: Be reasonable. We may formulate this third intuitive postulate thus: be tasteful, prudent, and discerning.

Finally, the need to coordinate intuitive and inferential perceptions of reality sanctions the postulate: coordinate the perceptions and judgements of your heart and head.

A full validation of appreciative forms of knowing within foundational thinking demands then that the operational postulates which govern a sound method be expanded to nine in all: be repentantly appreciative; be imaginative; be tasteful, prudent, and discerning; be attentive; be intelligent; be reasonable; be responsible; be loving; and coordinate the perceptions and judgments of your heart and head.

In the chapter which follows we will begin to explore the logical, inferential processes that shape foundational thinking.

CHAPTER V:

LOGIC, METHOD, AND LIBERATION IN FOUNDATIONAL THINKING

The two preceding chapters have reflected on the ways in which affective perceptions of reality color foundational method. These chapters drew on insights from narrative theology and from artistic and literary theory in order to describe how humans voice their appreciative grasp of the real. They contrasted rational and nonrational narrative, and pondered the challenge of coordinating logical and intuitive insights.

The present chapter focuses exclusively on the logical procedures that structure foundational thinking. It divides into five parts. The chapter begins by comparing Lonergan's understanding of method with Dewey's understanding of logic. We shall see that while Lonergan focuses on the analysis of intentionality, Dewey focuses on problematic situations. Section two analyses Dewey's account of the process of inquiry and the implications of what he calls "denotative method." Section three reflects on how Dewey's insights point to ways of generating the three "nests" of categories that function in the elaboration of foundational theology. Lonergan himself leaves this point obscure in *Method*. Section four will explore the applicability of Dewey's theory of logical inquiry to foundational speculation. The fifth and final section of this chapter will attempt to show that if one expands Lonergan's theory of method with insights from Dewey, one can begin to incorporate into foundational thinking the concern with social praxis that characterizes the method of liberation theology.

(I)

In *Method in Theology* Bernard Lonergan consistently contrasts the task of a method with that of a logic. He discovers two motivating ideals in all logical thinking: (1) the construction of a language of fixed terms whose use is regulated by accurate and immutable axioms and (2) the unified and absolutely rigorous deduction of all possible conclusions. He characterizes logic as superior to common sense thinking. Logic endows thought with clarity, coherence, and rigor unknown to both common sense and to literature. Logic, therefore, for Lonergan marks an important stage in the evolution of consciousness toward method, even though logic falls short of method itself. Nevertheless, even after the emergence of method, logic continues to function as an instrument of thought. It organizes and consolidates what inquiry has achieved, transforming the results of research and experimentation into systems (MT, 6, 64–67, 85, 92, 94, 138, 304).

Method, as Lonergan understands it, advances beyond logic by its discovery of "interiority." As we have seen, Lonergan defines method as "a normative pattern of recurring and related operations yielding cumulative and progressive results." Method does much more than systematize the results of research. It provides the context for collaborative creativity. It mediates between the systems logic organizes. Moreover, transcendental method unifies inquiry by revealing to the reflective mind the normative pattern of operations that lies at the basis of more specialized methods. As we have also seen, Lonergan describes that pattern as experience, understanding, judgment, and decision. Transcendental method thus insures that every specialized method be ruled by four imperatives: be attentive, be intelligent, be reasonable, be responsible.

Our reflections so far have led us to question some of these presuppositions. In the previous chapter, moreover, we concluded to the need to expand the imperatives of any sound method to include: be repentantly appreciative; be imaginative; be prudent, tasteful and discerning; and coordinate the perceptions and judgements of your head and heart.

As we shall soon see, we also need not acquiesce uncritically in Lonergan's definition of the term "logic." If we consult the American philosophical tradition, for example, we find very different conceptions of the logical enterprise. Indeed, John Dewey, used the term "logic" in ways reminiscent of Lonergan's use of the term "method." Dewey's logic, for example, repudiated logical formalism. In Dewey's eyes logic becomes purely formal when it studies the linguistic structures of thought in abstraction from the mental operations that employ them. For Dewey a sound logic constructs a theory of inquiry. As a consequence, Dewey's theory of inquiry, like Lonergan's method, focused on the operations that guide thinking.

Moreover, Dewey like Lonergan looked to modern science as a useful paradigm for sound method. He did so for the same reason as Lonergan: the manifest success of experimental, scientific procedures. Both men discovered an instrumental purpose in human thinking. Both acknowledged a relationship between controlled, scientific investigation and common sense thinking. Both discovered operational constants at work within human inquiry, and both allowed that our speculative understanding of those constants can evolve. Both believed that logical thinking advances best through social dialogue. Lonergan looked to method, Dewey to logic to control the processes of reflection and insight.

These parallels between Dewey and Lonergan suggest that an investigation of Dewey's theory of inquiry might offer an expanded insight into the operations that ought to guide any sound method. Where might such a suggestion lead?

(II)

Dewey believed that a sound logic advances autonomously and progressively by identifying fruitful procedures of investigation and by discarding sterile ones. The postulates of such a developing logic may therefore shift as insight into sound operational procedures advances. Logic achieves its purpose when it justifies warranted human assertions.[1]

Dewey's logic elaborates a theoretical account of inquiry. He conceives inquiry as organic, situational, and instrumental. Human organisms develop cognitively through ongoing interaction with their environments. That dynamic interchange is marked by identifiable rhythms. Restlessness betrays a state of imbalance between organism and environment. The restoration of equilibrium yields a new vital satisfaction. In a world of interacting, competing organisms, however, satisfaction never lasts forever. As a consequence, moments of satisfaction and the restless search for new satisfactions punctuate the life cycle of every developing, organically based mind (LTI, 23–36).

Dewey's concern to situate inquiry in an evolving, organic, environmental context also motivates his relentless attack on spectator theories of knowledge. We do not contemplate eternal verities. We achieve truth actively. Moreover, the achievement of truth changes any situation from an indeterminate to a settled one. Accordingly, Dewey defines inquiry as "the controlled or directed transformation of an indeterminate situation into one that is so determinate in its constituent distinctions and relations as to convert the elements of the original situation into a unified whole" (LTI, 104–105).

Situations contextualize the objects of inquiry. Moreover, culture and language partially determine human situations (LTI, 42–59). Problems arise out of situations which confront us either with our ignorance of forces we need to understand in order to direct events to a desirable satisfaction or with conflicting accounts of similar matters of importance. When that occurs a situation becomes problematic. (LTI, 105–107)

In identifying a problem we advance the first step toward rendering

---

[1] John Dewey, *Logic: The Theory of Inquiry* (N.Y.: Holt, Reinhart, and Winston, 1938). Hereafter this work will be abbreviated LTI.

an indeterminate, problematic situation determinate. "Without a problem," Dewey observes, "there is blind groping in the dark." (LTI, 107–
108) The identification of a problem engages deliberative judgment. We
deliberate over situations in which different courses of action with different corresponding consequences confront us. In instituting inquiry
the deliberating mind must first ask how the question should be posed,
how the problem ought to be conceived initially. The posed question sets
the goal of an inquiry. It indicates what needs to be learned, and it allows
discrimination between what we know in a settled manner and what we
need still to learn. Settled knowledge relevant to any given problem
provides the initial instruments which intelligence needs in order to
bring an unsettled situation to a satisfactory resolution. (LTI, 108–109,
158, 180)

As the inquiring mind gathers data relevant to the resolution of a
posed problem, possible ways of proceeding, possible explanations of the
problem begin to suggest themselves. We resolve a problematic situation
when through the instrumentality of thought every explanation but one
has been eliminated and when that explanation accounts for all the
relevant data. The final explanation transforms the situation into a
determined one by enabling the inquirer to use the settled elements in
an unsettled situation to bring about some desired result. The achievement of the desired result changes a disorganized situation in which any
number of things might happen into a unified one in which a rationally
predetermined eventuality is finally effected. (LTI, 108–119)

For example, when the United States decided to build the Panama
canal, epidemics of yellow fever among the workers threatened to undo
the project. The spread of a deadly disease of unknown cause transformed a situation of calculated risks into one that had gone out of
control. The directors of the project quickly identified the problem: they
needed to name the cause of yellow fever in order to eliminate it,
otherwise the entire enterprise would founder. Through a process of
elimination investigating scientists finally traced the virus which causes
the disease to the bite of a mosquito of the species *aedes*. Settled techniques of pest control could then be employed to eliminate the disease
bearing insect. The canal was eventually completed.

While Dewey regarded experimental science as a useful paradigm of
sound speculative method, he recognized that philosophical inquiry
could not reproduce every facet of scientific thinking. Scientific experimentation relies, for example, on precise mathematical measurement.
Philosophy does not. Philosophy could, however, he believed, imitate the
denotative character of scientific thinking.

"Denotative method" distinguishes the "crude subject matters in
primary experience" from "the refined, derivative objects" of reflective
thought. The crude, primary objects of experience set the problems for

inquiry, provide the data for its theories, and test its proposed solutions. Denotative method demands therefore that we measure the speculative importance of abstract theories by their capacity to change and enhance crude, macroscopic experience. For unless speculation can endow problematic situations with a new determinacy, thinking becomes divorced from living, and reflective persons begin to despise speculation that goes nowhere.[2]

Dewey believed that philosophy, like science, needs to employ a denotative method, but he set as the proper task of philosophy the critique of values. Philosophical thinking bears fruit in a settled judgment, a warranted assertion, a human belief. Philosophy critiques both belief and unbelief. It evaluates their causes and consequences and the values with which they deal. As a speculative enterprise, therefore, philosophy stands somewhere between literature and science. Like literature it comments appreciatively on nature, life, and the meaning of experience. Like science it attempts to render the human pursuit of goods more coherent, secure, and significant (EN, 323–331).

(III)

We have already noted the similarity between Dewey's understanding of logic and Lonergan's notion of method. Nevertheless, Deweyan logic and Lonerganian method also exhibit some interesting contrasts. Lonergan approaches method through an analysis of intentionality and of the "horizons" that structure human "interiority." Lonergan's understanding of the task confronting a method exhibits therefore a bias toward introversion, a preoccupation with one's own thought processes. Dewey's logic, by contrast, echoes the concern of the thinking extravert. It focuses not so much on the exploration of interiority but on the practical resolution of indeterminate situations.

A sound method, like any sound theory of knowledge, must, however, make room for both introverts and extraverts; and it must refuse to yield the field of speculation exclusively to either. Moreover, in the last analysis the two viewpoints complement one another; for an introverted concern with the structure of intentionality begins to take on methodological interest when it meets the extravert's demand that fine epistemological distinctions contribute to the satisfactory resolution of problematic situations.

Moreover, Dewey's insistence on the situational character of inquiry

---

[2] John Dewey, *Experience and Nature* (N.Y.: Dover, 1958). Hereafter this work will be abbreviated EN. For a critical assessment of Dewey's philosophy of religion, see: William M. Shea, *The Naturalists and the Supernatural: Studies in Horizon and an American Philosophy of Religion* (Mercer University Press, 1984).

also casts significant light on an obscure corner of foundational theological method. Lonergan demands that foundational thinking generate three "nests" of interrelated categories: transcendental categories, general theological categories, and special theological categories. He tolerates a pluralism of categories, insisting that not every foundational theologian need use the same ones. Unfortunately, however, he leaves the student of his method largely in the dark concerning the way in which foundational categories are generated.

Interiority alone does not provide an adequate generative principle. Viewed experientially, the designation of human evaluative responses as "interiority" could even occasion some philosophical misunderstandings by suggesting too sharp a contrast between the inner and outer worlds. Human evaluations from sensation to imagination to abstract thinking all respond to something or someone. Through our evaluative responses we become present (more or less adequately) to ourselves and to our worlds. Nevertheless, while evaluations lead experience, they do not effect anything. They do not generate themselves. Only selves, autonomously functioning agents, generate evaluations, and they do so through cognitive transactions with their worlds.

Nor can horizon analysis alone actively generate the categories of foundational thinking; for the mere differentiation of a speculative frame of reference does not determine the specific terms and propositions that ought to structure it.

If, however, neither interiority alone nor horizon analysis alone can generate the categories of foundational thinking, then how do they arise? Might not Dewey's preoccupation with situational indeterminacy offer some useful leads? Might not all three "nests" of foundational categories be generated by a problematic foundational situation?

It has been objected that situations should not be characterized as problematic but that doubtful theories about situations should. The objection presupposes fallaciously, however, that problematic interpretations of situations lie outside of the situations they interpret. In fact, of course, they lie within situations and help constitute their relative determinacy or indeterminacy. So do foundational interpretations of religious situations.

By a foundational situation I mean one which raises questions relevant to the pursuit of foundational theology: namely, questions about the scope, dynamics, and character of conversion. We have already identified four distinguishable moments in any conversion process: affective, speculative, moral, and religious. As we shall soon see, we also need to add a fifth moment: socio-political conversion. A foundational situation becomes problematic, therefore, when it raises questions concerning the causes and consequences of an integral conversion and when it raises questions concerning the kinds of realities encountered within conversion. Moreover, as we shall see, identifiable forces within a problematic foundational situation inevitably generate the three interrelated "nests" of categories that function in foundational thinking. Lonergan identifies the three "nests" as transcendental categories, general categories, and special categories.

In ancient and medieval logic transcendental categories function as predicates universally applicable in intent. Transcendentals can also be predicated of one another, although they do not mean identically the same. In Aristotelian logic "being," "true," and "good" all exemplify transcendental predicates. They do not mean exactly the same thing. "Being" means that which is. "True" designates being in its relation to the intellect; "good" designates being in its relation to the will. Nevertheless, while "being," "true," and "good" do not mean the same thing, we may nevertheless assert truthfully that every being enjoys truth and goodness and that whatever is true is good and vice versa.

We may view transcendentals logically not simply as predicates but also from the standpoint of the way they function within inquiry as a whole. Transcendental categories unify inquiry by providing a rubric under which any reality whatever may be thought. As mutually predicable they imply one another, and terms that imply one another endow any frame of reference with conceptual unity. Moreover, as mutually predicable, transcendental categories cannot be understood in isolation from one another. In other words, they endow any theory they structure with what Whitehead calls logical "coherence."

A problematic foundational situation generates transcendental categories because it raises religious questions. Religious questions seek both synthetic and normative answers. A warranted religious insight functions synthetically because it puts one into a life-giving relationship with one's God and with one's world. Any adequate response to a religious question demands therefore categories that will allow the inquiring religious mind to think the reality of self, God, and the world with logical coherence. In other words, in formulating the answer to any question generated by a problematic foundational situation, one will need to employ at some point transcendental categories. Besides enjoying coherence through mutual implication, such categories need to conceive reality in relational terms; for they seek to interpret relationships touched by religious ultimacy. Only philosophy supplies transcendental categories, for only philosophy of all the rational sciences attempts to understand the most generic traits of all reality.

The complexity of any problematic foundational situation also forces the formulation of general and special categories. Foundational theology ambitions a normative account of conversion. Religious conversion among other things effects the graced transformation of natural human growth. An adequate foundational theory of the dynamics of conversion

must therefore include an adequate account of natural human development. Other sciences than philosophy study natural growth and social
relationships; and other sciences than theology study religion. By "general categories" Lonergan means categories derived from some other
discipline than theology which nevertheless yield a normative insight
into the dynamics of conversion. Phenomenology, psychology, sociology,
history, and comparative religion all contribute insights into the dynamics of conversion. Moreover, the derivative character of general categories entails that the quality of foundational thinking must of necessity
depend on the state of those secular disciplines which supply the categories which the foundational theologian uses.

Foundational theology, however, studies more than natural processes. It also offers normative insights into their graced transformation.
Natural processes undergo graced transformation when they are informed and transvalued by religious faith. Any adequate theory of
conversion must, as a consequence, inevitably employ faith-derived categories. Faith-derived categories articulate an experience of divine encounter, of divine self-revelation. They integrate religious experience
but differently from transcendental categories. Transcendental categories integrate foundational theory in virtue of their abstractness, for they
must characterize any reality whatever. Special theological categories
integrate a foundational theory in virtue of their specificity, for they
claim to articulate the way in which God has come to be concretely,
historically, and normatively revealed.

Like all sound religious categories, special theological categories
attempt to communicate synthetic insights. They try to offer an integrated and integrating account of how a convert ought to relate to God,
to the world, to society, to oneself; but as categories they share the
specificity of the particular historical self-revelation of God which they
interpret. Categories derived from Christian faith, for example, do more
than invite a generic assent to God; they summon one to repentant
commitment to the God who has been historically self-revealed in Jesus
and in His Holy Breath. Special theological categories therefore create a
frame of reference for interpreting the graced transformation of natural
processes according to the specific demands of a particular historical
self-communication of God.

As historically specific, special theological categories also test the
adequacy of any proposed set of transcendental categories, for any
transcendental category which cannot interpret the specific way in which
God has chosen to reveal Himself falls short of the universal predi-
cability it ambitions. For example, classical theism lists "being" among the
transcendentals, and it characterizes "being itself" as absolute and unre-
lated. As a consequence, its metaphysical account of God fails to interpret adequately the revealed reality of a convenanting God who stands

in a loving relationship with His people. Similarly, the attempt of process theologians to use "experience" transcendentally but to define it as "dipolar" fails to interpret adequately a divine reality that stands historically self-revealed as triadic.[3]

We shall reflect in greater detail on the coordination and interpretative interplay of these three nests of categories in the chapter which follows.

The forces within any foundational situation which generate the categories of foundational thought coincide with the forces which render it problematic. Language and culture condition any foundational situation. That fact transforms the foundational situation into a potential source of categories. Two chief socio-cultural forces render foundational situations problematic: the forces of fragmentation and the forces of conflict.

Fragmentation results in part from conflict but only in part. It also results from finitude. Finitude, for example, forces the human mind to focus its attention and to specialize in different fields of investigation. Specialization inevitably fragments the pursuit of truth into autonomous disciplines that advance for the most part in disintegrating oblivion of one another. Intellectual specialization also secularizes thought. Legitimate specialized human inquiries create sources of information that develop independently from religious faith even when they do not directly challenge or contradict it. Because religious insight aspires to an integrated and integrating insight, foundational theology must find ways to counteract the fragmentation and secularization of knowledge which the finitude of the human mind spawns. Foundational thinking will succeed in this enterprise if it can create a religious frame of reference that successfully interprets the validated results of secular inquiry.

Foundational theory must also deal with conflict. Conflicts arise from either natural or sinful motives. Natural conflicts prescind from religious realities and values. Think, for example, of territorial battles among animals or the squabbling of small children. Sinful conflicts consciously violate the will of God. Think, for example, of every unjust war waged by Christians.

The dialectical analysis of unreconciled conflicts within both a religion and the culture in which that religion roots itself clarifies the way in which a given foundational situation has become problematic. Foundational theology must resolve the conflicts which the dialectician clarifies. Foundational theology tries to do so by creating an integrated and integrating frame of reference that preserves the truth in warring posi-

---

[3] For a discussion of this technical point, see: Donald L. Gelpi, S.J. *The Divine Mother: A Trinitarian Theology of the Holy Spirit* (Lanham, MD: University Press of America, 1984) 17–43.

tions while discarding errors and oversights. For example, in approaching reformation controversies a sound foundational theory will attempt to articulate a theology that builds on the best insights into human religious experience articulated by the embattled theologians of the period.

Dialectics, therefore, plays an important role in generating the categories that shape foundational thinking. Competing sets of transcendental categories proposed by different philosophers need to be examined and evaluated. The relevant results of secular science and scholarship should be scrutinized for points of convergence and conflict in their accounts of religious experience. The issues at the basis of religious squabbles need analysis and comparative elucidation.

In addition to philosophy, theology, and secular studies of religious experience, foundational theology may derive useful categories from three other scholarly sources: religious autobiography, religious history, and cultural history.

Foundational theology ambitions a normative account of conversion. As a consequence, only the converted can engage in foundational thinking; for one can expect little insight from normative reflection on an experience one has never undergone. Of necessity therefore pursuit of the foundational theological enterprise forces the theologian into self-criticism, and self-criticism systematically pursued bears fruit in religious autobiography. The dialectical significance of one's personal religious autobiography and therefore its potential fruitfulness as a source of foundational categories will depend upon the number of conflicting religious viewpoints one has endorsed in the course of one's personal development. At the very least, however, religious autobiography raises to consciousness in a preliminary fashion those religious and cultural forces that have moulded one's personal experience of conversion.

Cultural history, especially the history of ideas, offers another potentially fruitful source of foundational categories. At the very least cultural history will help identify the significant factors that shape a foundational situation. It uncovers the dominant motifs in civil religion and by dramatizing the evolution of a culture portrays in narrative the situation which an inculturated foundational theology must address. For example, a clear penchant for pelagianism rooted in a naive optimism about the integrity of human nature shapes secular attitudes in the United States from Benjamin Franklin through American Transcendentalism and naturalism all the way down to our own day. Any inculturated North American account of the dynamics of conversion would have to understand the roots of such deeply rooted cultural attitudes and summon them to repentance and healing.

One can also, of course, draw on legitimate insights in North American Culture to criticize in constructive ways the different religions it hosts. John Courtney Murray, for example, by reflecting critically on

Catholic tradition in the light of "the American proposition" successfully revised official Catholic perceptions of religious freedom. Similarly, one might draw creatively on the American experience of democratic pluralism in order to criticize religious fundamentalism in all the mainline churches.

Religious history too will contextualize the pursuit of an inculturated theory of conversion. Religious history anatomizes the complex motives that lie at the basis of religious conflicts, motives that often fail to find expression in the highflown rhetoric of theological antagonists. It helps the dialectician distinguish between merely ideological and authentically theological concerns. Moreover, the study of religious movements which characterize a given culture can within limits throw light on the authenticities and inauthenticities likely to surface in contemporary movements with past religious analogues. For example, a knowledge of the history of revivalism in this country in both its Catholic and Protestant expressions will aid any foundational theologian concerned to deal with the strengths and weaknesses of contemporary Catholic charismatic piety.

(IV)

Our dialectical comparison of Dewey's logic and Lonergan's method has then allowed us to clarify an obscure point in foundational method, one which Lonergan failed to discuss as such in *Method in Theology:* namely, we have been able to identify the generating source of foundational categories. We have called that source the foundational situation. We have described some of the processes likely to endow specific categories with more or less importance in different foundational situations: namely, fragmentation and conflict. Finally, we have noted the utility of dialectics in mediating between the foundational situation and the actual formulation of a normative theory of conversion. Finally, we have reflected on some of the major sources within the foundational situation of the categories that shape foundational reflection.

If truth be told, however, the foundational situation we have been describing differs in notable respects from the purely logical situation which Dewey describes. We shall find further insight into the specific character of foundational thought by contrasting the two. Moreover, we have not yet addressed a far more perplexing problem than the sources of foundational categories. That problem may be stated briefly: foundational theories attempt to resolve foundational situations rendered indeterminate by conflict and fragmentation. Can we then begin to describe the thought processes that produce the correct solution to a particular foundational problem?

First, let us contrast the foundational situation with the purely logical situation described by Dewey.

In all of his logical and epistemological speculations, Dewey's thought exhibits a central, driving concern: to keep the act of inquiry open by forestalling dogmatic attempts to close it arbitrarily. A similar concern surfaces in his ethical thought, especially in his polemic against fixed moral ends. In any moral situation one must, he believed, remain free to readjust one's ends to meet the novel demands of the unexpected. Concern with the open-endedness of inquiry also helped motivate Dewey's atheistic naturalism. He excluded theistic religion from his vision of the world in part because he believed that it encourages dogmatism and fundamentalism in both speculation and morality.[4]

A sound theology of conversion should join Dewey in unmasking the inauthenticities that motivate dogmatism and fundamentalism. Nevertheless, precisely because foundational theology attempts to understand an experienced encounter with the divine, it includes within it forces and values that do not function significantly in the problematic situations Dewey describes. Foundational theology would, for example, need to temper Dewey's hard-nosed preoccupation with problem solving by a counterbalancing openness to wonder, to contemplation, and to mystery. Similarly, unlike Dewey's naturalistic conception of the logical situation, any foundational situation would contain both realities and values that make religious claims of moral absoluteness and ultimacy.

Dewey, to be sure, recognized a religious dimension to human experience. Experience, he argued, takes on a religious character when it is shaped by ideals that organize it, integrate it, inspire it, and give it an ultimate direction. He, however, regarded such ideals as human creations and as always revisable (CF, 29–57).

A revealed religion like Christianity makes more specific moral demands. The God of Christianity claims the absolute and ultimate allegiance of those who believe in Him. Christians must cling to God beyond any other good in all circumstances of their lives. Moreover, Christian faith asserts that the incarnation reveals to us the reality of God and the moral demands He makes of us, demands that summon every human conscience to submission.

As an historical religion, Christianity looks back to the incarnation as the event that defines the identity of the Christian community. All Christians are called to live as the children of God in the image of Jesus and in the power of His Breath. We cannot change past events. They enjoy the eternal fixity of fact. Anyone, therefore, who consents to the event of Jesus' life and ministry as the normative, historical revelation of God and of the way humans are called by God to live acknowledges that the value system He incarnated makes perennial moral claims on the human conscience. We can and should revise inadequate accounts of the

---

[4] John Dewey, *A Common Faith* (New Haven: Yale, 1934). Hereafter this work will be abbreviated CF.

incarnation and the claims it makes on us; but, because it happened, it enjoys the fixity of fact.

Christianity does not, of course, claim to offer an exhaustive or comprehensive account of either God or human morality. In this life Christians glimpse both through a glass darkly. God reveals Himself to us in Jesus and the Holy Breath sacramentally. Sacramental events both disclose and conceal the realities they reveal. Consent to the religious imperatives intrinsic to a sacramental event of grace provides the Christian convert with cognitive access to God in faith. Because foundational theology only ambitions an account of religious experience as it actually transpires, nothing constrains it to offer an exhaustive account of the reality of God. It need only anatomize religious experience as it occurs by offering an applicable and adequate account of the limited historical revelation we have actually received. By the same token, however, foundational theory must also find means to explain how a partial, limited, and historically conditioned revelation of God can make absolute and ultimate normative claims.

Jesus of Nazareth lived at a particular time and place. His teachings reflect the cultural forces that shaped the eastern Mediterranean basin. We have historical access to His teachings through the collective memory of His disciples recorded in the New Testament. He proclaimed a specific understanding of God and modeled for His disciples their own stance to the divine. He demanded that they call God *Abba* (Papa) and place such trust in His providential care that they would never hesitate to share their goods with others. Like *Abba* they should place no conditions on their willingness to share. They should reach out to good and wicked alike and share on the basis of need not of merit only. Their sharing must reach across social barriers to the marginal and outcast. They should practice table fellowship with sinners. By such conduct they would inherit the kingdom of God, which should be founded neither on coercive violence, nor on power politics but on prayer whose authenticity expresses a mutual forgiveness that imitates the gratuity of God's forgiveness of all sinners, oneself included. The practical sharing which brings into existence the community of disciples seeks therefore to imitate the atoning love of Jesus for His own disciples.

The religious vision of Jesus begins to make absolute and ultimate moral claims only if one confesses Him as God incarnate, for the human mind of God incarnate reveals in its very historical uniqueness and concreteness what God thinks about the way humans ought to relate to Him. Anyone who does not confess Jesus as Lord and God can, if self-consistent, look upon his religious thought as only one fallible religious hypothesis among many. For the confessing Christian, however, the partial, limited, historically conditioned revelation of God in Jesus makes normative claims not only of moral absoluteness and ultimacy but of universality as well, for the self-communication of God in Jesus and His Breath reaches out to all people.

One can acknowledge the historical fact of such a revelation without arbitrarily closing off the path of inquiry. Dewey would concede willingly that inquiry does not advance in a vacuum and that facts define the realistic limits of speculation. Religious realism demands that theological speculation take into account not only the finite, concrete fact of the incarnation but the moral consequences that consent to that fact in faith makes upon the human conscience. Moreover, the fallibility of the theological mind demands that theology, no less than science and philosophy, advance through shared, systematic inquiry and that theological theories be tested not only against the facts of revelation but against their consequences for human conduct. Paradoxically, then, any purely naturalistic approach to religion like Dewey's inconsistently closes the door to religious inquiry by ruling out a priori any serious consideration of the fact of Christian revelation. In the process Dewey's thought lapses into the very dogmatism with which he faults religion.[5]

We cling to realities and values with moral ultimacy when we are willing not only to live but, if necessary, to die for them. We cling to them

---

[5] In his perceptive analysis of American Naturalism, William M. Shea discovers a potential opening to the supernatural in John Dewey's aesthetic experience of the whole. Shea correctly notes the analogy between religious and aesthetic experience, and argues that religious interpretations of experience, including Christian theologies of grace, invoke this felt sense of the whole of experience. We experience the whole, Shea further argues, as both unitive and unifying, on the one hand, and as dialectical and unsettling, on the other. We never possess or control the whole that we perceive. Instead, we belong to it. Shea suggests that if Dewey had pursued more systematically his reflections on this mysterious experience of the whole, he might well have discovered the presence of grace and the supernatural within experience itself. Cf. William M. Shea, *The Naturalists and the Supernatural: Studies in Horizon and an American Philosophy of Religion* (Mercer University Press, 1984) 117–141.

I am inclined to agree with Prof. Shea's criticism of Dewey's naturalism. I would only add two sets of observations. First, we need to distinguish three ways in which we humans perceive the whole. We have a vague felt sense of a reality that encompsses the persons and things with which we deal directly. In addition, we can apprehend the whole either intuitively or rationally. A vague felt sense of the whole needs intuitive and rational clarification. Intuitive perceptions of the whole invoke the archetype of the self, which mediates an imaginative sense of contextualizing wholeness. The rational mind constructs metaphysical theories of the whole whose applicability and adequacy, as Whitehead saw, need to be tested against reality. Second, all three perceptions of the whole—felt, intuitive, and rational—reflect the radical finitude of the human mind. Indeed, that finitude explains the mind's ability to deny aspects of the whole in the very act of imagining or conceiving it, as does Dewey's naturalism. Perceptions of the whole which remain open to the supernatural can, however, also fall victim to finitude by failing to account for some other dimension of the real. For reasons I have already explained, I would not discover in human perception of the whole Lonergan's unrestricted desire to know or the virtual infinity of the human mind.

with moral absoluteness when we acknowledge the ultimate claim they make on us in every circumstance. One cannot consent to such realities and values without confronting the mystery of living and dying, the fact of one's own finitude, the wonder of God and of the very world in which we live. The religious convert cannot as a consequence assume a purely instrumentalist approach to life and reality. Confrontation with the mystery of God, of life, and of iniquity introduces one into realms of experience that transcend mere problem solving without, however, excluding it.

Because the moral vision of Jesus makes absolute and ultimate claims, it constrains the Christian conscience to see to it that those values find embodiment in every situation and in every personal choice. Jesus' moral doctrine orients the Christian conscience toward a specific communitarian ideal, but it offers no easy formulas for realizing that ideal in the concrete. Indeed, in a world of finite, ego-centric, and sinful people, Christians may anticipate that Jesus' moral vision will never find perfect human embodiment in this life. Nevertheless, that vision constrains the Christian conscience to deal creatively with each situation in an attempt to advance it the next possible step toward the perfect realization of the ideal religious community that Jesus proclaimed.

The need for the Christian conscience to balance fidelity to the moral ideals Jesus proclaimed with realism and practical hope in confronting human finitude and sinfulness entails two important consequences for foundational method. First, any attempt to reduce a problematic foundational situation to satisfaction must lie open to the need for suffering and atonement, to the pain of rejection despite all efforts to reach across human barriers in forgiveness and love. Second, the human attempt to render problematic foundational situations determinate must constantly guard against the temptation to moral complacency. The moral vision of Jesus stands as a challenge to any human attempt to embody it. At no point can any disciple claim to have incarnated it totally and completely. The kind of divine love disclosed in Jesus simultaneously challenges His disciples to greater selflessness even as it assures them that their failures and limitations have already been comprehended and forgiven by an inexhaustible divine compassion.

Nevertheless, we can bring some problematic foundational situations to some measure of resolution. A foundational analysis of the charismatic renewal illustrates the process. This popular movement in ecumenical and lay spirituality poses serious questions concerning the moral consequences of Christian conversion. A blend of Protestant pentecostalism and Roman Catholic piety, the charismatic renewal sometimes inculcates a spirituality insufficiently attuned to values promulgated in the documents of Vatican II and to the best insights of contemporary theology. The very existence of the movement within the

Catholic Church poses a host of complex theological questions. Can one blend authentically Catholic and Penetecostal forms of worship? What does the New Testament mean by baptism in a Holy Breath? How does Breath baptism transform the conversion process? What role and function do the charisms play in human experience? How many kinds of charisms can we distinguish, and how do we authenticate their exercise? The charismatic renewal poses these and a multitude of other questions. In other words, the emergence of Catholic charismatic piety in the wake of Vatican II has created a problematic foundational situation within the Roman Catholic community.

One can provide a satisfactory foundational response to the questions the charismatic renewal raises. One can demonstrate that in a sacramental community everyone is called by the rites of initiation to experience Breath baptism, to live in lifelong openness to the sanctifying, charism-dispensing Breath of Jesus. One can demonstrate through an analysis of the dynamics of conversion that sacramental piety makes no sense and degenerates into empty ritualism when it is not completely informed by the charisms of the Breath. One can show that the charisms endow the church with primordial sacramentality and therefore provide the context that authenticates Christian rituals. In other words one can bring the problematic theological situation created by the charismatic renewal to resolution in principle.

Nevertheless, the successful resolution in principle of a problematic foundational situation does not automatically ensure its practical, pastoral resolution as well. Foundational theology can elaborate a normative account of the ways in which the charisms of the Holy Breath ought to lend dynamic shape to Christian conversion, but normative thinking appeals to human freedom. It cannot therefore offer an ironclad guarantee that people will abide by its norms. In point of fact, to this day inauthenticities do surface in charismatic communities as a consequence of the failure of both members and leadership to understand and implement a sound foundational theology of the gifts.

We have in this section been reflecting on the ways in which a problematic foundational situation differs analogously from the problematic logical situation which Dewey describes. Another vexing question faces us to which both Dewey and other North American thinkers have attempted indirectly to respond: namely, how does one go about formulating the hypotheses that will bring problematic foundational situations to theoretical and practical resolution?

No method guarantees or substitutes for creativity. It cannot supply or replace genius. It cannot provide sure-fire rules for coming up with the right answer to important questions. Within limits, however, methodological reflection can describe the creative process, can identify those things that foster creativity, and can provide criteria for evaluating the results of creative insight.

Arthur Koestler, for example, has argued both correctly and persuasively that creativity not only presupposes an affective matrix but that the character of human creativity derives in part from the kinds of affections it expresses. Comic creativity engages the aggressive-defensive emotions; tragic creativity, the sympathetic affections; and speculative creativity, a mixture of both.[6]

Similarly, Michael Polanyi has taught us that creative thinking engages "heuristic passion." The creative mind needs emotional engagement with a problem if it hopes to come up with the right solution. Creative thinkers fall in love with their work. Fascination with a problem stimulates the imagination to try different possible answers to vexing questions.[7]

So do stimulating environments in which every variety of solution can be proposed and discussed and then adopted or discarded on the basis of its merits. Moreover, dialectics endows the free discussion of problems with stimulating clarity by anatomizing the pros and cons, the strengths and weaknesses, the presuppositions and consequences of attempted solutions.

Deliberation guides the selection of proposed hypotheses. Here Dewey's logic offers additional illuminating insights. Dewey assigns deliberation a variety of tasks within inquiry. The deliberating mind ponders alternatives. Practical in its interest, it occupies the turf between free-floating fantasy and prudential judgment. Deliberation dispenses with too tight a control on the processes of thought and gives fantasy reign. Deliberation thrives on brain-storming. It blends receptivity to new ideas and new approaches with active interest and concern to find the right solution. Attuned to the complexity of any problem, the deliberating mind feels its way into problematic situations and in its investigation of the scope of a problem leaves no stone unturned. Deliberation distinguishes between the problematic and settled elements in any given situation. It transforms vague feelings concerning the unsettled character of a situation into an accurately stated problem.

The fact that deliberation engages human affectivity raises special problems for foundational thinking. While healthy affections can foster sound insight into the conversion process, disordered affections can subvert it. Emotional disorder can of course distort any thought process. When, however, conversion itself provides the subject matter for thought the need to deal with blinding passion assumes special impor-

---

[6] Arthur Koestler, *The Act of Creation* (New York: Macmillan, 1964).

[7] Michael Polanyi, *Personal Knowledge* (Chicago: University of Chicago Press, 1958).

tance. We will return to this question in discussing the criteria for a sound hypothesis. Suffice it to say here that the deliberating mind must deal with what Lonergan calls scotosis, that is, with neurosis that inhibits insight.

Having identified a foundational problem, the deliberating foundational thinker next needs to formulate a working plan to deal with it both speculatively and practically. Problems arise out of conflict and contradiction. The deliberating mind formulates a problem by identifying the points of apparent conflict as well as their apparent motives. Preliminary judgments about both will raise questions concerning the adequacy of the evidence adduced by the parties involved in the conflict. These questions will point in turn to the kinds of information that need to be gathered in order to resolve the conflict.[8]

In the process of gathering information the deliberating foundational thinker will need to deal disjunctively with facts, with goals, and with explanations. Deliberation employs disjunctions because it needs to identify alternative data, purposes, and interpretations of the problem it investigates and of the solution it seeks. The conceptual clarification of alternatives heightens consciousness of situational complexity and stimulates the creative imagination. In dealing disjunctively with facts, deliberation must determine what did or did not happen in order to make a situation problematic. In dealing with goals, it must examine alternative suggestions for resolving the unsettled situation. In dealing with explanations it must assess competing interpretations of the meaning and importance of relevant data. Moreover, the deliberations of the foundational theologian must advance in the light of a sound knowledge of Sacred Scripture, of tradition, of the history of doctrine, and of a dialectical analysis of the religious and cultural issues involved in a conflicted foundational situation.

The deliberative assessment of foundational situations must distinguish also between the problematic and settled elements of the situation. Settled insights into the exigencies of authentic conversion will provide the norms for discriminating authentic from inauthentic solutions. The foundational theologian will also need to distinguish religious realities and values that make morally absolute and ultimate claims from the contingencies of the situation that raise the problem. The former will provide a context for assessing alternative goals; but they will neither provide nor guarantee specific solutions to concrete problems.

In order to advance from an insight into the religious ideals that measure authenticity or inauthenticity in a conflicted foundational situation, the deliberating theologian must first repent of those disordered

---

[8] These reflections draw on insights in Dewey's logic; see LTI, 57, 162 ff., 170–171, 274.

affections that blind the heart to a sound appreciation of truly valuable elements ingredient in the problematic, foundational situation. Then one must affirm the need to preserve as far as possible those very elements. In addition one must repent of those attitudes, beliefs, and commitments that fall short of the ideal to which one is called by God. Finally, one must reach a prayerful, discerning judgment concerning the best way to advance the situation the next possible step toward the ideals to which one stands religiously committed.

Let us attempt to concretize these abstractions somewhat by returning to the example of the charismatic renewal. Let us assume the existence of a parish radically divided over the presence in its midst of a charismatic contingent. Let us assume that the pastor, who is contemplating forbidding the use of parish facilities to the charismatics, comes to you as a foundational theologian and seeks your advice. How should you go about the task of generating a possible solution to his problem?

Our reflections on the process of deliberation so far suggest that unless the problem engages your interest and excites you personally, you would be better advised to send the pastor to a competent consultant who experiences such involvement. You would also be well advised within the limits of time and resources to consult as broadly as you can in attempting to formulate a sound pastoral solution. You should also approach the question as far as possible without rigid preconceptions concerning the best way to resolve it. If anything about the situation threatens you, you should face your fears and anxieties and bring them to healing; otherwise they could betray you into misreading the situation or into imposing a solution out of fear or resentment rather than one that meets real needs.

The pastor has proposed to you a possible way of formulating the problem. He wants to know whether or not to exclude charismatics from use of church facilities. Before you can begin to address the problem you need to get your facts straight. You examine the pastor and discover that on being approached by some of his parishioners to start a charismatic group, he consented; but because of the press of pastoral duties as well as his lack of ease with charismatic forms of prayer, he himself attended the meetings only sporadically. He resisted, however, the efforts of extreme conservatives in the parish who urged him to condemn the charismatics as heretics, only to discover that several members of the charismatic group had begun to attend services at a nearby Classical Pentecostal church and had begun to imbibe beliefs and attitudes that from a Catholic standpoint seemed elitist, fundamentalistic, and authoritarian. On approaching the lay leaders of the charismatic group, he found them less than flexible. When he questioned several of their fundamentalistic interpretations of the Bible, they rejected his exegesis as unsound because, having never received the gift of tongues, he still needed to

receive the baptism of the Holy Spirit. The standoff between the charismatics and the conservatives had provoked a storm of controversy in the
parish and mounting pressure was being exerted on him to oust the
charismatics.

Having learned the salient facts of the case, you realize that the
situation contains many more problems than the pastor's dilemma
whether or not to eject the charismatics. As you probe further into the
situation, you discover that the conservative Catholics in the parish seem
to have little living, practical faith in the charismatic activity of the Holy
Breath and that the charismatics have bought blindly into an inadequate
understanding of the meaning and consequences of Breath baptism. In
other words, the conflict is motivated by inauthenticites in the religious
stance of both groups of adversaries.

As you ponder these basic facts in the light of a sound understanding of the dynamics of conversion, you begin to suspect that the pastor
has posed the problem too simply. The conflict has developed from
motives much broader and deeper than the allocation of parish facilities
to a particular group of parishioners. Communications in the parish
have broken down because serious inauthenticities mar the piety of both
the charismatics and their antagonists. You suggest to the pastor that
settling for a solution based on space allocation alone fails to do justice to
the pastoral complexities facing him. Tactfully, you invite him to examine
his own reluctance to involve himself actively with charismatic forms of
prayer and urge him not to let any such reluctance blind him to the
authentic values present in the piety of the charismatics. You urge him as
well to deal with any personal resentment he may feel at being called to
deal with an unwanted and sticky pastoral mess. All parties need to be
approached sympathetically with sensitivity to the authentic values that
each one cherishes.

As a foundational theologian you can also begin at this point to
identify some of the stable elements in the situation that might conceivably resolve the conflict. The New Testament offers abundant material on the activity and charismatic illumination of the Breath of Jesus. It
also contains important norms for discerning authentic and inauthentic
movements of the Holy Breath. All this material could be used to help
the charismatics reassess their own elitist, fundamentalistic tendencies.
Moreover, the Christian tradition, the councils of the church, the writings of the popes, and especially the documents of Vatican II contain
doctrines and principles which should challenge the animosity of the
traditionalists towards the charismatics. Foundational theology offers
sound insights into the dynamics of conversion which will facilitate a
pastoral assessment of the inauthenticities at the root of the troublesome
conflict.

You suggest to the pastor that together the two of you advance to a reformulation of the problem. Seemingly, the situation will not be brought to adequate resolution until both charismatics and traditionalists confront their own need for repentance and mutual reconciliation. Both need considerable pastoral instruction about a sound understanding of the authentic action of the Holy Breath in the hearts of individuals and in the shared life of a Christian faith community. Since the dispute has involved the entire parish, you offer the hopefully creative suggestion, that an opening has been made to invite a parish-wide reflection on this and other related questions.

With the collaboration of the pastor you begin to sketch a three dimensional catechetical program: one for the charismatics, one for the traditionalists, and one for the parish as a whole as an important component in the pastor's program for ongoing parish renewal. Your catechetical program attempts to inculcate sound moral and ascetical principles of discernment. It reminds all parties concerned of the moral exigencies of Christian discipleship. It instructs them in a sound theology of the gifts of sanctification and service. It shows the indispensable relationship between charismatic and sacramental piety. Your program attempts to rebuild the collapsed lines of communication among alienated parishioners by holding up to them the communitarian ideal every parish is bound in Christ to attempt to embody. After a repentant confrontation with personal responsibility for the disruption of community life, the members of the parish need to begin to move collectively to the next possible concrete approximation of the Christian ideal. In other words, having reformulated the problem in broader terms than the pastor originally posed it, the two of you sketch a possible solution, one that will be reached not simply by the administrative fiat of the pastor but by collective, parish-wide repentance, by a new discovery of the meaning of personal and communal openness to the Breath of Jesus, and by a process of shared decision making that could conceivably advance the parish to a new level of shared faith consciousness.

The preceding account of a fictional attempt to advance from a conflicted foundational situation, to the identification of the problem that motivates the conflict, to the imaginative formulation of a possible solution illustrates how deliberation could conceivably function in rendering an indeterminate foundational situation determinate. It describes the transition from the discovery of conflict to the formulation of a hypothetical solution. What, howver, constitues a useful hypothesis? Here the logic of Charles Sanders Peirce provides some useful criteria for identifying potentially fruitful hypotheses.

Peirce, Dewey's logical metaphor, can claim no small part of the credit for Dewey's resistance to formalistic logic. Peirce's logic emphasized more the fixation of belief than the resolution of problematic situations; but Peirce, like Dewey, understood logic as critical reflection on the operations of the mind. He acknowledged recurrent and interrelated patterns in the processes of human inference. Author of the pragmatic maxim, he judged the fruitfulness of an hypothesis by its capacity to generate verifiable consequences. In other words, Peirce's approach to logic shares the same fundamental characteristics as Lonergan's understanding of method.

Moreover, having distinguished more sharply than Lonergan between abductive (or hypothetical) inference and deduction (Lonergan lumps both under the rubric of understanding), Peirce devoted considerable reflection to the operations that give rise to sound abductions. He saw quite clearly that logic could provide no rules for generating the right answer to unsolved questions. He realized that in the creative advance of thought nothing replaces imagination and genius. He also realized that abductive thinking engages mind play, or "musement." At the same time he marveled at the human mind's capacity to hit with such frequency on the right hypothesis, on the single explanation among a virtually infinite number of speculative possibilities that unlock the riddles of a sphinxlike nature.

As he pondered the processes of hypothetical reasoning, its spontaneity and unpredictability, Peirce began to recognize that logic could finally find ways of serving abductive thinking despite the logical mind's overarching preoccupation with the control of thought rather than with mental playfulness. Logic, he realized, could supply criteria for deciding which hypotheses generated from the spontaneous creativity of mind play deserve the labor of deductive clarification and inductive testing. He suggested four such criteria: breadth, caution, testability, and instinctive simplicity.

The canon of breadth states that a good hypothesis will have many ramifications for other areas of human activity than the discipline in which it is formulated. The canon of caution states that we should select those hypotheses for inductive testing which we have in fact the available energy and resources to test. The canon of testability states that a good hypothesis should be able to be broken up into separate parts capable of independent verification. The canon of instinctive simplicity states that, all other things being equal, one should select for experimental testing that hypothesis which appeals most spontaneously to the educated mind. Have these logical canons any relevance to the conduct of foundational inquiry?

Although foundational theology does not employ exact, mathematical measurement, we can test its hypotheses to a point. Foundational hypotheses offer possible explanations of how human religious experience can and should develop. The consequences of conflicting accounts of the dynamics of conversion can be measured more or less systematically against the way religious people actually behave.

Here the distinction between explanatory and strictly normative thinking claims our attention. Explanatory thinking, as we have seen, offers an account about the ways in which realities around us can be reasonably expected to behave. To the extent that it tells how things ought to be expected to act, explanation provides a normative account of reality. In strictly normative thinking, however, the term "normative" begins to acquire other connotations that distinguish it from explanation. Strictly normative thinking deals not simply with predictable but with responsible behavior. It asks how I the thinker, or for that matter any other person, ought to act in the light of the intuitions, ideals, norms, and principles that govern responsible behavior.

Foundational theology must, as we have seen, produce both explanations and strictly normative hypotheses. It draws creatively on the philosophical sciences of esthetics, ethics, and logic in order to understand what kinds of habits ought to function in sound affective, moral, and intellectual development. In the process the foundational theologian generates strictly normative hypotheses that need validation not only in personal behavior but also in the results of the personality sciences and of social analysis. In exploring religious conversion, foundational theology generates theological hypotheses about human religious growth whose truth and adequacy can be measured both against the religious tradition it interprets and against the behavior of religious converts. Foundational theology deals not only with the growth processes of converts, it also measures the accuracy of their religious perceptions. It must offer a normative account of the way the realites encountered within conversion ought to be affectively and inferentially perceived. It will succeed in that task to the extent that it can predict how those same realities ought to be expected to behave. In other words, the foundational theologian needs to engage in both explanatory and strictly normative thinking.

The attempt to advance beyond the personal validation of its hypotheses confronts foundational theology with methodological problems analogous to those confronting empirical psychology. Both must rely to some extent on personal reflection on one's own experience. Both also need to acknowledge the extreme fallibility of such personal reflections and to check them against investigations of human behavior based on both interviews and impartial statistical surveys. In addition, the foundational thinker must consult the Christian tradition and test all normative insights into the dynamics of conversion against the historical revelation of God we have received.

We may then conclude that within the limits possible to scholarly thinking, foundational hypotheses should conform to the canons of caution and testability. If we can within limits validate inductively the relative merits of different foundational hypotheses, then caution suggests that we concern ourselves with those hypotheses that give the greatest promise of eventual validation, and prudence suggests that whenever possible we prefer foundational theories sufficiently complex to be broken down into a series of hypotheses capable of independent validation or invalidation; for even though negative conclusions can advance insight, a partially verified hypothesis points the way to an eventual solution to a problem in ways that a disproven one does not. Moreover, an hypothesis with independently testable clauses holds greater promise of at least partial verification.

Can we also apply the canons of breadth and of instinctive simplicity to proposed foundational hypotheses?

Because foundational thinking advances in the context of interdisciplinary collaboration, we can expect with some confidence that any promising foundational abduction will imply consequences that extend beyond the study of theology. At the very least it will suggest the ways in which the philosophical and general categories that structure foundational thinking need to be transvalued in faith. At the same time, since foundational method demands that theological ideas be validated against the proven conclusions of secular science and scholarship, suggestive foundational hypotheses will very likely suggest the need to adjust fallacious or inadequate religious presuppositions to the exigencies of hard fact. In other words, a promising foundational abduction should conform as far as possible to the canon of breadth.

The religious character of the foundational situation endows the canon of instinctive simplicity with connotations that go beyond Peircian logic. Peirce was led to formulate the canon of instinctive simplicity by observing the uncanny capacity of the scientific genius to select from a virtually infinite number of fallacious theoretical explanations the correct solution to a particular scientific problem. That astounding ability suggested to Peirce the existence of a kind of educated connaturality between the speculating mind and the realities it sought to understand. At the same time logical fallibilism cautioned Peirce to regard any such connaturality as an acquired talent. It resulted not from some innate, a priori tendency but from submitting the processes of thought to the stern discipline of facts, of sound methodological procedures, and of validated insights.

Lonergan's fallacy of the empty head points to a similar insight. The fallacy states that one should expect that individual to approach a problem with least prejudice who knows nothing about it. In other words, in order to ensure a completely unprejudiced opinion in any dispute, ask someone who has never thought about the contested question. In point of fact, of course, ignorance of facts and issues in the mind which formulates an opinion insures bias. Only prolonged consideration of a problem's ins and outs, minute and exhaustive examination of the relevant data, careful measurement and pondering of the evidence, and critical reflection on the relative adequacy of alternative explanations,— only disciplined processes such as these dispel prejudice and engender connaturality between the investigating mind and the problem it investigates. The mind that submits to such discipline and to the corrective of shared inquiry, ought, however, to trust its hunches; for such a mind has taken the pains to acquire a connatural feel not only for the scope and limits of a given question but also for the probable behavior of the realities it is attempting to understand.

The fact that the canon of instinctive simplicity counsels the educated mind to trust initially to its hunches in formulating hypothetical solutions to vexing questions raises, however, special procedural problems for the foundational thinker. In purely secular speculation, one may well trust the realities being investigated to educate the investigating mind to guess how they might well be expected to behave. After all, the investigating mind emerges from and is disciplined by its world. In the theological investigation of divine revelation, however, easy connaturality between the human mind and the reality it investigates should not be presumed naively. Theology investigates the transformation of natural realities in a supernatural one, of human realities in the divine. Only the gracious transformation of one's heart, mind, and commitment in the Breath of God endows them with a connatural feeling for divine things. The theological investigator acquires such connaturality only through the discipline of prayer, through the patient and painful ascent of the mystic spiral, through progressive purgation and illumination.

Cognitive connaturality with divine things advances at two interrelated levels. First, the charisms of the Holy Breath transform human ego processes and teach them the obedience of faith by endowing them with docility to the Breath's guidance. Second, infused contemplation progressively binds the heart to God in unitive love. Both processes advance progressively. One may then anticipate that foundational theological hypotheses emerge from a mind and heart only more or less attuned to the transcendent divine reality it attempts to understand. At the same time, theological thinking, like every other form of human reflection, needs to submit to the exigencies of hard facts and sound operational procedures. In other words, the foundational thinker will acquire authentic connaturality with the realities of faith only through the pursuit of a scholarship informed by prayer and of a prayer shaped by the scholarly pursuit of wisdom.

We may then conclude that the canon of instinctive simplicity can be implemented within foundational speculation only with proper theological qualification. In the study of divinity one acquires an instinctive feel for the reality under investigation through the repentant transformation of cultivated natural talents in submission to the charismatic anointing of the Holy Breath and to the purifying discipline of contemplation.

We can perhaps concretize the way in which the canons of caution and testability, of breadth and instinctive simplicity might shape abductive foundational thinking by returning to our earlier example of a beleagured pastor trying to hold together a parish polarized by a confrontation between a group of charismatics of fundamentalistic bent and a group of unreconstructed conservative Catholics.

The canon of testability would advise both you as a theological consultant and the pastor whom you are advising to invoke sound, verifiable criteria in both assessing the sources of conflict in the parish and in formulating possible solutions to those conflicts. Psychological criteria should enable you to distinguish emotionally healthy from neurotic and psychotic behavior. Doctrinal criteria should facilitate distinguishing sound from unsound beliefs. Moral criteria should help discriminate responsible from irresponsible behavior. Religious criteria should identify inauthenticities in the faith commitment of everyone involves. The social sciences should provide criteria for dealing with the dynamics of conflicted situations.

In addition the canon of testability would caution both you and the pastor against suggesting monolithic solutions to complex problems. Your pastoral strategies should deal independently with those facets of the situation capable of isolation and separate handling. Different pastoral strategies need to be designed for each of the groups involved in the conflict: for the charismatics, for the entrenched conservatives, for the parish as a whole. For problem individuals, individual strategies need to be concocted. Moreover, the relative success or failure of specific strategies will demand assessment and if necessary modification or replacement.

The canon of caution would suggest that before embarking on the complex and onerous task of attempting to bring peace to a badly divided community, both you and the pastor need to assess the community's resources to deal adequately with the problems facing it. If you have reason to suspect that the parish pastoral team would lack the skills to implement needed solutions to the conflict, then careful consideration should be given to bringing in outside help. In any case, before attempting to deal practically with the conflicted foundational situation, those responsible for the project need to assess the practical feasibility of the proposed pastoral solutions. When proposals exceed the bounds of practical realism, they should be modified accordingly.

The canon of breadth suggests that in formulating a pastoral solution adapted to the needs of this particular parish both you and the pastor needs to keep an eye on the pastoral needs of the Church as a whole. Not only should you prefer testing pastoral strategies that might have application in similar parish situations, but you should also have a care for the sound direction of the charismatic renewal as a whole and for assuaging the polarization between liberals and conservatives in the church as a whole. You should show a sensitivity to the implications of your pastoral experiment for religious psychology, for an understanding of human social dynamics, and for any possibility of advancing understanding of both these fields.

The canon of instinctive simplicity demands that both you and the pastor deal personally with any neurotic attitudes that might cause you to misread the situation or to propose inappropriate strategies and solutions. It would demand not only that your formulation of the pastoral problem and your attempt to resolve conflicts creatively proceed from a thorough knowledge of individuals and situations but also that it express as thorough a knowledge as possible of the theoretical and practical principles that govern sound pastoral praxis. Prayerful discernment flowing from a repentant heart should inform all.

We have thus far considered some of the operations and criteria that generate creative foundational hypotheses and some of the criteria for selecting sound ones. What of the verification and falsification of such hypotheses?

Inferential thinking first predicts the operational consequences of different hypotheses and then attempts to verify or falsify its predictions within experience. Hypothetical inference attempts to classify persons and things in ways that will allow the accurate prediction of their future behavior. If the hypotheses fail to do so, that fact calls into question the initial classification and the assumptions on which it rests. If the investigated realities perform as anticipated, that fact confirms the initial classification and the assumptions on which it rests. Because foundational theology studies the gracious transformation of human behavior, it predicts inferentially how persons and things may be expected to behave in a religious context.

At this point, we should perhaps recall a few logical basics. First, we never encounter the data of any inquiry raw. Second, the data of any inquiry always go beyond sense data alone and include perceptual evaluations of the kinds of forces operative in any given situation. Third, we experience all data as simultaneously significant and meaningful.

Anyone who would interpret the data of inquiry as "raw" in the sense of "uninterpreted" falls into self-contradiction. Events occur with or without human interpretation, of course; but for any event to be transformed from a mere event into data, it must be judged evaluatively as relevant to some unsolved problem. An event cannot be so identified without someone interpreting it. In other words, in order to become a datum for inquiry, an event must of necessity forfeit its rawness.

Moreover, data gathering must advance beyond the realm of mere sensation into the judgmental realm of perception. Sense qualities offer useful cues for identifying persons and things in a preliminary fashion. When, however, we transform sensed facts into the data of inquiry, we classify them abductively on the basis of initially hazarded perceptions of the laws that shape behavior. Intuitive judgments of feeling perceive the laws that ground factual transactions appreciatively; inferential perceptions grasp them abductively, deductively, and inductively.

Events signify. In other words, they possess a relational structure which the human mind can both sense and perceive. Events moreover acquire meaning by being sensed and perceived. They become meaningful through being evaluated. Meaning, therefore adds evaluation to the significant structure of events. When events acquire meaning for us we become present to them and they to us in a specific way, namely, in the way we sense and perceive them. We may sense and perceive them more or less adequately. As a consequence, the prudent mind takes pains to criticize the accuracy of its sensations and the truth and adequacy of its perceptions.

These basic logical principles impose a certain number of constraints upon anyone attempting to deal inferentially with unsettled foundational situations. For they suggest that no inferential approach to such situations will satisfy the logical criteria of accuracy and adequacy which fails to acknowledge the situation's specifically religious laws and tendencies. In order to understand such situations we must allow them to acquire religious meaning for us. We must recognize that forces and aspirations shape their significant structure which transcend mere spatio-temporal forces; and our foundational hypotheses must reckon with the ways in which those forces may be expected to behave.

Inferential thinking predicts. It measures anticipated performance against actual performance. We anticipate performance through hypothetical classification. We clarify our anticipations through deductive prediction. We verify or falsify our predictions inductively.

Foundational theology studies the graced transformation of human behavior through an encounter with God in religious faith. Its hypotheses attempt to classify the forces at work in any foundational situation, whether subhuman, human, or divine, in such a way as to allow their behavior to be predicted. Moreover, because foundational theology ambitions a normative account of conversion, it needs to anticipate not only those behavioral patterns that subvert any authentic religious commitment but also those which nurture it. It must also offer religious converts an explanatory account both of how the action of God can be expected to transform personal growth in faith and prayer and of how forces in one's environment foster and undermine authentic religion.

These reflections suggest yet another contrast between the foundational situation and the logical one described by John Dewey. Dewey's instrumentalism causes him to value the rational control of events. He tends to assume that given the time, energy, effort, and intelligence, systematic inquiry can bring any indeterminate logical situation under control. Indeed, for Dewey, the verification of an hypothesis establishes control over a situation previously out of control.

Among the forces that shape a foundational situation, however, anyone seeking a normative account of the conversion process must factor in God. As a consequence, the ideal of control functions less significantly in foundational speculation than in purely logical thinking. Only God exercises complete control over problematic foundational situations. Those attempting to bring such situations to practical, pastoral resolution function as the instruments of the Breath of Christ. Not only, therefore, do they need to submit prayerfully to Her gracious inspirations, but they may also anticipate that their pastoral strategies may well be upset by what Thomas Aquinas calls the Holy Breath's surprises.

Nevertheless, the fact that humans can serve as the instruments of God in bringing the peace of Christ to troubled foundational situations entails that foundational method enjoys something like the denotative character that Dewey discovered in both scientific and philosophical speculation. Foundational theories derive from problematic situations and attempt to resolve those situations successfully. Moreover, every prudent foundational theorist should take care to distinguish between the macroscopic situation that both poses problems and judges the accuracy and adequacy of proposed solutions and the fallible interpretations and strategies concocted by foundational theory.

Dewey's description of the denotative character of human inferential thinking shares with the North American philosophical tradition as a whole an orientation toward the future and a concern with practice. Nevertheless, unless the human attempt to grapple rationally with reality tempers a concern with the future by a parallel and counter-balancing concern to learn from the insights and mistakes of the past, it runs the risk of repeating blunders out of ignorance.

Because foundational theology advances in the light of a systematic retrieval of the historical development of both a religion and the culture in which that religion roots itself, it provides the needed counterbalance to too exclusive a concern with the future. In the process, it offers means to liberate North American theological speculation from a brand of pragmatism that focuses somewhat narrowly on the future.[9] As we shall see, in the process foundational theory can also offer a useful corrective to a narrow concern with political praxis in the resolution of conflicted

[9] The pragmatism of William James falls victim to this fallacy. He interprets the pragmatic maxim as orienting the mind away from concern with the past toward concern with consequences and with the future; cf. William James, *Pragmatism* (New York: Meridian 1960) 71–79.

foundational situations. To this problem we now turn in the final section of this chapter.

(V)

The reflections of the preceding four sections of this chapter have given us reason to question the adequacy of Lonergan's notion of logic. No one need restrict the term "logic" to the purely deductive operations which he ascribes to logical as opposed to methodological thinking. Our reflections have also provided grounds for questioning whether the turn to the subject with its concomitant analysis of intentionality alone can ever suffice to ground foundational method. This last point deserves further consideration, for, as we shall see, if systematically pursued, it opens Lonergan's method to the possibility of a fruitful dialogue with liberation theology.

In our comparison with Dewey's theory of inquiry, we found that the former stresses the analysis of intentionality, while the latter emphasizes the analysis of problematic situations. We cannot equate simplistically these two kinds of analysis. No amount of philosophical exploration of the meanings I intend, however detailed, will disclose to me the significant structure of the problematic situations that confront me. Hence, any sound method needs to balance critical reflection on the evaluative processes that shape human judgments of feeling and of inference with an analysis of the forces that shape situations out of control. Situational analysis can engage both explanatory and strictly normative thinking. In confronting any situation as a foundational theologian, I not only desire to understand how the forces that shape it may be expected to behave, but I also seek to determine how a fully responsible person ought to attempt to direct the course of events in ways that accord with gospel living.

To the extent that it attempts to deal with both a religion and a culture, Lonergan's method ambitions at least implicitly the analysis of problematic social, cultural, and political situations, although his own reflections on method fail to deal in detail with such problems. Contemporary liberation theology, however, offers some significant resources for developing the concern with situational analysis latent in Lonergan's description of the fundamental task of theology. Lonergan, as we have seen, assigns theology the task of mediating between a religion and a culture. In expanding Lonergan's method to include situational analysis we will find particularly suggestive the concern of liberation theology to root the pursuit of theology in a political commitment that finds methodological expression in social analysis and social praxis.

Dewey, moreover, provides a useful bridge between Lonergan's methodological concerns and those of the Latin American liberationists.

Dewey's theory of knowledge displays greater sensitivity than Lonergan's to the affective, appreciative grasp of reality; and his account of the intentional structures that shape inferential thinking converges at important points with Lonergan's own. At the same time Dewey's concern to incorporate situational analysis into the process of inquiry links him solidly to a liberationist commitment to praxis as an indispensable key to sound method.

Indeed, even though Latin liberation theologians derive their concern with praxis from Marxist theory, when they describe what they mean by praxis they sound very much like Deweyan instrumentalists. Both praxis and instrumentalism repudiate philosophical dualisms: the artificial separation of theory from practice, of mind from body, of speculation from social transformation. Both insist on the need for situational analysis. Both attempt to extend the life of the mind into the political arena. Indeed, the convergence between liberating praxis and instrumental logic suggests that were Latin liberationists able to overcome their understandable repugnance for the culture of a nation whose policies contribute significantly to their economic oppression, they would find in the logic of both Peirce and Dewey insights that would enhance anything they themselves have written heretofore about the method of praxis. That same study could also help free the term "praxis" from the Marxist connotations it now possesses, connotations that tend to produce more rhetorical and ideological passion than insight into the operational procedures of theology.

In summoning theologians to conscious concern with social and political praxis, liberation theologian Gustavo Gutierrez tempers his challenge to traditional theological method by endorsing the legitimacy of more sacrosanct approaches. Political involvement, he argues, should never blind theologians to the fact that systematic study of the word of God seeks to instill wisdom and nourish the well-springs of Christian spirituality. Nor should the concern with praxis prevent theologians from serious historical research or discourage them from rigorous rational and systematic thinking. Rather, Gutierrez proposes praxis as an important and indispensible supplement to more traditional theological methods.[10]

Gutierrez roots theological concern with praxis in the constraints of Christian charity, in the contemporary need to develop a spirituality for activists, in the moral demands of new convenant religion which tempers love of God with practical concern for others, in the social concerns of Vatican II, and in the need for theologians in the wake of the council to develop a theology sensitive to the signs of the times. Gutierrez cites two

---

[10] Gustavo Gutierrez, *A Theology of Liberation*, translated by Sr. Caridad Inda and John Eagleson (New York: Orbis, 1973) 3–6. Hereafter this work will be abbreviated TL.

philosophical sources that support his concern with praxis: Maurice Blondell's philosophy of action and Marxist political theory. Christian eschatology, he also argues, commits theologians to a defense not only of orthodoxy but also of orthopraxis; for Christians fall short of complete fidelity to their tradition when they fail to strive to ensure that God's will be done on earth as in heaven (TL, 6–10).

Any attempt to grapple critically with gospel living in a contemporary context Gutierrez insists, forces one to face political as well as individual realities and problems. Politics pervades the whole of human life; and, granted the human condition, political involvement inevitably leads to political conflict (TL, 45–50). At the same time, the Christian's entry into the political arena poses the gravest questions concerning the meaning of the gospel, its relevance to the contemporary world, and the self-understanding of the Christian community. In imitation of Christ, a theology committed to critical reflection on social and political praxis takes a stand with the oppressed who struggle for freedom. From within the unsure and often confusing battlefield of contemporary politics it attempts to understand how Christians committed not only to preaching but living the gospel ought to behave (TL, 81ff).

Juan Luis Segundo has transformed Gutierrez's irenic attempt to open traditional theological method to critical reflection on political praxis into a polemic challenge to the "academic" pursuit of theology. No theology, Segundo argues, which fails to "close the hermeneutical circle" can claim operational adequacy. For Segundo the very existence of a "hermeneutical circle" in theology presupposes two conditions: (1) the questions which arise out of contemporary concerns should be rich, general, and basic enough to challenge customary presuppositions about reality and (2) those who pursue theology must remain open to the possibility that new questions can change traditional interpretations of Christian faith and practice.[11]

---

[11] Juan Luis Segundo, *The Liberation of Theology,* translated by John Drury (New York: Orbis, 1976) 8–9. Hereafter this work will be abbreviated LOT.

Segundo's further reflections on theological method offer a formula for confusion. In *The Liberation of Theology* he distinguishes between faith and ideology. Faith, he suggests, orients the human person to the absolute. He then argues that since the absolute transcends history, faith in the absolute lacks concrete truth content (LOT, 108). An ideology he defines as "some idea. . . . of the goal of the revolutionary process and the proper means to be used to achieve it" (LOT, 102). Faith in the absolute frees one, he believes, *for* ideologies; for without an ideology to endow it with practical consequences faith dies (LOT, 106–110). Segundo also regards the historical realm of ideology as purely relative. As a consequence, his contentless faith in the absolute supplies him with *no norms whatever* for choosing among ideologies; and it leaves him floundering in moral and situational relativism, where the end justifies the means (LOT, 154–182).

In *Faith and Ideologies* [(New York: Orbis, 1982); hereafter this edition will be abbreviated as FI] his position has not improved significantly. He now defines faith as an ordering consent to the realm of value which necessarily subordinates every other value of an absolute value (FI, 25). Unfortunately, he offers no convincing proof of the fact that in ordering their values humans are forced of necessity to consent to an absolute. He also broadens his definition of ideology to mean all human knowledge about efficacy. He defines the realm of efficacy as devoid of value; and he assigns to scientific thinking the systematic exploration of this valueless realm (FI, 27). He even equates ideologies with the sciences (FI, 105–106).

In *Faith and Ideologies* Segundo also distinguishes anthropological faith, understood as human consent to absolute value and its subordinate values, from religious faith. Anthropological faith, he suggests, becomes religious faith through the transmission of transcendent data "decisive for a realm of value" and through adherence to the tradition of witnesses that transmits the "transcendent data." "Transcendent data" in his sense of this paradoxical term, can be neither experienced nor empirically verified (FI, 73), but they supply a religious tradition with its dogmas (FI, 76–77). Segundo, for example, regards the resurrection of Jesus as a transcendent datum (FI, 165). By a "datum" Segundo means "what is." "Transcendent data" enjoy moral rather than empirical verification and falsification. Empirical verification transpires in the here and now; moral verification, only "in the end" (FI, 155). "Transcendent data" tell us what reality can offer us in the last analysis (FI, 167). In the here and now "transcendent data" function as the premises that structure value systems (FI, 157); and reality tends to confirm them (FI, 265–267).

Segundo regards values as undefinable (FI, 17). They therefore can be communicated only by the use of "iconic" rather than "digital" language (FI, 155). Digital language is fixed by social convention. In iconic language the instruments of meaning and the meaning they communicate cannot be separated, as, for example, in the case of animal gestures (FI, 135). But Segundo also believes that we mix digital and iconic language and that the biblical use of poetry, myth, and history all communicate transcendent data (FI, 163).

I will not tax the reader with a detailed discussion of the confusions in Segundo's discussion of the relationship between faith and ideology, but I shall mention a few. Segundo's assertion that the Absolute cannot reveal itself in history overlooks the fact that the Absolute has chosen to do precisely that. The incarnation means that a concrete segment of human history has in fact taken on universal, absolute, and ultimate significance because God has lived it. As a consequence, Christian revelation has both historical and moral content; and Christian faith consents to that content. The consent of faith incudes consent to the moral demands of discipleship. And those demands include commitment to establishing God's just reign on this earth. Biblical justice means the order that God wills for redeemed creation. The Christian discovers through faith the nature of that order in the moral teachings of Jesus. And Jesus demands that we labor to bring about a social order in which we share the physical supports of life freely with others as an expression of our faith in God's providential care for us. It demands the creation of a social order in which the sharing proceeds on the basis of need, not of merit only, in which no one is excluded in principle from the sharing, and in which the sharing of goods expresses a mutual forgiveness in the name of God and in the image of Jesus.

The fact that Christian love makes specific moral claims provides a norm for evaluating the moral acceptability of different courses of action. Among others it excludes Segundo's own situational and moral relativism. As Christians we consent to the moral vision of Jesus with ethical absoluteness and ultimacy. As a result it binds us in every moral situation we face.

Nor need we wait until the parousia to verify or falsify every moral or religious claim, as Segundo seems to suggest we do. We can and do define values using "digital" language. Segundo's contention that only iconic language expresses moral values illegitimately reduces moral options to mere esthetic preferences in the here and now. Moreover, while religious predictions about the next life must obviously await the next life in order to find

In addition, four factors must shape theological thinking if theologians expect to avoid closing the hermeneutical circle prematurely. (1) They must experience reality in such a way that they begin to suspect the ideologies present in the contemporary situation. (2) They must subject all ideologies to systematic critique, including theological ones. (3) This ideological critique should produce further suspicions that traditional interpretations of the Biblical witness have failed to take important data into account. (4) Finally, theologians must construct a new frame of reference for interpreting the Biblical witness which takes into adequate account the new relevant data (LOT, 9).

Moreover, like Gutierrez, Segundo insists that the hermeneutical circle will never find completion unless those who pursue theology take a clear political stand against social injustice. Without political commitment no theologian can aspire to an authentic interpretation of the gospel message and its demands. Apolitical theologians tacitly and fallaciously assume the ahistorical character of theological reflection and end by discoursing about "eternal verities" irrelevant to the world in which they live and to the plight of the socially and politically oppressed. (LOT, 81–95) Liberation theology unmasks the inauthenticity of such academic theology and plunges the contemporary theologian irrevocably into the center of the social struggle for political and economic justice (LOT, 3–6).

Black liberation theology originated in the United States quite independently from its Latin counterpart. A black theology of liberation sprang from the black radicalism of the late sixties. Martin Luther King's Christian pacifism offered the black community a church-based form of social activism that placed ordained, Christian ministers in the forefront of the black struggle for freedom and justice. The split between King's southern-based National Christian Leadership Conference and Stokley Carmichael's northern, urban, ghetto-hardened Student National Coordinating Committee replaced King's original idealistic search for the integration of blacks and whites in racial harmony with a more politically aggressive search for Black Power. Black Power demanded the end of racism as well as social, economic, and political justice for the black community; but it rejected any immediate search for racial integration. Instead it asserted black culture and identity aggressively.

While the Black Power movement secularized black social and politi-

---

verification or falsification, we can verify or falsify here and now theological hypotheses about the actual revelation of God we have recived historically.

In other words, apart from his insistence on the need to complete the hermeneutical circle, Segundo's project for the liberation of theology offers more obfuscation than freedom.

cal radicalism, the Black Muslim church offered another threat to the influence of black Christian clergymen hopeful of leading the more radical wing of the North American black community. The Black Muslim church offered blacks in this country a religious alternative to Christianity. Solidly rooted in the African continent, the Muslim religion would, the Black Muslims argued, allow blacks to reclaim their original African heritage while espousing a religious creed that sanctioned the use of violence, when circumstances required it, in order to vindicate the rights of the blacks.

James Cone launched black liberation theology as a movement in 1969 with his book *Black Theology and Black Power*. As the title suggest, in its earliest formulation black liberation theology represented an attempt on the part of concerned black churchmen to reassert intellectual leadership of the political left wing of the black community. As it has developed, black liberation theology has not only produced an immpressive body of literature, but it has also exhibited a growing catholicity in its concerns.[12]

Black liberationists in this country have entered into a fruitful dialogue with Latin liberationists. That dialogue has produced two significant developments. First, it has led the more radical black theologians of liberation to espouse a form of Christian Marxism. Moreover, the initial application of Marxist analysis to the situation of blacks in the United States has forced recognition of the fact that besides white racism, economic and political forces also conspire to deny blacks their most fundamental human rights. That realization has also bred a sense of solidarity between the black community and other oppressed minorities in the United States and elsewhere. Feminism too has begun to impinge on black theological awareness.

[12] James H. Cone, *Black Theology and Black Power* (New York: Seabury, 1969), *A Black Theology of Liberation* (Philadelphia and New York: Lippincott, 1970), *The Spirituals and the Blues* (New York: Seabury, 1972); *God of the Oppressed* (New York: Crossroad, 1975), *For My People: Black Theology and the Black Church* (New York: Maryknoll, 1984); *Speaking the Truth: Ecumenism, Liberation, and Black Theology* (Grand Rapids: Eerdmans, 1986); James Deotis Roberts, *A Black Political Theology* (Philadelphia: Westminster, 1974), *Roots of a Black Future: Family and Church* (Philadelphia: Westminster, 1980), *Liberation and Reconciliation: A Black Theology* (Philadelphia: Westminster, 1980), *Black Theology Today: Liberation and Contextualization* (New York and Toronto: Mellen, 1983); Cornel West, *Prophesy Deliverance* (Philadelphia: Westminster, 1982); Major J. Jones, *Black Awareness: A Theology of Hope* (New York and Nashville: Abingdon, 1971), *Christian Ethics for Black Theology* (New York and Nashville: Abingdon, 1974); Cecil Wayne Cone, *The Identity Crisis in Black Theology* (Nashville: AMEC, 1975); Michelle Wallace, *Black Macho and the Myth of the Superwoman* (New York: Dial, 1978); Lawrence Lucas, *Black Priest/White Church* (New York: Random House, 1970); Albert B. Cleage, *The Black Messiah* (New York: Sheed and Ward, 1968); Gauraud S. Wilmore, *Black Religion and Black Radicalism: An Interpretation of the Religious History of the Afro-American People* (New York: Maryknoll, 1983); Joseph R. Washington, *Black Religion: The Negro and Christianity in the U.S.* (Boston: Beacon, 1964).

Besides broadening the scope of black liberationists' social concerns, the dialogue between black and Latin liberation theologians has produced a second important speculative result. In the thought of James Deotis Roberts it has motivated both an appreciation and a criticism of the methods employed by Latin liberation theology.

In *Black Theology Today: Liberation and Contextualization* Roberts acknowledges Segundo's contribution to the method of liberation theology by his insistence that contemporary Christian theology complete the "hermeneutical circle" by deriving from a creative reading of the gospel in the light of social analysis a practical program for forging a new and more just social order. Roberts, however, criticizes Segundo for failing to take into adequate account the contribution which personal spirituality makes to the theological enterprise. (Gutierrez, as we have seen, shows more sensitivity on this specific point.) Roberts calls for an approach to the theological enterprise less narrowly focused on social transformation, one that reaches out to the entire human race. An adequate theological method, Roberts argues, must show more sensitivity to the concerns of narrative theology than liberation theology has done heretofore. A theology adequate to the needs of the black community must summon people to a vision of wholeness and integration of life, it must evolve a symbolism that interrelates the sacred and the secular, it must affirm the fecundity of life and the importance of community, and it must bridge this life and the next. Black theology in Roberts's estimate needs to incorporate in its thought patterns both poetry and philosophy. It must deal with all the complex challenges offered by the culture in which the gospel is preached. It must speak with an inculturated idiom. The universality of its concerns demands too that it deal with the issues raised by the ecumenical dialogue. Though creatively reconstructive, black theology needs, Roberts believes, to keep in close contact with the needs of black people, but with all their needs, including their need for a just social order.[13]

Have the reflections of liberation theologians on theological method anything to teach the foundational theologian? By the same token, have Lonergan's reflections on method anything to teach liberation theology? Finally, has our attempt to set Lonergan's method in dialogue with a North American philosophy any light to throw on these important methodological questions?

An inculturated North American approach to foundational thinking can, as we have seen, legitimately invoke "experience" as a central, unifying category. The construct of experience developed in these pages shares many traits in common with Dewey's. Both recognize the organic

---

[13] James Deotis Roberts, *Black Theology Today: Liberation and Contextualization* (New York and Toronto: Mellen, 1983).

basis of human experience. Both portray experience as the rhythmic alternation of activity and receptivity. Both acknowledge that we perceive reality both affectively and inferentially and that we judge it both emotionally and rationally. Both affirm that we come to know our world by having a transaction with it. We also interact with symbolic structures and in the process gradually clarify what we want to say about ourselves and reality. We employ symbol systems instrumentally both in order to communicate insights and in order to resolve as far as possible problematic situations. Both constructs of experience acknowledge the finitude of the human mind, the social, dialogic character of thinking, the abstractive character of both affective and inferential perceptions, and the possibility of social collaboration.

As we have already seen, the construct of experience defended in these pages differs in three notable respects from that defended by Dewey. It defends the possibility of experiencing supernatural realities when we respond in faith to some historical self-communication of God. It distinguishes more sharply than Dewey does three distinct realms of experience: the realm of value (or of Quality), the realm of action (or of Fact), and the realm of tendency (or of Law). Finally, unlike Dewey, the construct of experience we have proposed includes within experience itself the realities that are experienced. Dewey, as we have seen, restricts the term "experience" to human evaluative responses, which he then contrasts with "nature," the object of human experience. Our own construct sides with Whitehead in speaking of experienced realities as elements that function within experience itself. They shape experience more or less consciously and make it into a specific kind of experience.

The world we experience defines the realistic limits of all human evaluative responses. Whether we respond affectively, speculatively, morally, or religiously, we always respond to something and must respect its own capacities for evaluative and decisive behavior if we are to avoid dwelling in a world of pure fantasy.

The world we experience also confronts us with a whole realm of dynamic tendencies distinct from those that shape our personal responses. The tendencies present in our world condition our personal responses for good or for ill. We acquiesce all too easily in the attitudes, biases, prejudices, beliefs, and value systems of the society in which we live. We imbibe its bigotries: its racism, sexism, class prejudices, tacit inequities, and injustices. We absorb its belief systems as if by osmosis: its jingoism, its social elitisism, its inflated and myopic conceptions of reality, its skepticism and unbelief. We are tainted by its false values and ideals: its capitalism, commercialism, materialism, militarism, egotism.[14]

---

[14] The following studies call attention to the darker side of North American culture: Robert N. Bellah, Richard Masden, William M. Sullivan, Ann Swidler, and Stephen M.

The neurosis, error, moral evil, and sin which infect the environments that shape us as experiences set the agenda for Christian repentance. Through repentence we assert personal autonomy and freedom over against the autonomy and freedom of the forces that people our environment, and we resolve to stand against dehumanization and sin in subsequent personal choices.

Having declared responsible independence through personal conversion from the sick, deceptive, unjust, and religiously unbelieving forces that shape experience, we still face, of course, the ongoing purification of ingrained habits and attitudes that conflict with our new-found freedom before God. The Catholic theological tradition calls the forces of dehumanization and unbelief that continue to shape a baptised convert's world "concupiscence." Prior to conversion it calls them "original sin."

Not every force that shapes the experience of converts dehumanizes or perverts it. Communities which foster and support integral conversion before God provide a realm of grace that invites and nurtures both initial and ongoing conversion.

We have identified three ways in which the immanence of the world to human experience shapes the process of conversion significantly. (1) The sinful and dehumanizing forces at work in the world set the agenda for repentance. (2) Those same forces inhibit the healing of concupiscence. (3) Environments that foster integral, personal conversion offer realms of grace that counteract the forces of dehumanization and sin. The immanence of the world to human experience shapes the dynamics of conversion in yet another way. It creates the possibility for socio-political conversion.

As we have seen, distinguishable networks of habits ground the distinction between affective, speculative, moral, and religious conversion. In each instance the decision to convert creates a new conceptual frame of reference because it commits the convert to understanding the laws that govern these four distinct but interrelated realms of human experience.

The habits that shape personal experience differ, however, from the

Tipton, *Habits of the Heart: Individualism and Commitment in American Life* (Berkeley: University of California Press, 1985); John A. Schiller, ed., *The American Poor* (Minneapolis: Augsberg, 1982); Suzanne C. Toton, *World Hunger: The Responsibility of Christian Education* (New York: Orbis, 1982); Robert Lekachman, *Greed is Not Enough: Reaganomics* (New York: Pantheon, 1982); Tom Barry and Deb Preusch, *The Central America Fact Book* (New York: Grove Press, 1986); Richard J. Barnet and Ronald E. Mueller, *Global Reach: The Power of the Multinational Corporations* (New York: Simon and Schuster, 1974); Angela Y. Davis, *Women, Race, and Class* (New York: Random House, 1983); Carl N. Degler, *Neither Black Nor White: Slave and Race Relations in Brazil and the United States* (New York: Collier, 1971); Manning Marble, *How Capitalism Underdeveloped Black America* (Boston: South End Press, 1983).

habitual tendencies present in one's world. They differ in their autonomy; for while converts interact constantly with their worlds, the two function within experience as distinct sources of evaluation and decision. One may then over and above personal conversion also assume personal responsibility for attempting to influence the decisions that shape one's world; for those decisions occur independently of personal choice.

Moreover, because we function autonomously within personal conversion, gorwth in self-mastery need not affect significantly the course of events in the world about us. In the last analysis, however, integrally converted Christians must take responsibility not only for the course of their personal human and religious growth but also, as far as possible, for the course of events in the world in which they live. Let us, then, define socio-political conversion as the decision to renounce social, political, and economic irresponsibility and to see to it in so far as it lies within one's power that not only one's personal choices but also the choices that shape one's world and its institutions spring from motives that express integral conversion before God.

The choices which shape the convert's world find embodiment not only in individual personal choices but in the social, economic, and political institutions of human society. The politically converted commit themselves therefore to transforming not just individuals but also institutions according to the exigencies of conversion itself. Personal conversion commits one to understand the dynamics of one's own affective, rational, moral, and religious development. Political conversion, however, introduces the convert into the realm of social analysis. The political convert needs to understand how human institutions are born, develop, and decline, how they condition human behavior for better or for worse, and how they can be both humanized and Christianized. The personally converted take charge of their own decisions; the politically converted seek to influence the decisions of others in ways that improve human society.

The integrity of the conversion process demands political conversion. The moral inevitability of political conversion flows from three distinct but interrelated sources: the potentially corrupting influence of social, political, and economic structures, the need to create saving realms of grace, and the missionary impulse proper to Christianity.

The institutions and persons in our social environments stand within us as experiences and shape us either consciously or unconsciously. They can foster the life of grace within us, sensitize us to legitimate human values, or corrupt us affectively, intellectually, morally, and religiously. We sin by commission or by omission. We commit sin when we act in ways that we know contradict the will of God. We sin by omission when we opt not to prevent some evil we might have averted by acting. Faith consciousness as it grows heightens sin consciousness. Converted Christians who refuse to act when they could do something to counteract the destructive impact of sinful decisions and institutions on the lives of other people sin by omission. Through preferring inaction to the prophetic denunciation of evil, they allow themselves to be corrupted by the very evil they see corrupting others. Those therefore who deliberately choose to ignore social sin and its impact on their own lives and the lives of others inevitably succumb to its blandishments and adulterate the authenticity of any commitment to personal conversion.

Humanizing, gracious environments, on the other hand, result from collaborative effort. In order to exist and survive they need the active support of the very persons who benefit from them. Moreover, the moral consequences of Christian conversion commit the convert to active participation in communities of faith sharing in which both the material blessings of life and the charisms and graces of the Breath of Christ are dispensed freely, not on the basis of merit alone but also and especially on the basis of need. Active participation in such a community pits the Christian convert prophetically against the forces of antichrist. As a consequence, personal conversion to Christianity culminates in the gracious transformation and transvaluation of political conversion. Christian converts who fail to dedicate their lives to the creation of communities of faith that incarnate the mind of Christ refuse irresponsibly and inauthentically to accept fully the moral consequences of personal Christian conversion. At the same time, dedication to the humanization of social environments springs in part from political conversion, from the decision to nurture integral conversion not only in oneself but in others. Christian conversion transforms and transvalues political conversion by ensuring the creation of life-giving human environments imbued with gospel values.

Finally, every Christian community lives bound by the command of the risen Christ to proclaim the good news to every creature. Among those creatures who need to repent and submit to the good news we must number those who make the administrative and policy decisions that shape human society. The Christian community who contents itself therefore with converting only private individuals to Christ and exempts those in positions of power from the need for conversion disobeys the divine command to proclaim the gospel to every creature. Every proclamation of the gospel seeks to transform the minds, hearts, decisions, and lives of other people. Fully effective gospel preaching presupposes, therefore, political conversion in those who proclaim the good news by word and by deed.

A sound insight into the dynamics of conversion demands, then, that foundational method incorporate into itself the kinds of concerns eloquently voiced by contemporary liberation theologians. It must extend critical reflection on Christian practice into the social, economic, and political arenas. In order to do that effectively, it needs to supplement insights into the dynamics of personal growth with social analysis.

At the same time, Lonergan's understanding of the task and methods of theological thinking offers liberation theology a frame of reference in which it can reconcile its preoccupation with praxis with some of the more traditional concerns that have motivated theological thinking. More specifically, Lonergan's concern to ground revisionist theological thinking in a sound understanding of the dynamics of conversion tries to ensure that theological speculation will nurture Christian spirituality. Every spirituality offers practical wisdom for approaching God; and at the heart of every sound spirituality lies an equally sound insight into the dynamics of an authentic and integral conversion. Similarly, Lonergan's theory of functional specialties and his distinction between mediating and mediated theology together ensure that the systematic reformulation of Christian faith rest not only on sound spiritual doctrine but also on the systematic scholarly retrieval of the history of the Christian tradition.

Moreover, a sound foundational analysis of the complexities of the conversion process suggests that liberation theologians would be well advised not to focus too narrowly on political conversion. As we saw in Chapter II, the different moments in the conversion process mutually condition one another. Exclusive preoccupation with social analysis and with the transformation of social structures could lead any theology of liberation to ignore or give short shrift to the personal affective, speculative, moral, and specifically Christian elements that shape any human and Christian effort to effect social and political transformation.

A more systematic implementation of Lonergan's method in a Latin American context could also advance the further inculturation of theological thinking in the Latin church. To date not only many of the theological categories but many of the strategies for liberation proposed by Latin liberationists have been imported from Europe. A foundational analysis of situations of injustice in Latin America would draw systematically on the ongoing retrieval not only of Christian tradition as a whole but also of the cultural traditions of the Latin American people themselves. A dialectical analysis of the contradictory forces that have shaped Latin culture could provide Latin theologians with a richer indigenous vocabulary for pursuing a theology that fosters a liberating praxis.

As we saw in the course of Chapter II, a reflection on the dynamics of personal conversion can generate practical insights into the operational procedures of foundational thinking. The inclusion within converted behavior of a political moment distinct from personal conversion opens an entirely new frame of reference for foundational thinking and introduces new complexities into the dynamics of conversion. Can these new complexities offer further insights into the operational procedures of foundational theology? Here we face two interrelated questions: (1) How does personal conversion condition political conversion? (2) How does political conversion condition personal? The answers to both questions will yield further insights into the practice of foundational speculation.

We discovered five dynamics within personal conversion: (1) Religious conversion mediates between affective and moral conversion. (2) Intellectual conversion seeks to inform affective, moral, and religious conversion. (3) Religious conversion graciously transvalues affective, intellectual, and moral conversion. (4) Moral conversion orients affective and intellectual conversion practically to realities and values that make absolute and ultimate claims. (5) Affective conversion animates intellectual, moral, and religious conversion.

From these five dynamics we derived the following operational procedures: (1) Foundational theology must unmask the inadequacy of any account of the human conscience which fails to invoke religious values and must also elaborate procedures for reaching moral decisions in the light of divine revelation. (2) Foundational thinking must submit to sound logical and methodological procedures. (3) Foundational theology must offer two accounts of affective, intellectual, and moral conversion: one which details normatively their development in abstraction from religious conversion and another which details normatively their transmutation and transvaluation in faith. (4) Foundational theology must integrate a moral element into its account of sound affective and speculative development. (5) Foundational theology must identify and develop sound criteria for distinguishing true from false hopes. (6) Foundational theology must resolve dialectical conflicts among appreciative perceptions of the real. (7) Foundational theology must resolve dialectical conflicts between appreciative perceptions of reality on the one hand and inferential perceptions on the other.

Do these insights into the dynamics of personal conversion and their operational consequences illumine the foundational exploration of the dynamics of political conversion?

Every kind of conversion, political conversion included, can occur in abstraction from the other forms of conversion. By the same token, socio-political conversion, like affective, speculative, or moral conversion, can also occur only naturally, in complete abstraction from religious conversion. The political activist who lacks personal conversion confronts society as a potential menace. Effective leaders riddled with neurosis, convinced of falsehood, and devoid of personal or personal moral or religious ideals can lead others down the primrose path of demagoguery and chaos. Think of Adolf Hitler.

Personal conversion authenticates socio-political by providing it with affective, speculative, moral, and religious norms for distinguishing between sound and unsound policies and official decisions. One form of conversion authenticates another by enabling those who have experienced the second form of conversion to act with the kind of responsibility to which they as converts ought to aspire. Human institutions ought to express and foster integral conversion before God. They can instead foster neurosis or psychosis, replace the search for truth with rhetorical and ideological obfuscations, corrupt consciences, or pervert religious aspirations. When that occurs those personally converted at an affective, intellectual, moral, or religious level can recognize such intitutions as unjust and oppressive by judging them in the light of the insights which personal conversion yields.

Socio-political conversion, on the other hand, authenticates personal conversion by deprivatizing it. It does so in two important ways. First, it forces the personally converted to deal with the needs, aspiriations, hopes, beliefs, cultures, and life styles of unfamiliar or even alien individuals and social groups. Socio-political conversion thus forces the personally converted to face and deal with the limitations of their own individual experience in a challenging social context. Second, socio-political conversion motivates those who experience it to espouse specific social, economic, or political causes. Institutional change results from social collaboration. Socio-political converts need first to decide which situations of institutional injustice make greatest claims upon their consciences and then make common cause with others who share similar aspirations.

Let us then begin to reflect in greater detail on the ways in which these two forms of conversion transumte and transvalue one another.

The morally converted individual who undergoes political conversion advances from privatized to socially responsible morality. The fact, then, that religious conversion mediates between affective and moral conversion has important consequences for any religiously motivated search for social justice. The Christian in search of a just society understands justice in the light of Jesus' moral vision. The politically converted Christian seeks to mobilize others to establish the reign of God on earth as in heaven. Such an individual submits to the moral exigencies of life in the kingdom by freely sharing with the deprived on the basis of need not of merit only and seeks actively to bring about a world in which all people live in mutual reconciliation and peace. Jesus' vision of the peaceable kingdom gives as a consequence a dynamic orientation to the Christian search for a just social order. This fact imposes an important constraint on foundational thinking and provides us with an eighth operational procedure to supplement those just cited: namely, (8) Foundational theology must not only describe the process of personal transformation in the image of Jesus, it must also elaborate practical strategies for advancing human society even closer to the most perfect embodiment of the kingdom of God on earth possible in any given circumstance.

Similarly, the fact that intellectual conversion seeks to inform all the other forms of conversion means that the socio-political convert must submit to sound logical and methodological procedures. When this methodological exigency is read in the light of the insights already sketched in this chapter, it suggests other important operational consequences for foundational thinking. (9) Foundational theology must concern itself with unsettled social, economic, and political situations that pose significant questions concerning the dynamics of conversion. (10) Foundational theology must derive its categories in part from a social analysis of the conflicts that destabilize such situations. (11) Foundational theology must seek ways of transforming socially, politically, and economically unsettled situations into settled ones. Let us reflect briefly on the implications of these three operational principles.

First of all, we should observe that a human situation can enjoy even a healthy measure of social, economic, and political stability and still qualify as unsettled from a foundational standpoint. I speak of course of situations of entrenched institutional oppression. From the standpoint of foundational speculation, no situation counts as settled which fails to incarnate integral conversion before God. Oppressive situations need to be destabilized, the shackles of oppression need to be removed or at least seriously mitigated if one is to resolve it in ways that begin to measure up to the exigencies of conversion.

As we have already seen, foundational theology derives its categories from unstable foundational situations. Political conversion forces the foundational thinker to take into account the social, economic, and political forces that destabilize foundational situations. As a consequence, foundational thought stands helpless before the institutional and corporate dimensions of unstable foundational situations without the assistance of sound social analysis.

Moreover, in attempting to convert such situations into foundationally settled ones, a sound theology of conversion must deal not only with social, political, and economic injustice but also with the neuroses, errors, false values, and religious idols that re-enforce injustice.

The fact that religious conversion transvalues not only affective, intellectual, and moral but also political conversion entails that (12) foundational theology must judge the ultimate adequacy of all social, economic, and political strategies by their ability to incarnate and foster gospel living.

The fact that moral conversion orients the other forms of natural conversion to realities and values that make absolute and ultimate claims entails that (13) foundational thinking should assess the social, political, or economic resolution of unsettled foundational situations by sound moral norms as well as by the moral demands of gospel living. The recent pastorals of the North American bishops, *The Challenge of Peace* and *Economic Justice for All,* illustrate this methodological principle admirably. Both letters subject the policies of the Reagan administration to careful scrutiny and judge them unacceptable not only in the light of gospel values but also in the light of sound rational principles of morality.

Finally, the fact that affective conversion seeks to animate political conversion along with the other forms of conversion demands that (14) foundational theory attempt to distinguish true from false political hopes. In addition, (15) foundational theology must seek to resolve the emotional conflicts that destabilize social, economic, and political situations. It must unmask the irrational fears, neurotic guilt, and sadistic bigotry that oppress people and summon them to repentant healing. At the same time, (16) in resolving social, economic, and political conflicts a sound foundational account of the dynamics of conversion must ensure that the judgments of the head and of the heart agree, that the voices of prophecy, of genuine prudence, and of discernment sanction the policy decisions that shape people's lives.

We have been exploring the ways in which personal conversion conditions socio-political and the operational consequences of such conditioning for foundational speculation. How then does socio-political conversion condition the other forms of conversion? Moreover, what operational consequences flow from that conditioning?

Political conversion deprivatizes personal piety. The logic of Christian conversion leads in the direction of political conversion to the extent that it demands the creation of communities of grace that embody the mind of Jesus and the repentant submission of every individual to the obedience of faith. Individuals personally converted to Christ can, however, fail to perceive or endorse the world-transforming consequences of their personal religious conversion. Political conversion sensitizes the religious convert to important economic, social, and political concerns and in the process helps rescue the religious convert from the inauthenticities of privatized piety. As a consequence, (17) foundational theory needs to explore the ways in which political conversion transforms individual believers and religious communities into prophets of socio-political transformation. It needs to elaborate a spirituality for social activists and practical strategies for mobilizing the Christian community in order to address pressing social needs.

Political conversion ensures that affective healing and the dark night of sense transpire in active confrontation with individuals and groups with whom one stands in a shadow relationship. In Jungian theory the shadow functions as the archetypal symbol of the dark side of the psyche which needs to be brought to consciousness and healing integration into the rest of the personality. We stand in a shadow relationship with individuals or groups that either trigger within us unacknowledged fear, resentment, and guilt or symbolize for us undeveloped or unwelcome aspects of our own personalities. Individuals who fail to deal effectively with their own shadows tend to project them onto other individuals or groups. Racial bigotry illustrates the tendency. Bigots project onto the members of a hated race their own violence, lasciviousness, ignorance, and unconscious guilty desires.

Political conversion can also plunge one into social conflict. Conflicts can in turn trigger anxiety, animosity, feelings of inadequacy and of helplessness. In the give and take of political confrontation, political conversion forces individuals in need of affective healing to deal socially with difficult and threatening relationships. It forces collaboration with individuals whom one might never normally choose as companions. We may then conclude that (18) foundational theology needs to provide sound norms for understanding the psychodynamics of affective healing through social interaction.

Political conversion rescues intellectual conversion from academic futility. When human speculation disassociates itself from the challenge of social transformation it can degenerate into a sterile academic debate utterly divorced from human life. Scholarship and speculation must, of course, always serve more than purely political needs and constituencies. Foundational theology in particular stands constrained to explore all the dimensions of converted experience, both personal and political. When, however, the search for truth ignores the all-pervasive impact of social, economic, and political institutions on human life and conduct, it easily succumbs to institutional manipulation and political naivete. Political conversion challenges the theoretical mind to deal practically with problematic social, economic, and political situations. As a consequence, (19) foundational thinking can never rest content with resolving problematic religious, social, economic, and political situations in principle; it must also devise practical strategies for resolving them in fact to the extent that it can.

Finally, political conversion demands commitment to specific causes and collaboration with others of similar moral persuasion to right social wrongs and to create just social structures. Hence, (20) foundational theology needs to develop practical social, economic, and political strategies for the collaborative resolution of pressing public and social problems.

We may then conclude that when one ponders the methodological concerns of liberation theologians in the light of a foundational theology sensitive to the challenges and opportunities inherent in the North American philosophical tradition, these two strains in contemporary theology illumine one another. When foundational theology expands

Lonergan's construct of conversion to include a socio-political moment, it can complete successfully Segundo's hermeneutical circle. It can also attend to the more universal theological concerns voiced by liberationists like Gutierrez and Roberts.

American pragmatism offers a broader philosophical understanding of praxis than does Marxist theory. American pragmatists concur with Marx in insisting on the close relationship between theory and practice. A pragmatic theory of praxis avoids, however, some of the unacceptable connotations of Marxism: dialectical materialism; the sacrifice of freedom to inexorable, historical laws; and belief in the inevitability of class conflict. Peirce's pragmatism shows how orthopraxis serves the interests of orthodoxy by forcing the clarification of beliefs. Dewey's instrumentalism addresses unsettled political and economic situations but extends its concern to other kinds of indeterminate situations as well.

Black theologians in this country must judge the relevance of these observations on method to the theological needs of the black community. They seem to me, however, to address all of the methodological concerns voiced by James Deotis Roberts: his universalism; his desire to incorporate into liberation theology a poetic, a narrative, and a philosophical component; his insistence that theology must promote human wholeness and integration; his sensitivity to the need for an inculturated Christian theology that faces the challenge of contemporary culture; his ecumenical openness; his passion for social justice.

I am inclined to think that the foundational method I have proposed can also deal with the kind of issues raised by Cornel West. West has advanced further down the road of Marxism than most black liberation theologians. West criticizes Marxist theory for a number of speculative blunders. He finds that Marxism collapses human nature and practice into history and fails to take adequate account of relegous transcendence. Marxism, West believes, exaggerates naively the promethean possibilities of humanity, focuses too narrowly on socio-political reality, and blinds itself both to new social configurations in the post-capitalist world and to religion's revolutionary potential.

Nevertheless, West discovers three potentially fruitful points of contact between black liberation theology and Marxism: dialectical method, concern with liberation, and social critique of racism and classism in western culture. West identifies finally with what he calls a progressivist strain in contemporary Marxism which stresses the self-organiazation and self-guidance of the working classes and which encourages individuality and democracy.[15]

West recognizes pragmatism's potential to encourage social criticism

----

15 Cornel West, *Prophesy Deliverance* (Philadelphia: Westminister, 1982) 19, 99–100, 108–117.

and reform, although he faults the pragmatists for failing to take into account class struggle. At the same time, West looks to pragmatism to protect liberation theology from lapses into dogmatism.[16]

The failure of American pragmatists to deal with class struggle does not mean that one cannot apply a pragmatic logic of consequences to the problem of class conflict wherever one encounters it. In my own opinion, however, a Deweyan concern to keep open the paths of enquiry within social analysis would require that one distance oneself from the interpretation of class struggle which one discovers in classical Marxist theory. Classical Marxism presents class conflict as an economic necessity. If one regards class conflict as a necessity rather than as a fact, then one has little choice in selecting a strategy for resolving that conflict. One must join the revolutionary struggle to overthrow one's oppresors. A consistent application of pragmatic logic to the problem of class struggle would, by contrast, treat it as a contingent fact rather than as a demonstrated necessity within a problematic economic situation; and it would allow for a variety of strategies for resolving the conflict. In other words, pragmatic logic gives some promise of liberating liberation theology not only from questionable religious absolutes but also from questionable Marxist absolutes.

We began these reflections by comparing and contrasting Lonergan's theory of method with Dewey's logical theory. We concluded that foundational method ought to conform to the canons of denotative method in Dewey's sense of the term and concern itself with the successful resolution of problematic situations. We identified such situations as the generating source of the three nests of categories that structure foundational thinking. We explored then the analogies between problematic logical and foundational situations. On the basis of these insights we have attempted to put Lonergan's method into dialogue with liberation theology and to incorporate into it a conscious concern with politically committed praxis. Finally, we have probed the methodological consequences of distinguishing political from personal conversion.

One final complex task remains. We will address it in the chapter which follows. We must examine the ways in which the three nests of categories that structure foundational thinking interplay with one another. We must at the same time devise methods of coordinating the three nests of foundational categories both among themselves and with one another.

---

[16] Ibid., 21.

CHAPTER VI:

THE COORDINATION AND INTERPLAY OF CATEGORIES IN FOUNDATIONAL THINKING

A problem began to surface in the preceding chapter to which we must now attend. As we have seen, Lonergan prescribes three "nests" of categories for foundational thinking. He distinguishes the notions from the categories needed to formulate any normative theology of conversion. Transcendental notions correspond to "our capacity for seeking and, when found, for recognizing instances of the intelligible, the true, the real, the good" (MT, 282). In Lonergan's theory of knowledge, transcendental notions express the spontaneous, dynamic drive of intentional consciousness toward Being. They raise to consciousness the human mind's virtual infinity, its insatiable thirst for intelligibility (MT, 73–74). As a consequence, Lonergan's transcendentals relate intentionally to any cognitive object of human questioning. They also relate to the correct answers to those same questions, for the transcendental notions designate the reality, the truth, the existing good that motivates any given human inquiry. They also designate that same reality, truth, and good interpreted in true judgments.

The transcendental notions make questions and answers possible, but Lonergan holds that they themselves cannot provide the answers to specific questions. That interpretative task the categories perform (MT, 282). Categories provide the conceptual grist for both science and scholarship. Moreover, the formulation of a normative theology of conversion, Lonergan argues, demands two distinguishable kinds of categories. Foundational thinking derives a set of general categories from speculative disciplines other than theology which study human religious experience. Among these disciplines, we should number philosophy, clinical and experimental psychology, social psychology, sociology, cultural anthropology, comparative religion, and others. In addition to these general categories, foundational theology needs a set of categories that arise from religious faith itself. Lonergan calls this second set of categories "special categories." They designate the objects of knowledge proper to theology as such.

In the preceding chapters we have found reason to question both the virtual infinity of the human intellect as well as its spontaneous orientation to Being as such. In the process we have also implicitly challenged

Lonergan's account of the interpretative function of transcendental notions, for that account presupposes both the intellect's infinity and its insatiable thirst for Being.

In the preceding chapter we have, however, discovered an important and different interpretative function within foundational thinking for descriptive categories universally applicable in intent. These categories endow any normative theology of conversion with coherence, with synthetic unity. Categories universally applicable in intent must achieve this goal at a high level of abstraction; for they seek to interpret any reality whatever encountered within conversion. Moreover, when viewed as descriptive concepts, categories universally applicable in intent function interpretatively more in the way that Lonergan's categories function rather than like "notions" in his sense of that term, for descriptive transcendental categories ambition a verifiable account of any reality whatever encountered within experience. Descriptive transcendentals perform, then, an important service within foundational theology, for a normative theology of conversion ambitions a synthetic insight into the reality of God, of oneself, and of one's world. Without an integrating set of descriptive transcendentals at least analogously applicable to God, self, and the world, foundational theology will fall short of the speculatively synthetic account of religious experience which it ambitions.

In the experiential approach to foundational method developed in these pages, therefore, three distinguishable sets of categories lend conceptual structure to a normative theology of conversion. First, foundational thinking employs a fallible but integrating set of transcendental categories, universally applicable in intent. Metaphysics, the speculative philosophical discipline which reflects on the most generic and universal characteristics of the real, supplies this first set of categories. It does so by using the insights of the normative sciences in order to distinguish true descriptive and explanatory accounts of the real from false ones. In addition, however, philosophy also contributes to the pool of general philosophical categories supplied by the other scholarly and scientific disciplines whose results illumine religious experience. Finally, theology itself supplies a third set of special categories derived from reflection on the experience of faith.

The fact that a normative theology of conversion employs simultaneously three sets of categories derived from a variety of speculative disciplines each with its own distinctive method poses a severe challenge to foundational method. The challenge may be simply stated: how should foundational theology go about the task of integrating these contrasting sets of categories? Should foundational speculation even ambition such an integration? Would not prudence rather counsel that philosophy, theology, and other disciplines go their separate methodological ways? Does not the history of ideas teach us that the empirical sciences fare ill when subjected to artificial philosophical or theological constraints?

Certainly foundational speculation needs to respect the autonomy of any discipline from whose findings it attempts to benefit. The history of thought, however, teaches other lessons besides the fact that philosophy and theology can cramp the progress of empirical science. History also teaches that empirical or clinical accounts of religious experience rest on tacit philosophical or theological presuppositions. Such presuppositions invite legitimate philosophical and theological criticism. A normative theology of conversion would seem to provide a useful context for pursuing such a critique. Moreover, philosophical and theological generalizations that ignore the results of scholarly, empirical, or clinical investigations of human experience risk running roughshod over important facts that can validate or invalidate philosophical and theological hypotheses.

No. Whatever the difficulty, foundational method must face the challenge of at least attempting to coordinate the three sets of categories that shape any normative theory of conversion. To this thorny question we turn our attention in the present chapter. Our reflections divide into four parts. First, we must attempt to understand the difference between the coordination of categories and their interpretative interplay. Second, we shall attempt to illustrate how these procedures function within foundational thinking. Here two distinct problems will face us. On the one hand, we must reflect on the problem of coordinating among themselves each of the three sets of categories foundational speculation employs. On the other hand, we must also understand how to coordinate all three sets of categories with one another.

In the preceding chapters we have attempted to set Lonergan's method into dialogue with the North American philosophical tradition. That dialogue has forced us to question some of the presuppositions that ground his method and has allowed us to articulate a more detailed account of the operational procedures that structure foundational thinking than Lonergan himself. Unfortunately, however, the American philosophical tradition will offer no answers to the question that faces us in the present chapter, for no classical American philosopher has ever engaged in foundational speculation on the precise methodological terms that Lonergan has suggested. One can reach a sound insight into the coordination and interplay of categories within foundational speculation only by actually exploring conceptually the dynamics of conversion as a prelude to reflecting critically on the ways in which the three sets of categories employed in foundational theology interpret reality and one another.

I have to date used foundational method to complete three such explorations into Christian conversion: *Experiencing God: A Theology of*

Human Emergence, (1978), *Charism and Sacrament: A Theology of Christian Conversion*, (1976), and *The Divine Mother: A Trinitarian Theology of the Holy Spirit*, (1984). In the present chapter I will attempt to explain as clearly as I can the ways in which I have attempted to coordinate the transcendental, general, and special categories which I have employed in these three studies. I shall also attempt to describe as well the interpretative interplay of all three sets of categories.[1]

(I)

First of all, let us distinguish between the coordination of categories and their interpretative interplay. Categorial coordination engages the relationship between categories and the realities they interpret. We may distinguish four basic techniques for effecting categorial coordination: agreement, complementarity, convergence, and dialectical reversal. The interplay of categories, on the other hand, looks not to the relationship between categories and the realities they interpret but to the relationship of categories and of sets of categories to one another. As we shall see, within foundational thinking philosophical categories, especially transcendental categories, interpret and contextualize general and special categories. Moreover, philosophical logic validates the methods of scholarship and of science by providing them with sound operational principles. Theological categories verify, falsify, and transvalue certain kinds of philosophical and general categories. They also endow foundational thinking with concrete integration. Finally, general categories verify, falsify, and amplify certain kinds of philosophical and special categories. The implications of this distinction between the coordination and interplay of categories should become clearer in the course of the reflections which follow.

Let us begin to reflect in greater detail on the techniques of categorial coordination. We have named four such techniques: agreement, complementarity, convergence, and dialectical reversal. These techniques function in other contexts than foundational speculation. Let us then illustrate how each technique functions in more familiar frames of reference before we attempt the more complex task of illustrating its use within foundational thought.

We coordinate categories on the basis of the ways in which they relate

---

[1] The fact that this chapter attempts to reflect on my own pursuit of foundational theology explains its lack of footnotes. In the course of this chapter, I attempt to illustrate the co-ordination and interplay of foundational categories with examples from my own writings. I could, of course, have referred the reader in footnotes to the places in my writings where those examples occur. Since, however, the reader would find there nothing more than what the text of this chapter already contains, I deemed the documentation redundant and omitted it.

to the realities they seek to interpret. Categories agree when they assert the same thing about the same reality. Sometimes their agreement appears in the very act of assertion. One person may describe a summer day with record tempertures and humidity as "extremely hot and muggy," another as "sweltering." No one, however, who understands the meaning of what each has said could seriously doubt that both agree fundamentally in their assessment of the weather.

We recognize real agreement less readily when differences in terminology obscure identity of intent. An American visiting England for the first time may not, for example, realize that the helpful hotel clerk who suggests taking a lift is really recommending an elevator. Similarly, rival candidates who actually stand together on a particular issue may misinterpret one another's position out of mutual suspicion or rhetorical excess.

Categories complement one another when they interpret accurately two different but interrelated kinds of reality. Solid geometry complements plane geometry. Insight into artistic creativity complements a sound theory of logic. In business an understanding of sound techniques of personnel management complements a shrewd reading of the fluctuations of the stockmarket.

Categories converge when they assert different but non-contradictory things about the same reality. A historian's assessment of the place of Beethoven's ninth symphony in the development of western music might well converge with a careful analysis of the musical structure and form of that masterpiece. An accurate factual account of important world events converges with a sound news analysis of the significance of those same events. The testimony of eyewitnesses to a complex historical occurrence yields a convergent insight into the forces that conspired to cause it.

Categories that agree, complement one another, and converge do not contradict one another. Either they assert the same truth, or they articulate insights into interrelated realities or into different facets of the same reality. When categories contradict one another, we must resort to dialectical reversal in order to coordinate them. Dialectical reversal employs three basic techniques for coordinating contradictory categories. (1) It endorses some categories as true and valid and discards other categories as false and invalid. In this case, coordination is accomplished by eliminating from discourse the misleading contradictory categories. (2) Dialectical reversal may endorse a particular set of categories (i.e., frames of reference) as adequate and dismiss other sets of categories (i.e., frames of reference) as inadequate. In this case, dialectical reversal eliminates contradiction by demonstrating the inadequacy of frames of reference that motivate the contradictions. (3) Contradictions arising from inadequate frames of reference may also be overcome by the creation of a more comprehensive frame of reference that takes into account the best insights of those frames of reference it supercedes. In this case contradiction is overcome by redefining in the novel frame of reference the meaning of formerly contradictory terms in such a way that they cease to contradict one another. Let us reflect in more concrete detail on each of these techniques for coordinating contradictory categories.

We employ the first technique every time we endorse one account of reality as true and set aside one or more contradictory accounts of reality as false. During the Watergate investigations, for example, contradictory versions of the Nixon administration's involvement in the Watergate break-in flooded the press, but as the investigating committee amassed more and more evidence in the case it was able to distinguish truth telling from lies. In this particular instance, the first technique for resolving categorial contradictions resulted in the resignation of a president and the imprisonment of a number of federal officials.

We endorse particular propositions as true and valid and set aside others as false and invalid; but we cannot either verify or falsify frames of reference as such. We can validate and invalidate only what we assert. Frames of reference, however, provide the context within which assertions can be made or denied; but while frames of reference are presupposed, they themselves are neither asserted nor denied as such. We can, however, choose between frames of reference on the basis of a judgment concerning their relative adequacy. An adequate frame of reference allows one to account for all the data relevant to the resolution of a given question. An inadequate frame of reference does not.

The history of science illustrates the way in which less comprehensive frames of reference give way to more comprehensive. Shortly before Copernicus revolutionized astronomy with his theory of a heliocentric universe, careful observation of the movement of the heavenly bodies had turned up several anomalies for which Ptolemaic astronomy, the then accepted theory, could not account. Copernicus's theory explained some of those anomalies and promised to explain others. As a consequence, within a short time scientists abandoned Ptolemaic astronomy as the less adequate of the two theories.

Analogous evaluative processes occur at the level of common sense thinking. The civil rights movement, the black power movement, the feminist movement, and similar social protests challenge the limitations and biases in popular perceptions of reality that blind individuals, groups, and whole societies to the needs of ignored minorities in their midst. Such social protests demand that inadequate ways of ordering a given society yield to a more just and more humanly comprehensive social system.

The third technique for resolving contradictions among categories poses the subtlest challenge to the dialectical mind. The third technique presupposes that contradictory perceptions of the same reality have been motivated by inadequacies in the frames of reference that generated the perceptions. The third technique proposes to resolve the contradiction by creating a more adequate frame of reference capable of taking into account the best insights of those less comprehensive frames of reference it replaces.

The debate over the relationship between population control and world hunger illustrates the way in which this particular technique of dialectical reversal operates. In the early stages of the debate some held that poverty rather than expanding populations explained the growth of world hunger. Those who defended this position pushed therefore for the redistribution of the earth's collective wealth in such a way that the needs of present and of future generations could be met. Others insisted that unjust social structures rather than poverty accounted for the growth of world hunger. Those who defended this second position pushed therefore for the reconstruction of the social and economic order as the most effective means for eliminating world hunger. Still others defended the position that the population explosion itself has produced world hunger. Those defending this third position pushed accordingly for the stringent limitation of future births through appropriate methods of birth control.

A closer examination of the relationship between population and world hunger suggested, however, that none of the three proposed theories had taken adequate account of the complexity of the problem. As a result some students of the problem proposed yet a fourth position which attempted to take into account the best insights of the theories it attempted to replace. The new proposal conceded that expanding populations pose a serious challenge to contemporary society but questioned whether birth control alone provides an adequate solution to the problem. Indeed, a mounting body of evidence points to the fact that the birth rate tends to decline spontaneously in more affluent countries where hunger poses less of a threat. The new approach encouraged the ongoing development of food resources to meet expanding population needs; but it also insisted that only by reforming the political, economic, and social structures that produce starvation could the challenge of world hunger be effectively addressed. In other words, the new proposal suggested a more comprehensive frame of reference for addressing the question of the relationship between population growth and world hunger, one which would allow the claims of earlier, less adequate theories to illumine different facets of a complex problem.

(II)

We have identified four common techniques for coordinating categories: agreement, convergence, complementarity, and dialectical reversal. As we have seen, these techniques may be employed in other frames of reference than foundational theology, but the four techniques also facilitate the coordination of all three sets of foundational categories.

Two different and interrelated tasks of coordination confront foundational thinkers. First they must coordinate its philosophical, general, and special categories among themselves. Second, they must coordinate all three sets of categories with one another. Let us reflect on these two processes of coordination in order. We begin with the coordination of philosophical, general, and special categories among themselves.

Although philosophy, like other disciplines, displays a broad variety of viewpoints and methods, philosophers can on occasion agree with one another. Moreover, any foundational theology which ambitions an inculturated account of conversion would, as we have already seen, be well advised to derive the philosophical categories it employs from the specific culture it addresses. Philosophical traditions result from the speculative interchange of the thinkers that generate them. In the course of that interchange philosophers teach one another. As a consequence, despite the personal idiosyncrasies that diversify their various systems, one may in examining a particular philosophical tradition discover broad areas of consensus that endow it with a distincitve cultural character.

As we saw in the first chapter, an analysis of the North American philosophical tradition reveals some areas of broad and developing consensus. We have identified six such areas. As the American philosophical tradition grows, its principal thinkers display an increasing repugnance to dualistic conceptions of reality. They tend to question the speculative utility of the category "substance." They focus attention on the dynamic structure of experience and tend to use the term "experience" itself as a central integrating category. North American philosophy consistently assimilates religious and esthetic experience. It insists on the finitude, on the fallibility, and on the social, dialogic character of human reason. Finally, North American philosophy shows a preoccupation with consequences and with the dynamic interrelation of thought and action. Needless to say, not every North American philosopher develops all these themes or treats them in the same way; but one may find areas of genuine agreement among them. The technique of agreement can, then, be effectively employed in order to coordinate among themselves the philosophical categories that structure foundational thinking.

The foundational theologian can also identify broad areas of agreement among the general categories that shape a normative theory of conversion. General categories, the reader will recall, derive from scientific and scholarly disciplines other than theology which illumine human religious experience. Among those disciplines we should number experimental and clinical psychology. Developmental psychologists, for example, propose different theories about the stages of human psychic growth, but they all agree that some kind of developmental construct offers the most fruitful way to generalize about human behavior. Sometimes, too, developmental schemes build on one another. Lawrence Kohlberg's theory about human moral development, for instance, presupposes and endorses Jean Piaget's account of the stages of human cognitive development. James Fowler's description of cognitive religious development builds on the work of Kohlberg, Piaget and Erickson.

Different theological traditions also exhibit broad areas of consensus. Medieval theology, for example, substituted for an Augustinian theory of human depravity a more benign interpretation of human nature which concedes to sinful humanity the possibility of performing naturally virtuous actions without the help of divine grace. During the sixteenth century the Catholic and Protestant traditions divided on this issue, Luther and Calvin siding with Augustine and the Council of Trent siding with the medieval scholastics. As Protestant theology has evolved, however, it has tended to repudiate an Augustinian theory of depravity and to endorse an understanding of human nature that approximates more closely Tridentine anthropology.

Clearly, then, agreement offers one useful means for coordinating the three sets of foundational categories among themselves. So does complementarity. Categories complement one another, as we have already seen, when they interpret accurately two different but interrelated kinds of reality.

For example, in John Dewey's philosophy of experience, his esthetic theory complements his logic. The former describes the irrational thought processes that create artistic and literary creations of beauty; the latter describes the logical pursuit of truth. Both Dewey's esthetic theory and his logic presuppose the same relational, transactional construct of experience. Both presuppose the instrumental character of symbolic behavior. Both illumine distinct but interrelated moments in the growth of experience. Logical thinking, Dewey argues correctly, endows with rational precision the kinds of cognitive transactions that shape artistic thinking.

The insights of two different philosophical minds may also complement one another. For example, William James's insights into the dynamics of religious affectivity in *The Varieties of Religious Experience* converge with Josiah Royce's reflections on the rational, moral, and social dimension of religion. Both men say insightful things about the human encounter with the holy; but while James attends primarily to individual feelings, Royce focuses primarily on the social processes that motivate rational religious beliefs and choices.

General foundational categories may also complement one another. In the field of developmental psychology, for example, Jean Piaget has studied primarily the stages of intellectual development; Lawrence Kohlberg, the stages of moral development; James Fowler, the stages of faith development; and Eric Erickson, the stages of affective development. By exploring distinct but interrelated aspects of human growth, these four men have articulated a complementary portrayal of human development which other thinkers have correlated and consolidated.

Special foundational categories complement one another also. A sound theological anthropology both grounds and complements sacramental theology and Christology. If, moreover, one is willing to conceive the triune God on an analogy with human social experience, it can ground trinitarian theology as well. Systematic theological thinking complements biblical exegesis.

Besides complementing one another, the philosophical categories which shape foundational thinking also converge with one another. Categories converge when they assert different truths about the same reality. For example, within the North American philosophical tradition different thinkers focus on different facets of the same moment within human experience. Dewey, Royce, and Peirce all assert the fallibility of rational thought processes as well as the social, dialogic character of human reason. Peirce argues this thesis on logical grounds. Dewey insists on the transactional, instrumental character of rational thought. Royce explores the conditions for the possibility of shared rational awareness. Each thinker offers a sound insight into the experience of rational reflection, but each approaches human rationality with a different set of concerns. As a consequence, together they paint in many ways a convergent portrait of logical thinking.

We also discover convergence among the general categories that shape foundational thinking. Jean Piaget argues, for example, that until about the age of eight most children cannot engage in abstract, rational thinking. He characterizes pre-rational thought as transductive. Transductive thinking proceeds by trial and error, it indulges in fanciful portrayals of reality, and it engages the child's felt apperceptions of the real. Piaget describes in a general way the processes of transductive thought, but he leaves one largely at a loss to analyse its conceptual processes in any detail. Fortunately, however, Jungian archetypal theory converges with Piaget's analysis at this precise point and offers techniques for organizing the otherwise chaotic patterns of human imaginative thinking. Both men agree that pre-rational thinking eschews logic. Both look upon transductive thinking as an attempt to deal with reality. Archetypal theory, however, advances beyond Piaget in that it discovers recurring imaginative patterns within transductive thought. Moreover, Jungian archetypal theory endows those patterns with symbolic significance for understanding the process of human psychic maturation. Jungian theory lacks the systematic empirical validation of

Piaget's developmental hypothesis; but the clinical utility of Jung's thought endows it with a measure of validation. In their descriptive accounts of the pre-rational patterns of evaluation, therefore, Jungian and developmental theory converge.

Strictly theological categories may also converge among themselves. The first Vatican Council denies, for example, that supernatural faith results from rational argumentation. Jonathan Edwards, on the other hand, asserts that faith results from an irrational, affective consent to divine beauty incarnate, a consent motivated by the supernatural illumination of the Holy Breath. Both assertions offer convergent accounts of the dynamics of Christian conversion. Similarly, a careful examination of the first two stages of faith development described in Teresa of Avila's *Interior Castle* will show that they converge remarkably with the graces sought during the first two weeks of *The Spiritual Exercises* of Ignatius Loyola. Teresa describes accurately the attitudes that characterize two distinct but interrelated steps toward contemplative union with God, but Ignatius offers practical strategies for leading an individual through prayer from step one to step two.

Categories invite dialectical reversal when they make contradictory assertions about the same reality. Moreover, we have distinguished three dialectical techniques for resolving contradictions: the elimination of false categories, the elimination of inadequate frames of reference, and the reintepretation of initially contradictory categories in a more adequate frame of reference that resolves their contradictions. Let us reflect on the way in which each of these techniques can be employed in order to coordinate among themselves the three kinds of categories that structure foundational speculation.

In the development of the North American philosophical tradition, transcendental speculation proposed more than one unverifiable theory of knowledge. Ralph Waldo Emerson, for example, believed with many other Platonists that the human mind encounters truth, not in material sensible things, but by ascending to a transcendent realm of eternal, immutable Being. Theodore Parker believed that the human spirit possesses faculties that allow it within subjectivity to grasp both objectively and self-evidently the existence of God, the immortality of the soul, and the universal principles of moral conduct. Both men believed that the mind grasps truth with intuitive self-evidence. In the latter half of the nineteenth century, however, C.S. Peirce refuted decisively such fallacious claims to self-evident intuition. By invalidating the epistemology of both Emerson and Parker, Peirce enabled the student of the North American philosophical tradition to resolve the dialectical conflict between his theory of knowledge and theirs by abandoning the latter.

The study of a particular philosophical tradition also allows one to prefer more comprehensive to less adequate frames of reference. Process theology, for example, has attempted to construct a metaphysics of experience. It has proposed a dipolar construct of experience. In process theory experience grows through the ongoing integration of its concrete, physical pole with its abstract, conceptual pole. In *The Problem of Christianity*, (1913), however, Josiah Royce demonstrated the inadequacy of such a dipolar construct of human cognition. Although Royce was attacking the epistemologies of William James and Henri Bergson, his objections apply to Whitehead's epistemology as well. For Whitehead, like James and Bergson, equivalently conceived of human cognition as the ongoing interrelation of concrete percepts with abstract concepts. In such a theory of knowledge, one cannot, however, account for a fundamental act of knowing, namely, the act of interpretation, in which one individual explains another reality to another individual. In order to account for such an interpretative experience, Royce correctly argued, we must with Peirce and in opposition to James and to Bergson (and I would add to Whitehead as well) conceive human cognition as triadic rather than as dipolar in structure. Royce concluded, soundly in my opinion, that all dipolar constructs of human experience must be set aside as inadequate and replaced by a more adequate triadic construct.

On occasion, philosophical speculation can resolve dialectical contradictions by subsuming them into a larger frame of reference which redefines the contradictory terms in such a way as to eliminate the contradiction. For example, as we have already seen, Emerson defended the position that Being, reality, is grasped in a privileged way by irrational, imaginative intuitions. Bernard Lonergan by contrast held that inferential, logical thinking enjoys privileged cognitive access to the real. John Dewey, however, constructed a more comprehensive epistemology than either Emerson or Lonergan. Dewey held that the human grasps reality both through inference and through nonrational, artistic intuitions. Dewey's more comprehensive theory of knowlege thus eliminates the dialectical contradiction separating Emerson and Lonergan. As we have also seen, his insights find an echo in the work of Bernard Meland.

The three techniques of dialectical reversal also facilitate the coordination of general foundational categories. The science of psychology studies human experience, and some of its conclusions cast light on human religious experience as well. As psychology has advanced, moreover, a certain number of contradictory accounts of the human psyche have been definitively set aside as false and invalid. For example, the James-Lange theory of human emotions interpreted the experience of affectivity as the sensation of physiological processes. Other theorists offered different and contradictory interpretations of human affections. Eventually, experimental evidence forced the psychological community to abandon the James-Lange theory as false and to prefer empirically verifiable accounts of how the emotions work and what they perceive.

As the behavioral sciences have advanced, thoreticians have also been able to identify interpretative frames of reference as inadequate. The development of clinical psychiatry illustrates the process of identification. Freud deserves great credit for having discovered the unconscious mind, but critical reflection on Freud's ideas has caused subsequent theorists to question the adequacy of Freud's conception of the psyche. Humanistic psychology faults Freud for focusing too narrowly on the pathological psyche to the neglect of healthy emotional development. Logotherapy faults Freud for failing to take into adequate account the human search for meaning. Jung criticizes Freud's failure to value sufficiently the archetypes of the unconscious mind. All three critiques concur in asserting the inadequacy as such of Freud's original construct of the psyche.

Scientific and scholarly investigation of human experience has also produced more comprehensive frames of reference capable of reconciling contradictions generated by less comprehensive contexts. Both Freudian and behavioristic psychology, for example, propose atheistic interpretations of human religious experience; but other psychological theories offer a more comprehensive description of the psyche that validates the human ecounter with the holy. James's psychological phenomenology of the varieties of religious experience, logotherapy, Jungian archetypal theory, and other schools of psychology all make room for theism. They offer, therefore, a more comprehensive frame of reference for dealing with human personal development.

As scientific and scholarly interpretations of human psychic development have advanced, they have also on occasion formulated more comprehensive frames of reference that reconcile the conflicting insights of earlier, less adequate theories. Jung, for example, attempted to formulate a personality typology broad enough to allow him to incorporate the conflicting psychological theories of both Adler and Freud. Freudian theory, he argued, cast significant light on the neuroses of extraverts, while Adler's will to power illuminated the neurotic conflicts of introverts. In the process Jung constructed a more adequate typology than either Freud or Adler, one that helped resolve at least some of the conflicts between their two competing theories.

The techniques of dialectical reversal also reconcile conflicts among special foundational categories. The human attempt to articulate the experience of an encounter with the holy labors under the constraints of radical finitude, bias, and sinfulness. As a consequence, every religious tradition produces a certain number of contradictory accounts of God and of the ultimate meaning and purpose of life. When those contradictions defy reconciliation, the religious tradition in question and the living, religious community that transmits it fragment. Think of the fragmentation of the Christian community that occured at the time of the Protestant reformation. Religious contradictions, however, can be resolved by eliminating false religious doctrines, by discarding inadequate theological frames of reference, and by casting more adequate frames of reference which allow the redefinition of formerly contradictory terms in such a way that the contradictions disappear.

As we have already seen, we test the truth or falsity of Christian doctrines against the historical data of revelation, for incarnational theology creates the possibility of approaching God empirically. If indeed the divine Word became flesh in Jesus of Nazareth, then His life, teaching, and destiny provide us with facts, with data, about who God is and about how the deity chooses to relate to us and to our world. Every Christian theology must test its affirmations about God against the historical data of Christian revelation. So too must any normative theology of conversion. The empirical testability of theological propositions entails the possibility of validating or invalidating them inductively.

Similarly, theological propositions that express beliefs about human nature and the world in which we live can be validated or invalidated in the behavior of humans and of nature either as we experience it directly or as we reconstruct it from the evidence of the past.

The empirical testability of theological hypotheses against the data of revelation and of experience allows theological method to approximate at a scholarly level the methods of the empirical sciences. We cannot, of course, ordinarily quantify theological propositions in the manner of the hard sciences, but within limits we can reach judgments about the truth or falsity of specific faith affirmations and about the relative adequacy or inadequacy of the frames of reference in which they occur.

For example, sacramental theology prior to Vatican II attempted to show that Jesus of Nazareth had defined the matter and form of all seven sacramental rites of the Catholic church. Contemporary biblical exegesis as well as the history of Christian ritual have however demonstrated the anachronistic character of such a theological hypothesis, and it has been correctly discarded by theologians as invalid and unverifiable. History and exegesis also call into question, however, the proposition that only baptism and the eucharist can trace their origins to the ministry of the historical Jesus. The eucharist repeats the prophetic gesture that Jesus used to explain to His disciples the meaning of His passion, but the other rites of the church give symbolic access to other facets of His ministry. By rejecting mosaic divorce practices and by demanding of his disciples a mutual love and forgiveness that imitates God's own love for us, Jesus transformed the meaning of marriage and redefined its terms for those who would enter the kingdom. His proclamation of the Father's unconditioned forgiveness came to ritual expression in the Christian community not only in the rites of initiation but in the formal reconciliation of backsliders. Jesus' ministry of healing foreshadowed the Christian rite of anointing. His baptism by John, His visible possession of the Holy Breath, His revelation as a "lifegiving Breath" in His resurrection, and His visible mission of the Pentecostal Breath to the Christian community all ground the rituals that eventually evolved into the rites of Christian intiation. Finally, His appointment of the twelve as judges in the new Israel and His appearance to and commissioning of the apostles in the resurrection laid the foundation for the rite of orders. Besides the eucharist, then, all the rites of the church can trace their roots to some facet of Jesus' ministry. That fact lends, then, some historical plausibility to the belief that He "instituted" the seven sacraments, even though He lived in total ignorance of medieval canon law.

Not only can dialectical contradictions in theology be resolved by validating or invalidating theological hypotheses, but we can also invoke the data of both revelation and of human experience to assess the relative adequacy of theological frames of reference. The development of the sciences of archeology and of anthropology has, for example, forced a theological reinterpretation of the historicity of the adamic myth. Instead of interpreting the biblical story of the sin of our first parents with the naive historical objectivity that frequently characterized both patristic and medieval exegesis, contemporary theology has been forced to reassess the presuppositions that grounded such interpretations and to set them aside as methodologically inadequate. Contemporary exegesis looks upon the story of Adam and Eve as an accurate myth about the religious singificance of all human history rather than as a factual account of what occurred at the dawn of human history. In effect, therefore, contemporary theology has set aside one exegetical frame of reference as inadequate and preferred another that better suits the data of revelation and of experience. Similarly, theological abandonment of a strict Augustinian doctrine of depravity or of antecedent predestination expresses a judgment not only on the truth or falsity of specific propositions he defended but also on the inadequacy of the frame of reference in which Augustine's thought advanced. We recognize today gnostic influences on his conception of human nature and stoic influences on his notion of providence. We have also correctly questioned the adequacy of either frame of reference to interpret divine revelation.

Finally, as theological speculation advances more comprehensive frames of reference can emerge which allow for the reconciliation of contradictory theological positions. Christian Aristotelianism eventually replaced Christian Platonism as a more adequate way of approaching Christian self-understanding in faith. In the twentieth century, Christian existentialism seemed to many to offer a still more comprehensive context for understanding the gospel than Christian Aristotelianism. Since Cathlics and Protestants had divided during the reformation in part over

the stance they took toward Christian Platonism and Christian Aristotelianism, the emergence of Christian existentialism provided a neutral
territory for discussing and beginning to resolve some of the doctrinal
contradictions that split the church in the sixteenth century. In this
country a Christian experientialism could perform a similar function if
developed and pursued systematically.

(III)

We have been reflecting on the first operational challenge that faces
any foundational theologian: namely, the coordination among themselves of the three different sets of categories that structure foundational
speculation. We have identified four fundamental techniques for effecting such a coordination: agreement, complementarity, convergence, and
dialectical reversal. A more complex task, however, faces any would-be
practitioner of foundational speculation: namely, the coordination of the
three sets of foundational categories with one another.

As I have already indicated, study of the North American philosophical tradition has convinced me that one can use the four techniques of
agreement, convergence, complementarity, and dialectical reversal to
derive from it a fairly comprehensive metaphysics of experience, one
that provides a promising and potentially fruitful frame of reference for
discussing the dynamics of conversion. That construct of experience has
grounded the preceding reflections on foundational method. It supplies
my own practice of foundational speculation with its transcendental
categories. I conceive all reality as experience in some form. I define
experience as a process composed of relational elements called feelings. I
discover three kinds of felt relations in the higher forms of experience:
values, actions, and tendencies.

A colleague schooled in a more traditional hylemorphic metaphysics
has asked me why he should equate being and experience. I myself know
of only one reason to adopt any proposition: its verifiability. While I do
not regard the equation of reality and experience as a self-evident belief
or as the only way to define Being in a non-tautologous fashion, I myself
have yet to encounter any reality that cannot be described as an experience in the sense in which I have defined that term.

"Experience," then, provides my foundational thinking with its basic
transcendental category. We have reflected in a previous chapter on
some of the implications of conceiving Being as experience. Let us now
turn to the more complex task of understanding the operational procedures that sanction the simultaneous coordination within foundational
thinking of its transcendental, general, and special categories.

The same four techniques that coordinate the three sets of foundational categories among themselves also coordinate them with one another. Let us reflect on how this occurs.

Categories agree when they assert fundamentally the same thing about the same reality. The philosophical construct of experience which I defend discovers an evaluative continuum within human experience stretching from sensation through affection and images to abstract inference. It recognizes two ways of grasping reality judgmentally: one affective and irrational, the other inductive and logical. It acknowledges the developmental, transactional character of experience as well as its organic basis. A similar construct of experience shapes not only the psychological theories of Jean Piaget and other developmental psychologists that build upon his insights but also the clinical, neo-Freudian psychology of Karl Menninger and of Paul Preuser. That same construct also makes sense out of Carl Jung's theory of psychological types. In all these instances one may detect a fundamental agreement between the transcendental and general categories I have employed in constructing a normative theology of conversion.

Moreover, when the philosophical construct of experience I have proposed has been validated and amplified by data from experimental and clinical psychology, it provides a useful frame of reference for reflecting on a Christian faith experience. For example, John of the Cross in *The Ascent of Mount Carmel* and in *The Dark Night of the Soul* speaks of the healing of disordered affections that occurs during the dark night of the senses. John describes disordered affections only in the most generic terms as darkening, defiling, and enslaving. Clinical psychology also attempts to deal with disordered human affections; but it describes them in greater symptomatic detail than John. In other words clinical psychology allows us to articulate a detailed symptomology of disordered human affections, but that symptomology agrees with John's more general description of their effect upon the human psyche. Moreover, the transcendental category "experience" properly defined interprets both.

In other words, a metaphysics of experience, experimental and clinical psychology, and Christian theology can on occasion agree in their portrayal of reality. Such agreement facilitates the coordination of all three sets of foundational categories with one another.

The three different sets of foundational categories complement one another when they offer an accurate account of distinct but interrelated realities. A sound philosophical analysis of human esthetic experience complements Lawrence Kohlberg's account of the stages of human moral development. Both analyses complement a theological explanation of the moral consequences of Christian conversion. All three complement a social analysis of economic injustice. The four speculative analyses complement one another even though they are derived from four different disciplines because each focuses on a distinct but interrelated facet of the experience of integral conversion. The first targets experiences proper to affective conversion; the second, experiences proper to moral conversion; the third, experiences proper to religious conversion; the fourth, experiences proper to socio-political conversion.

The different kinds of categories which structure a normative theory of conversion converge when they say true but different things about the same reality. A philosophical analysis of the symbolic articulation of intuitive insights converges with Jungian archetypal analysis. Each analyses human imaginative activity from a different persepective. The former throws light on artistic and literary forms of expression; the latter on the psychological significance of dream images. Jungian artistic and literary criticism illustrates the complementarity of these distinct sets of categories.

Moreover, both a sound philosophical description of human affectivity and Jungian archetypal analysis converge with a theological account of the healing of the human heart accomplished in the dark night of the senses, for that account describes affective and imaginative healing in faith. Insight into the dynamic growth effected in the dark night springs from a Christian encounter with God in faith and prayer. Philosophical aesthetics and clinical psychiatry do not; but both cast light on the mystics' accounts of their encounter with God in prayer.

Finally, dialectical reversal can also effect the coordination of the three sets of foundational categories with one another. When philosophical, general, and special theological categories contradict one another, the contradiction can sometimes be set aside by rejecting one or more sets of categories as false and invalid while endorsing another set of categories as true. For example, a philosophical description of human experience which contradicts the hard evidence furnished by careful empirical investigations into human development should be discarded as false. Similarly, philosophical, scholarly, or scientific hypotheses which contradict the data of revelation ought also to be set aside as religiously false and misleading.

A comparison of the different frames of reference employed by philosophy, scholarship, the empirical sciences, and theology can also on occasion motivate a sound judgment concerning their relative adequacy and inadequacy. For example, Lawrence Kohlberg's theory of human moral development prescinds for all intents and purposes from the religious realities and values that enter into human ethical choices. Kohlberg, then, presents one possible way of understanding natural moral development; but an ethical theory which would take into account the impact of both rational and faith values upon the development of the human personality would offer a more comprehensive ethical frame of reference than Kohlberg's.

Sometimes, too, contradictory affirmations dividing the various disciplines that contribute categories to foundational speculation can be resolved by creating a more comprehensive frame of reference that takes into account the best insights of the conflicting theories. In a sense, the creation of such a frame of reference describes the fundamental challenge of a normative theology of conversion. Certainly, a construct of conversion that acknowledges an affective, an intellectual, a moral, a socio-political, and a religious moment within the process of both initial and ongoing conversion provides a potentially fruitful frame of reference for evaluating the more focused results of philosophical, scholarly, scientific, and theological insights into human experience.

Moreover, foundational theory can on occasion resolve the apparent contradictions that seem on first examination to divide disciplines from one another. For example, Kohlberg proposes an account of rational moral development that seems to contradict the ethics of discipleship inculcated in the New Testament. For Kohlberg, reason judges the ultimate morality or immorality of human actions. In the New Testament faith, not reason, stands as the ultimate arbiter of moral decision. A sound theology of Christian conversion offers a way of avoiding an arbitrary option between faith and reason in making moral choices. Foundational theory suggests that religious conversion provides a context of faith which transvalues the moral insights of natural reason without abolishing them. Christian conversion requires that the filial ethics of discipleship which Jesus preached and incarnated inform the moral decisions of every convert, but New Testament morality does not provide a solution to every human moral dilemma. Christian ethics needs also therefore the best insights of a moral reason informed by prayer and illumined by the action of the Breath of Christ.

(IV)

The attempt to coordinate the three sets of foundational categories among themselves engages their interpretative interplay. Coordination, as we have seen, differs from interplay. Coordination evaluates categories on the basis of the way they relate to the realitities they seek to interpret. Interplay focuses on the way in which categories interpret one another. The formulation of transcendental categories invokes philosophical insight. General categories emerge from disciplines other than theology whose conclusions illumine religious experience in some way. Special categories are engendered by faith and by theological speculation. Within the total enterprise of foundational thinking, how, then, do these three sets of categories relate interpretatively to one another? In the final section of this chapter, I shall attempt to show that within a normative theory of Christian conversion philosophically derived categories interpret, integrate, and contextualize general and special foundational categories; that theological categories validate and transvalue certain kinds of philosophical and general categories; and that general categories validate and amplify certain kinds of philosophical and theological categories. Let us reflect on each of these kinds of interplay in turn.

Philosophy seeks to understand in a rational manner lived, day-to-day, human experience. It uses language as its tool. Philosophers engage in three identifiable kinds of thinking: they describe what appears in experience, they engage in normative reflection of affective, intellectual, moral, socio-political, and religious development, and they make generalizations about the nature of reality. We may, then, distinguish seven major philosophical disciplines: phenomenology, esthetics, logic, ethics, political philosophy, philosophy of religion, and metaphysics. All these philosophical disciplines can contribute insights to a normative theology of conversion. Metaphysics, however, supplies foundational speculation with its trascendental categories.

Philosophical speculation begins descriptively because a descriptive exploration of the different facets of any reality under investigation alerts one to the complexity of the issues with which one must deal in making normative or metaphysical judgments about it. Strictly normative philsophical thinking formulates criteria which allow one to distinguish between a sound and an unsound evaluative response to reality. Philosophical generalizations about the nature of reality whether descriptive, strictly normative, or explanatory labor under the same fallibility as attends any other human hypothesis. Nevertheless, every systematic philosophical account of the real aspires to applicability and adequacy. An applicable account of the real will make sense out of some entities encountered within experience. An adequate theory of reality will encounter no entities for which it cannot account. Philosophy also lives by precise definition and by logical self-consistency. As a consequence, logical inconsistency also forces the revision of philosophical theories.

Philsophy differs from both theology and positive science. Theology invokes both reason and faith in its judgments about the nature of reality. Philosophy invokes reason alone. Positive science uses complex instrumentation and precise measurement and tests its theories against systematically assembled data. Philosophy uses no instrument besides language, concerns itself more with value than with precise mathematical measurement, and tests its theories against lived, day-to-day experience.

Nevertheless, precisely because philosophy attempts to make rational generalizations about the nature of reality, it stands accountable to theology, science, and scholarship; for a sound philosophy must interpret correctly the validated results of all three of these disciplines. Philosophical categories will interpret those results if they apply to them in the sense in which they have been philosophically defined.

Needless to say, any philosophy which contradicts divine revelation or the validated results of scholarship or of empirical science stands judged by them as false. Any philsophy which fails to account for every facet of divine revelation or for the validated conclusions of science and scholarship stands judged by them as inadequate. When, however, philosophical categories do apply to the results of theological speculation, science, or scholarship,they interpret them philosophically. Interpretation, therefore, provides the first instance of interpretative interplay between the philosophical categories which structure foundational speculation, on one hand, and between its general and special foundational categories, on the other.

Moreover, when within the enterprise of foundational speculation transcendental philosophical categories do apply to the results of theology, positive science, and human scholarship, they can also help to integrate those results. For example, in the three foundational studies I have written, I have tried to show that the category "experience" can be legitimately invoked to understand the dynamics of personal development in faith, the experience of shared Christian worship, and the reality of the triune God. We can, I believe, invoke the same category in order to interpret Christ, the church, or any other reality encountered within an experience of integral five-fold conversion. In other words, when used transcendentally, the category "experience" yields a conceptually coherent insight into Christian revelation. When the same philosophical category interprets the foundationally relevant results of scholarship and of the empirical sciences, it integrates conceptually all three nests of foundational categories.

Moreover, an adequate philosophical description of the complexities of human experience can also provide an overarching frame of reference for ascertaining and effecting the agreement, convergence, complementarity, and dialectical reversal of general and special foundational categories. As we have seen, a sound philosophical construct of human experience will distinguish sensations, affective and imaginative perceptions of reality, logical perceptions, and moral deliberations. Within such a descriptive, philosophical construct, one can begin to situate the results of different clinical and empirical studies of human experience. Neo-Freudian psychology, for example, focuses its attention primarily on human affections. Jungian archetypal theory targets the imagination. Piaget explores the whole spectrum of cognitive development and attempts to determine empirically at what age different kinds of evaluative responses become possible. Kohlberg attends primarily to moral cognitive development.

By situating the results of clinical or empirical investigations of human behavior within a descriptive philosophical construct of experience, one can more readily determine whether or not any two theories address the same moment in the growth of experience. Once that has been determined, one can proceed to ascertain whether or not they agree, converge, complement, or contradict one another. In other words, the philsophical categories that shape foundational thinking help contextualize both general and special categories and in so doing facilitate their coordination.

Finally, by supplying the normative principles of logic to science and scholarship, philosophy validates their operational procedures.

We have, then, identified four ways in which philosophical categories interplay with other foundational categories. They interpret general and special categories when they apply to them in the sense in which they have been philosophically defined. Transcendental categories integrate general and special categories by providing an abstract rubric for thinking any reality whatever. Descriptive transcendental categories can also be used to contextualize other general and special categories in such a way as to facilitate their coordination within foundational speculation. The principles of logic validate the methods of science and scholarship.

General foundational categories supplied by science and scholarship, on the other hand, help to validate philosophical and special categories not by sanctioning their operational procedures but by supplying the data that verifies or falsifies philosophical and theological generalizations about created reality.

Besides validating some of the generalizations of both philosophy and theology, general foundational categories can also help amplify both. The philosophy of human nature, for example, has much to learn from both personality theory and from the social sciences. The focused and precise character of scientific mensuration can, moreover, raise to consciousness facets of realities that both science and philosophy investigate, facets that philosophical reflection on lived, day-to-day experience overlooks. For example, philosophy describes the same spectrum of cognitive responses that developmental psychology studies; but developmental psychology advances beyond a mere philosophical description of human knowledge by supplying evidence that human cognition develops in identifiable stages. Not until the age of two do children develop the capacity to imagine a world. Only much later do they manifest a capacity for logical thinking. These validated results of detailed, empirical studies of human cognitive development amplify the insights of a philosophical phenomenology of the human. They also cast light on a theological understanding of Jesus' human experience.

We have, then, identified two ways in which general foundational categories interplay with philosophical and special categories. General categories help to amplify the other foundational categories, and they also help validate them by providing data concerning human nature and the world in which we live.

Special foundational categories derive not from reason but from faith. They interplay with transcendental and general foundational categories in three significant ways. First of all, since special categories articulate an experience of God's historical self-communication, they validate or invalidate philosophical, scientific, or scholarly affirmations about the nature and activity of God by providing historical evidence that verifies or falsifies human statements about the divine.

Second, faith-derived categories transvalue the results of philosophy, science, and scholarship reached in abstraction from divine revelation. We transvalue categories by shifting them from one frame of reference to another. The shifted category retains some of its originally intended meaning but acquires new implications and connotations from its use in a novel frame of reference. When we invoke philosophical, scientific, or scholarly categories to formulate a theological theory, we necessarily transvalue them by religious faith. When transvalued in faith those same categories begin to acquire new interpretative capacities to the extent that they now begin to shed light on a human encounter with God.

As we have seen, transcendental categories integrate the other foundational categories by providing an abstract rubric for thinking any reality whatever. Because special categories articulate a religious insight, they also contribute to the integration of foundational thinking by expressing a unified and unifying vision of God's relation to the world and of it to God. Because special foundational categories derive that insight from a concrete, historical event of divine self-disclosure, they accomplish the integration of foundational thinking in a concrete rather than in an abstract manner, for they interpret the specific conditions historically determined by God for advancing toward personal, social, and cosmic integration in and with the deity. Special foundational categories, therefore, also interplay with transcendental and general foundational categories by endowing them with concrete integration.

We have, then, identified three ways in which special theological categories interplay with transcendental and general categories. They articulate the data of revelation that validate or invalidate philosophical, scientific, or scholarly affirmations about God. They transvalue transcendental and general categories developed in abstraction from divine revelation but subsequently employed within theology. They endow foundational insight with an integrating concreteness.

In the course of this chapter we have been attempting to understand the coordination and interplay of foundational categories. We have reflected on the operational procedures that shape foundational method and have identified four techniques of coordination: agreement, convergence, complementarity, and dialectical reversal. We have concluded that the transcendental and philosophical categories employed within foundational speculation interpret, integrate, and contextualize general and special categories. To the extent that philosophy provides other speculative disciplines with sound operational procedures, it also validates their results. General categories, we also concluded, help to verify, falsify, and amplify the other two sets of foundational categories. Special foundational categories interpret a concrete, historical encounter with the divine. They help verify or falsify philosophical, scholarly, or scientific affirmations about God and articulate a conceptual frame of reference created by religious faith that transvalues the other kinds of foundational categories. They also endow foundational thinking with integrating concreteness.

We began these reflections as an experiment in foundational method. We decided to test the claim of Lonergan's method to foster inculturated theological thinking. The time has come to assess the results of that experiment. We shall do so in the short afterword which follows.

AFTERWORD:
ASSESSING THE RESULTS

We began these reflections as an experiment in theological method. We proposed to test the ability of Lonergan's method to produce an inculturated North American theology. We decided to use the method in order to expand Lonergan's own account of the operational procedures that generate foundational theology. On this point Lonergan himself, as we have seen, displays considerable reticence. While his method attempts to root revisionist theological thinking in an experience of conversion and assigns to foundations the task of formulating a normative account of Christian conversion, *Method in Theology* leaves the reader largely in the dark concerning the concrete operations that are supposed to generate and coordinate the three nests of categories employed in foundationaal speculation. We proposed therefore to address the question: what operations generate a normative theology of Christian conversion? As a way of testing the ability of Lonergan's method to foster theological inculturation, we also decided to examine foundational method in dialogue with the North American philosophical tradition.

The time has come to assess the results of our experiment. It has caused us to call into question some of the presuppositions that lie at the basis of Lonergan's method as he originally formulated it. Lonergan quite correctly suggests that any theory of method ought to focus on the operations that shape inquiry. Careful attention to the operations of inferential thinking convinced us of its radical fallibility not only when it concerns itself with empirical data but also when it reflects on the operations of the mind itself. We therefore questioned Lonergan's claim to have articulated an unrevisable account of the terms and relations of all human thinking. We decided that far from yielding unrevisable insights into the dynamics of conscious thought, transcendental method can only produce fallible working hypotheses about the way people ought to think. Our subsequent explorations of foundational method further convinced us that the theory of knowledge that underpins Lonergan's method actually needs revision at a number of key points.

We found reason to question Lonergan's claim that at the basis of human culture lie transcultural cognitive dynamisms of thought. Rather, because the realm of culture and the realm of human symbolic cognitive behavior coincide, we concluded that the human attempt to formulate either appreciative or inferential insights transpires within culture. Human cognitive activity and the learned tendencies that ground it may advance or undermine culture, but they never transcend culture.

We also found reason to question the unrestricted character of the human desire to know. Indeed, at the basis of Lonergan's portrayal of the human mind as an insatiable thirst for Being lie several uncriticized Thomistic assumptions about the way the human mind works, assumptions that close empirical investigations of human cognitive behavior call into question. Empirical and clinical studies of human thought processes suggest that finitude, ego-centrism, and ego-inertia characterize human thinking with more spontaneity than some fictive "unrestricted desire to know." That insight led us to the further conclusion that any explanatory interpretation of human thought processes needs empirical validation.

We also found reason to question Lonergan's use of the term "experience." We found other, more comprehensive uses of that term in the North American philosophical tradition. We decided with Whitehead to employ the term "experience" as a descriptive category universally applicable in intent. With help from Peirce's phenomenology we described experience as triadic rather than as dipolar in structure.

In addition, we found reason to question Lonergan's handling of appreciative cognition. We discovered within intuitive thinking judgments of feeling that grasp the real as truly and as fallibly as inferential judgments. We decided that Lonergan had illegitimately attempted to restrict the knowledge of reality to an inferential grasp of the virtually unconditioned. Finally, we found reason to question the introverted character of Lonergan's method. We decided that his turn to the subject focuses too narrowly on the analysis of intentionality and fails to take into sufficient account the results of social psychology. Moreover, we found that the term "experience" when conceived in triadic terms and used transcendentally could accommodate both types of analysis.

Nevertheless, while our investigations have caused us to question some of the presuppositions that ground Lonergan's method, they have validated others. They have validated his definitiion of method as a set of recurring and related operations yielding cumulative and progressive results. We may legitimately measure the validity of any definition of method by its ability to foster criticism of the presuppositions that ground it. Paradoxically, then, our very revisions of Lonergan's epistemology have contributed to that validation; for those revisions have flowed directly from his definition and its clear focus on the operations that structure thought.

Our reflections on Lonergan's method have also indirectly lent support both to his distinction between mediating and mediated theology and to his theory of functional specialties. Foundational theology, as we have seen, grounds the three other specialties that comprise mediated theology. By explicitating its operational procedures in greater detail than Lonergan has, we have placed the pursuit of mediated theology on a sounder footing and simultaneously distinguished more clearly the operations of an important functional specialty.

We have also in the course of our experiment expanded our insight into the scope of foundational theology itself. We have added two kinds of conversion to Lonergan's original list of three. We have concluded that in addition to investigating intellectual, moral, and religious conversion foundational theology must also explore affective and socio-political conversion as well.

Moreover, in approaching conversion experientially we were forced to investigate the ways in which the different moments within the conversion process mutually condition one another. As a consequence, we have identified seven distinct dynamics within Chrisitan conversion. (1) Christian conversion mediates between affective and moral conversion. (2) Intellectual conversion seeks to inform affective, moral, religious, and socio-political conversion. (4) Moral conversion orients affective, intellectual, and socio-political conversion to realities and values that make absolute and ultimate claims. (5) Affective conversion seeks to animate intellectual, moral, socio-political and religious conversion. (6) Socio-political conversion authenticates affective, intellectual, moral, and religious conversion by deprivatizing them. (7) Personal conversion authenticates socio-political conversion by providing affective, speculative, moral, and religious norms that judge socio-political activity.

The identification of five moments and seven dynamics within the total experience of conversion provides a collaborative frame of reference for pursuing foundational speculation. All five moments within the conversion process together with the seven dynamics that interrelate the five moments need to be explored in much more descriptive and normative detail and illumined by empirical and clinical investigation.

Reflection on the five moments and seven dynamics of conversion has also allowed us to identify a number of specific tasks for future foundational theologians to perform. If one approaches foundational speculation in the experiential manner suggested by North American philosophy, one needs to expand descriptively the categories "experience" and "religious experience." Moreover, that same philosophical tradition offers considerable resources for effecting both expansions. In addition, foundational theory must elaborate a strictly normative account of Christian conversion. If in addition Christian foundational speculation hopes to engage in meaningful ecumenical dialogue with the other great world religions, it will need to elaborate a strictly normative account of the kind of religious conversion that authenticates other religious traditions as well. Moreover, foundational speculation needs to formulate two accounts of human growth and development. The first account focuses on natural growth processes, which occur in abstraction from God's historical self-revelation and self-communication to humanity. The second account must show how the experience of faith transmutes and transvalues natural forms of conversion.

Foundational theology must also differentiate true from false hopes and adequate from inadequate ones in order to encourage converts to true and adequate human aspirations. A strictly normative theory of conversion must also resolve dialectical conflicts among appreciative perceptions of reality by coordinating sound judgments of feeling with one another. Such a theology needs to elaborate sound norms for understanding the psychodynamics of healing through social interaction. An integrated account of the conversion process must also reconcile the convert's head and heart. It must coordinate intuitive and inferential perceptions of reality. More specifically, foundational theory needs to coordinate myths with world hypotheses, scholarly and biblical narratives with one another and with theoretical and practical inferences, prophetic and lyric visions with logical accounts of the real, and judgments of feeling with judgments of belief. In the process of doing all of this a sound and balanced foundational theory must observe nine operational postulates: be repentantly appreciative; be imaginative; be prudent, tasteful, and discerning; be attentive; be intelligent; be personally responsible; be socially responsible; be religiously loving; and integrate the judgments and perceptions of your heart and head.,

Any adequate explanation of the dynamics of conversion needs not only to account for the processes of personal conversion but also to elaborate practical strategies for advancing human society ever closer to the most perfect embodiment of the kingdom of God possible in any given circumstance. It must resolve conflicting claims made by the Christian religion and by the particular culture in which it roots itself. Foundational speculation must examine unsettled social, economic, and political situations within the church and within secular society that pose significant questions for converts. It must show the relationship between moral development and, on the one hand, the other forms of personal and socio-political growth on the other. A socially adequate theory of conversion seeks especially to transform politically and economically unstable situations into foundationally settled ones that submit not only to sound moral norms but also to the moral demands of gospel living. The effective foundational theologian must settle unresolved foundational situations not only in principle but as far as possible in fact. Foundational theory will therefore also need to develop strategies for the collaborative resolution of pressing public, social problems. Foundational theory must differentiate true from false political hopes and resolve the emotional conflicts that destabilize social, economic, and political situations. It must also ensure that the judgments of the healed and repentant heart sanction the policy decisions that shape people's lives. A strictly normative theory of Christian conversion must also examine the ways in which socio-political conversion transforms both individual believers and entire communities of faith into prophets of social, economic, and political betterment. Foundational theory must demonstrate the inadequacy of any account of the human conscience which fails to invoke religious values. Finally, just as in dealing with personal conversion, foundational theory needs to draw on the best insights of contemporary personality theory, so too in dealing with problems of social transformation it needs to profit from the best insights of the social sciences.

Besides providing a context for the future pursuit of foundational speculation by identifying some of the important kinds of questions which foundational thinkers need to address, the preceding reflections have also allowed us to identify some of the logical criteria that validate any given foundational hypothesis. Every account of conversion needs to be tested against the criteria of logical consistency, coherence, applicability, and adequacy. We have examined the role of deliberation in the formulation of foundational hypotheses and examined criteria for selecting among formulated hypotheses. Foundational thinking must submit all its theories as far as possible to deductive clarification and to inductive testing against the data of revelation and of natural experience. In formulating hypotheses foundational thinkers need to alternate between focused investigations of specific problems and an integrating theory of the whole.

Finally, our experiment in foundational method has allowed us to identify techniques for generating and coordinating the three sets of categories employed in formulating a strictly normative theory of conversion. We have also identified the unsettled foundational situation as the generating source of categories; and we have identified four techniques for coordinating them: agreement, complementarity, convergence, and dialectical reversal. We have seen how these techniques can be used not only to coordinate each set of categories among themselves but also to coordinate all three sets with one another. Finally, we have reflected on the ways in which the coordination of all three sets of categories with one another engages their interpretative interplay.

Moreover, we have good reason to believe that a systematic pursuit of foundational speculation along the lines we have suggested would indeed foster the inculturation of theology in this country. It would advance the two major goals of inculturated theological thinking. It would draw systematically on the speculative resources which North American culture provides in order to elaborate a theory of integral five-fold conversion. It would also use that construct to challenge the inauthenticities that mar our American way of life. It would devise strategies not only for fostering personal responsibility but also for resolving in both principle and fact unresolved foundational situations.

An experiential approach to formulating a normative theology of conversion would also foster the minor goals of theological inculturation. Our method endorses the empirical notion of culture which Lonergan describes and respects cultural pluralism. It encourages dialogue among different Christian denominations about the experience of conversion that validates Christian belief and practice. It acknowledges that different world religions embody different kinds of religious experience and invites a dialectical examination of the truth and relative adequacy of their accounts of religious conversion. The approach to foundational thinking we propose also avoids narrow nationalism. While it draws critically on the specific culture in which it roots itself it remains in dialogue with the Christian tradition as a whole and with theological movements in other lands. It thus strikes a balance between church unity and local cultural diversity. Finally, by taking into account the methodological insights of liberation theology, our foundational method ensures that the voices of deviant or minority groups within any given culture can contribute to the resolution of indeterminate foundational situations.

I originally undertook these reflections on foundational method as an exercise in speculative integrity. Having attempted three studies in foundational theory, I wished to step back from them and reflect critically on the relative adequacy of my own operational procedures. I publish them as an invitation to creative collaboration. The formulation of an inculturated theology of conversion that addresses the significant issues of North American culture poses such an enormous challenge that only a fool would undertake the task alone. If the preceding observations on the procedures of foundational thinking succeed in encouraging others to take up that challenge, then they will have justified the sweat that produced them.